Exploring Rural
SPAIN

Exploring Rural
SPAIN

JAN McGIRK

CHRISTOPHER HELM
London

© 1988 Jan S. McGirk
Line illustrations by Lorna Turpin
Maps by David Henderson
Christopher Helm (Publishers) Ltd, Imperial House,
21-25 North Street, Bromley, Kent BR1 1SD

British Library Cataloguing in Publication Data

McGirk, Jan S.
    Exploring rural Spain. — (Exploring
    rural).
    1. Spain — Description and travel —
    1981- — Guide-books
    I. Title
    914.6'0483   DP14

    ISBN 0-7470-2203-8

Typeset by Leaper and Gard, Bristol
Printed and bound in Great Britain by
Billings and Sons Ltd, Worcester.

CONTENTS

To Tim
and the boys, who share my road

Spain — the regions and the routes

INTRODUCTION

Spain will sear itself into your imagination. The light is clear and some-times cruel, and cool dim places become precious. Winds are capricious, and most regions have mocking nicknames for theirs. One pilot who rode these Iberian air-currents was puzzled by the odd round clearings she kept seeing, even in isolated mountain villages. Once she landed her biplane, she found the answer: bullrings. The Apollo astronauts, viewing an 'earth-rise' from their lunar landing, radioed back that while Europe seemed aswirl with clouds, 'Spain is different'.

It is much more than a sun-drenched tourist destination beckoning from the south of a European map. Still, it has cashed in on its reliable climate to such an extent that visi-tors equal the number of Spaniards in the country each year. Don't be put off by such a statistic: most of these hordes stay resolutely on the coast, with a few venturing into nearby cathedrals and museums. Spain is huge, nearly as big as France with only two-thirds as many people.

Heading for the Fería

Once you venture off the usual tourist circuit, you will uncover a contradictory country. Many pre-conceptions can be justified (yes, it has Moorish rose gardens and gypsies, thousands of castles and fighting bulls, slow waiters who serve food that can be laced heavily in olive oil and garlic, and it can be noisy, hot, austere and oblivious to animal suffering). At the same time, it has unexpected pleasures: ancient cave art and modern trog-lodytes, formal French-style gar-dens and bleak deserts, an erotic church, even a village monument dedicated to the human liver —

1

an organ subjected to much abuse with the marvellous cheap wine and potent spirits. Extraordinary seafood restaurants exist hundreds of kilometres from the coast. Eagles spiral between high crags. Flocks of flamingos gather in the southern saltmarshes. Wild horses run loose in misty mountain pastures, and Galician witches threaten to turn into swarms of bees. Medieval towns seem to have walled out the 20th century until you spy the video game in the corner of the local tavern. Rural Spain is not necessarily bucolic, and rarely boring. The Spaniards themselves are friendly, excitable, courteous, un-snobbish and generally fine company. Knowing Spanish is a big bonus, but smiles and sign-language go a long way towards understanding.

With such startling variety, Spain defies a single definitive guide. This book offers a personal selection of drives through rural regions which are too often ignored in a mad rush to the coast. None the less, not all of the beautiful beaches are scorned. Monumental places which might be dismissed as tourist traps also are given their due. Lists of city sights are outside the main scope of this book and are consequently sketchy. On average, there are three tours per region. The travelling time estimates are generous, allowing for languid lunches, unexpected conversations, sudden stops for stunning views, and even an occasional bout of travel sickness on those winding roads. There are hundreds more potential trips out there for adventurers. Milk the places you do visit for all they're worth: when possible, go on foot and go inside. Given the choice, spend time instead of money.

Regions

Since Franco's demise and the reassertion of democracy within this venerable kingdom, Spain's old ethnic divisions have been officially recognised as 17 autonomous regions within a federation. These echo the proud domains whose rivalries kindled battles and strategic marriages in times past. The touring zones in this book are based on my own feel for the lay of the land, my map-reading struggles on the road, geographical boundaries, plus the government's groupings of these historical communities. The Canary Islands have been left out, since it is doubtful that the independent driver from abroad would make it there. Likewise, the enclaves in North Africa — Ceuta and Melilla — were skipped.

The Balearic Isles, with good ferry connections, are covered even though they seem like a demi-world of their own. Northern provinces, with mossy coastlines and rock spires that outdo the grand Cathedral at Santiago de Compostela, comprise Cantabria/Euskadi (or Basque Country), and Galicia/Asturias, which will strike you as the antithesis of travelposter Spain. Andalucía and Extremadura, both in the sun-baked south, affirm most of the clichés of castles and castanets yet somehow seem the most alien and intriguing. Catalonia/Aragón, on the flanks of the Pyrenees, is as known for wine within Spain as Rioja/Navarra, and the landscape offers as many surprises as the resilient people. The Levant Coast is much more than rice and oranges, and retains a surprisingly strong Moorish feel. Old Castile/León and New Castile/La Mancha, on the daunting central plain, preserve much of the medieval past in villages of desolate beauty and by bizarre rites and festivals. All ten sections are distinct and many now spurn Castilian Spanish on their maps and road-signs as an assertion of independence. This can be monstrously confusing, and I've used Spanish place-names for consistency and indicated the alternative in brackets if it is widely used.

Entry Requirements

A valid passport is necessary, and motorists need an international drivers' licence. Cars should be marked with the regulation nationality plate. These are the rules, though enforcement can be sporadic. Be prepared. Australians and New Zealanders need a visa for entry, obtainable from any Spanish consulate. British, Canadian and Irish citizens are allowed a 3-month stay without an extension visa; US citizens are entitled to 6 months. Don't count on a short trip over the frontier for instant renewal. Though this usually works, new laws aimed at controlling illegal residents on the 'Costa del Crime' insist that an extended stay be premeditated, with an extension visa obtained on the first entry and then produced at the local police station for validation. Most of officialdom is still muddled over the matter, but life can be made difficult if you are a lawbreaker, even unintentionally. Cars in the country over 6 months can be required to show import papers.

Officially you are required to carry your identification papers with you at all times; some wily types, once stung by a pickpocket, take to carrying a photocopy of the passport's front pages plus the page stamped with the Spanish entry date. Then they leave their passport in the hotel safe. The papers are perfectly acceptable to police and a good idea, if you remember to reclaim the real thing before checking out.

Insurance

Best to check current regulations through an automobile club. Spain's main automobile club is the RACE, but it is advisable to make arrangements in your home country. Minimum requirement is a green card proving limited liability. These are usually on sale at a main border and definitely need to be endorsed for Spain. Because of the high price of litigation in Spanish courts, you're wise to beef up coverage for driver and passengers. Seat belts are mandatory, together wih an official warning triangle in case of breakdown. British drivers shouldn't forget to give way to traffic on the right and to drive on the right (wrong) side of the road. This seems obvious, but is a leading cause of accidents, particularly at the start of fly-drive schemes. Danger points are pulling out of a drive onto a fairly empty road and the instinct to swerve to safety in the usual direction. If an accident does happen, you must get full details from the other driver: name, address, phone, occupation, vehicle registration number, insurance company and policy number. Any injury (even slight) must be reported to the police, and the law requires that an injured person be whisked promptly to an emergency room. Hail a passer-by if you are alone, for you shouldn't leave the accident until the details are settled.

Getting There

The direct car link from Britain is the Plymouth-Santander ferry, operated twice a week by Brittany Ferries. The 24-hour journey costs almost as much as the cheapest charter flight (22 July-16 September is high season). Child discounts can make it work out a bargain: under 4s are free; under 13s go half price. The journey isn't as rough as the Bay of Biscay's reputation would have you fear, and it is quicker than the average 36 hours of solid driving it takes to get through France. Details from travel agents or Brittany Ferries, Milbay Docks, Plymouth PL1 3EF (0752 21321) or Estación Maritima, Santander (942 21 4500). The Pyrenees mountains still form quite a barrier, and there are only a few viable routes through the high passes. Puigcerdá and Somport-Canfranc is a particularly scenic route, and Andorra is another. If you have plenty of time, follow the traditional Road to Santiago through Roncesvalles, Vall d'Aran or else by way of Tarbes and Aragnouet before taking the tunnel to Parzan. The quickest trip is to shoot down to Catalonia via Calais, Paris, Bordeaux and La Jonquera.

To reach Spain's lovely green Atlantic coast take either the Portsmouth ferry to St Malo or the Plymouth ferry to Roscoff before motoring down France's west coast. It can work out quite inexpensively to go on a fly-drive package. Special deals are available through Iberian or British Airways. Even cheaper would be a good London bucket shop ticket combined with a hire car from a charter airport (Gerona and Málaga both have outrageously cut-price flights). A budget-conscious traveller from the USA should consider the advantages of a two-stage flight: transatlantic bargain to London with a day layover to find a cheap charter round trip to Spain.

Roads and Driving

At times, *en route* between small towns, out-of-the-way roads become major thoroughfares for the transportation of farm goods. Even major roads in Spain often have but two or three lanes, which means that many large and overladen trucks must be passed. If your car is right hand drive, this may place a strain on the one in the navigator's seat (though if you motored down from France and are still on speaking terms with your travelling mate, you will have this down cold). Truck drivers are often helpful and will signal with their lights when it is clear to pass. But do rely on your own judgement. On multi-lane highways, the speed limit will be posted at 100 or 120kph; this drops down to 90kph on a two-lane road. Within town limits, it is only 60kph unless otherwise marked. While it seems that limits are ignored with impunity, speeding fines are stiff when enforced and payable on the spot. Also remember that Spaniards will often slow, stop or turn unexpectedly, with nary a signal, and that double or even triple parking is the rule. Be prepared for aberrant driving and for motorscooters and even pedestrians to weave through slow traffic. In Madrid, particularly, stopping at red lights seems to be optional. Though usually well marked, dangerous curves sometimes appear without warning, despite the previous dozen being painstakingly indicated. Don't be unduly alarmed if a car goes past waving a white handkerchief from the window and blaring the horn constantly. All you must surrender is the right of way; the car is on an emergency run to the hospital. *Ruta Turista* sometimes will be marked on roadsigns by the local government and these routes are almost always a worthwhile diversion, providing you have enough time left to finish before nightfall. When you are passing through a large city, be aware that due to the afternoon siesta, there are often four 'rush hours' when commuters clog the roads, and that they do not correspond to the British or American equivalent. If possible, avoid driving in or near a metropolis at 9 am, or 2 pm, 4.30 pm and 8 pm. Fridays can be a trial, with residents fleeing the cities for weekends in the country.

Maps and Directions

Coming armed with detailed Michelin or Automobile Association maps is a good idea and can prove a timesaver, but locally available maps are, on the whole, equally reliable. The best are from MOPU (the government highway department) or Firestone. CAMPSA, the petroleum distributors, publish *Guia España*, an excellent atlas with road maps and a detailed, easy-to-read index (in Spanish). It can be bought at many bookstores and some petrol stations. One trip-soothing feature is succinct street maps of largish cities, right in the index. There is nothing more exasperating than struggling around a maze of one-way streets, trapped in a place that's *en route* from A to B. On the other hand, if temper is kept in check, it's a fine way to discover an unanticipated delight. Keep track of the stumpy stone kilometre markers at the roadside (they measure distance from a central point in Madrid's Puerto de Sol) to help avoid losing your way. Many ventas (roadside inns) and hotels quote their addresses by this distance and directions often refer to them. For ultra-detail, the maps and atlases put out by *Ediciones Almax* cannot be bettered, for they list even the alleys in the most remote villages. For many, though, the density of information causes confusion.

In many towns, especially in the south, you may be misled when asking directions. This isn't out of spite, but more out of perverse pride. Not wanting to disappoint the lost traveller, the passer-by may invent a route if he doesn't know it. More frequently, in the smaller villages, you will be personally escorted to your destination. Also, quite a few street names (and even town names) are reverting back to their pre-Franco designations, and references older than 10 years may no longer exist.

Cartography has been linked with Spain since distinguished mapmakers made it an art in the 12th century, and the free maps from most tourist offices reflect this tradition. Beware that some are over-simplified for beauty, and once you get off the magic route there are no indications how to get back on again. ICONA, less potent now that the local regions control ecological policies, is the national conservation agency and printed some fine no-nonsense maps of the more forested regions — heavy on the detail, light on the rapturous descriptions. These are worth asking for specifically. Two points to avoid frustration: with a straight-forward phonetic logic, Spaniards consider certain sounds, spelled with a combination of two letters, as letters on their own and alphabetise accordingly. For example, 'Chinchón' won't be found between 'Calatrava' and 'Ciudad Real' as you might expect; it will follow all the 'c' entries, starting a new 'ch' category. Other Spanish letters to remember are 'll', 'ñ' 'rr'. Numbers are also written differently, with a decimal point setting off the thousands and a comma used to mark the decimals. Thus 35,000 written the English way could be construed as just 35.

About Dining

On the road, a venta (roadside inn) is your best bet, as is the more casual *cafetería* where Spaniards get snacks (*tapas* or *raciones*, normally displayed in a glass case at the bar) to stave off the hunger pangs based on their most unusual dining hours. Most restaurants do not serve lunch until 1.45 or 2 pm, and dinner isn't in full swing until 9 pm, or more usually 10 or 11. In town, due to the increase of middle-class week-end homes, the big night to dine out now is Thursday, and restaurants can be surprisingly crowded. A venta can provide good yet inexpensive food and is apt to have more flexible hours. If trucks are pulled up in front, it is often a sign that it's worth stopping there: value for money. Do try the regional cuisine: seafood is excellent and ordering anything grilled (*a la plancha*) sidesteps worries about meals drowned in olive oil (though some of the olive oil is marvellous). Spanish food is spicy, but not Hispanic (there is not a jalapeño pepper to be seen!). Also, in Spain a *tortilla* is a plain potato omelette, not the same thing as a Mexican *tortilla*. Bland inter-national cuisine or simple roast chicken is often on offer, but it would be a shame to shy away out of mere squeamishness from specialities like partridge in chili and chocolate sauce or baby eels. There are probably more medium-range restaurants in Spain than anywhere else, and the ranking by numbers of forks rather than hotel stars is a guide to the trap-pings and price range, not necessarily linked to the food's quality. In many unpretentious establishments, a surprisingly good *Menu del Día*, with three courses plus wine, need not cost more than about 600 pesetas. Tips are nominal, as service is normally covered in the bill, and shouldn't be more than 5 or 10 per cent. IVA (the Spanish Value-added Tax) should be included in the menu prices or mentioned at the bottom. One caution: lobster and langoustine (prawns) are luxuries here, and usually sold by weight. Often the price quoted is per 100 grams, with a standard serving being many times that (those shells and claws are heavy!). The bill could add up to six times what you expect if you are caught unaware. Ask the price of *una racion* (a serving) for these items, and avoid costly surprises.

The Spanish meal is an occasion for talk — albeit often simultaneous monologues — and for sharing with friends. Children are welcome in most places, even long past midnight, and babysitters (*canguros* or kangaroos) are scarce except in swank hotels or university cities. Meals are rarely rushed, so if you are in a great hurry to make time on an itinerary, stand at a *tapas* bar, in a sea of paper napkins lapping at your ankles, or bring along provisions for a picnic. Markets are fun and the fresh local produce is usually delicious.

Accommodation

Ignore the horror stories of Spanish plumbing and explore the full range of lodging in this country. Top ranking (with prices to match) are the highly reputed government *parador* hotels. The word means stopping place, and there are now 86 of these luxury hotels that have been installed in an assortment of converted castles, monasteries or palaces (plus a few purpose-built modern edifices). They are extraordinarily well-sited in scenic or historic spots and furnished with appropriate antiques as well as modern conveniences. Stays are limited to a fortnight and the chain is plotted out so each is a comfortable day's drive away (by the old-fashioned 1920s motorcars operating when the scheme first came to light). Reservations in high season are advisable, and if you don't order the regional dishes in the restaurant, you're apt to be disappointed by mediocre cooking. *Albergues* are wayside inns, also government run, which allow a traveller a maximum stay of 2 nights. Both paradors and albergues are marked on most highway maps and are indicated by road-signs. Rustic mountain refuges (*refugios*) are maintained in many of the national parks and government hunting preserves. Less organised, but especially applicable to rural routes, are the *Casas de Labranza* which are operated along similar lines to the French *gîtes*. These provide lodging in private farmhouses, sometimes in separate quarters but also alongside the clan in a number of the smaller places. Some require that you pitch in with chores as part of the experience; others treat you as complete guests. A detailed guide obtainable from the National Tourist Board, or regional tourist offices (marked *Turismo*), can provide information on local ones.

Private accommodation is carefully ranked by the government on pale blue signs posted near the main entrances. With tourism a major industry, this is serious business. Alas, there are so many categories it's hard to keep them all straight. A *Casa de Huespedes* (CH) or *Fonda* (F) is the lowest on the scale, usually clean but with a shared bath down the hall. Next come *Hostales* (Hs) or *Pensiones* (P), which are rated with 1–3 stars. The difference is that *pensiones* serve meals. A 3-star *hostal* approaches being a 1-star hotel, but is usually a little less prepossessing. Hotels, at the top end, are ranked on services rather than price and range from 1–5 stars. Most paradors are at least 3-star hotels, usually 4-star. By law, room prices must be displayed in the lobby and on the door of each room. *Hotel Residencia* (HR) or *Hostal Residencia* (HosR) means that there is no dining room. Electricity normally is 220 volts, but it can vary so it's best to make sure before plugging in any appliances.

In addition, *habitaciones* (rooms) or *camas* (beds) to hire are often indicated by a small sign. These small places are unofficial, but often cheap and satisfactory. In the villages, a landlady may rent out a room or two in her *casa particular* (private home), but you would never know unless you bother to ask at the local bar. Staying in somebody's house is intimate and makes you feel like a traveller rather than a tourist. There are also an abundance of well-equipped campsites in Spain, marked on special Tourist Board maps. Should you ever end up just 'sleeping rough', it's best to obtain permission from the landowner or risk being roused in the morning by a bull or a hunter. Finally, many monasteries and convents are reviving their *hospederías* (traditional guest houses) and provide well-lit private rooms and communal meals to wayfarers who wish to retreat from the world awhile. The nominal price ranges between 900 and 1,500 pesetas, and most accept only male guests, though Montserrat is a Barcelonan honeymoon retreat.

Monday, Monday …

A non-day for most museums and monuments plus many restaurants. If you can, plot the longer driving portions of the trip for Mondays, when the countryside is all you want to be open.

Fiestas and Holidays

Celebration is part of Spanish life, and you'll find that festivals are not self-conscious events cooked up by an overzealous Tourism Board, but genuine events. Local saints, heroes, annual harvests: almost any excuse will do, and some go back over centuries and the original reason is forgotten. Public holidays are taken quite seriously and, throughout the country, everyday life shuts down on: New Year's Day, 6 January (Three King's Day), Holy Thursday, Good Friday, Easter Sunday, May Day, Corpus Christi (late May or early June), 25 July (Santiago), 15 August (Assumption), 12 October (Columbus Day and Hispanidad), 1 November (All Saints), 6 December (Constitution), 8 December (Immaculate Conception) and, of course, Christmas Day.

Each village and town also has its own patron saint with special community festivities, and these can spin out for a fortnight of fun. Jumping through bonfires, dancing on stilts, leaping over mattresses covered with babies, dousing the rival town with wine, battling mock Moors: there is a wide, weird variety. Ask for the current booklet about 'Festivals of Special Interest to Tourists' (*Fiestas de Interes Turistico*) at any tourist office. It gives a monthly run-down of all fairs, fiestas and festivals, which tend to be movable feasts with a date that switches yearly. It's so popular that supplies forever run short, but keep trying.

Siestas

One Andalucian friend calls it 'Iberian yoga', and the practice of a snooze after a heavy lunch in hot weather, especially after staying up till the wee hours of the morning, is utterly sensible. It must somehow recharge the psyche. But siesta can play havoc with the plans of foreigners who are unused to it. A sudden switch to summer hours will confuse even experienced travellers. Generally, things shut down between 2 and 5 and reopen in the evening until 8. In summer, everything gets going in the early morning cool and comes to a halt around 3. Bank hours are usually 9–2. The result is an incredibly long morning: afternoon won't begin until siesta starts. And you'll overhear Spaniards greeting each other with 'Good Afternoon' as late as 10 at night! Many Spanish people hold down two jobs with the benefit of a long siesta, and others waste much of it away in incredibly clogged traffic. In many of the monuments tucked away in small villages, opening times are sporadic. It is always worth looking around for the bearer of the key. Church sacristans are rarely far away and don't mind being roused. A small tip (50-100 pesetas) will be expected.

Water

Generally the tap water is fine for drinking, though it has enough chlorine to kill a goldfish. Stick to bottled water if you feel uneasy, and do avoid well water. Traveller's tummy anywhere is often put down just to a change in background microbes or a sudden increase in alcohol intake. If the worst comes to the worst, don't be shy about heading into any restaurant or bar to use the lavatory (*servicios*), even if you're clearly not a customer. This is standard Spanish practice due to their lack of public conveniences, and it won't raise an eyebrow. Ask the pharmacist for *vacuosa*, tablets that come in a bright yellow package. They are thin wafers of absorbent charcoal, have absolutely no interference with other medication and ease the symptoms of queasiness or diarrhoea very quickly.

Health

If you speak Spanish, discuss ailments with the village pharmacist, who will advise whether a visit to the doctor is necessary. Spanish pharmacists are highly trained para-medicals and can save you much grief. Also, if you have a chronic problem and know which medicines remedy it, many prescription drugs are available over-the-counter in most of the country. Obtaining contraceptives is not the obstacle it was during the Franco era, though some devout Catholic chemists won't stock them. Since Spain joined the Common Market, some private health plans and the NHS have begun working out reciprocal agreements. Check with the Spanish Consulate and your own health plan for details. Before leaving the UK, obtain an E111 Form for treatment at state clinics and hospitals abroad. Even with this, you will need to hoard all receipts and wait patiently for reimbursement. The simplest thing is to take out travel health insurance to make things more straightforward.

Climate

Don't believe that 'The rain in Spain stays mainly on the plain'; it's mostly up on the northeast coast, creating a pocket of almost Irish weather, only with more warmth and brighter rainbows. Quite a bit is caught on the peaks as snow. Probably the best time to do a general tour is spring or autumn. Soria and Teruel suffer the bitterest winters on their exposed plains, even though the sky can be a brilliant blue. Since buildings are designed to cope with the extreme summer heat, it may actually be colder inside than out. Do open the window a crack if you're in a room heated by an old-fashioned charcoal brazier (*bracero*), usually hidden beneath a long felt cloth on a circular table. Without fresh air, fierce headaches are common. Winter is mild in the Balearic Isles, most of the Levant and Andalucía. Still, skiers can take to the slopes of the Sierra Nevada near Granada from late December through May. Summers can be oppressively hot, yet are bearable on the flat Meseta, the central plateau region, because they're not humid. Seasides (especially in the little-visited north) or mountains — no shortage of these — are the best destinations for this season. Drivers should come equipped with strong sunglasses any time of year, and polarised lenses are a must for the sudden contrasts of shade and dazzle. The range of temperatures can be great within a single day in spring or autumn, especially in central Spain. A drop of 15 degrees Farenheit is common after the sun goes down. Pack at least one sweater along with the sunscreen. Hayfever sufferers would be wise to tour in autumn rather than spring, since there's little rain to damp down the pollen.

Telephones

Should you wish to call home from some remote pueblo, you will need to go to the central *telefónica*, where you can dial from a partitioned booth. Even in a large town, this is far less expensive than phoning from your hotel room, where a large surcharge (up to 25 per cent) is added on. To reverse the charges, you ask the operator for *cobro revertido*. But you must ring reverse charge from the central *telefónica* in town, not from a public booth. Telephone boxes operate on coins, which you line up to roll down a slot, and most new ones have directions in English. No change is given, so come prepared with plenty of 5 and 25 peseta coins. If you are making a local call, you're wise to put in an initial 25 peseta coin to avoid being cut off in mid-sentence. Often, bars have public telephones, but there's no guarantee that you'll be heard above the din. Some petrol stations also are equipped with telephone boxes. There are a number of spots in Spain which remain off the line altogether, especially in the Las Hurdes region and even in mountain villages that are an easy commute from Madrid. If you want to, it is possible to evade the 20th century in rural Spain.

Information

THE SPANISH TOURISM BOARD offers a wealth of detailed maps, brochures and pamphlets, mostly for free. Now that the autonomous regions have asserted independence in tooting their own horns, there can be some confusion about literature from select areas. Generally, though, the service is unmatched. The new tourism minister has particular enthusiasm for promoting the interior, and a request for information on rural areas will be seized on with pleasure. A new booklet called 'Visiting the Paradores', from the 'Viajes y Cultura' (Trips & Culture) collection, describes each of the parador hotels in an historical context and suggests outings in the immediate surroundings. 'Fiestas of Special Interest to Tourists' details all important festivities which happen in Spain, giving monthly and regional listings. 'Vacations in Casas de Labranza' lists all the *gîte*-style accommodation offered in the provinces. There are also innumerable bright brochures on individual cities and museums, bold posters, and surprisingly detailed regional maps. Their *Mapa de Comunicaciones* is a good general map of the nation. Visit or telephone their offices abroad to pick up information before you go.

Spanish National Tourist Offices:
57/8 St James's Street, London SW1 (01-499 0901)
665 Fifth Ave, New York, NY 10022 (212-759-8822)
845 North Michigan Ave, Chicago, ILL. 60611 (312-944-0215)
4800 The Galleria, 5085 Westheimer, Houston, TX 77056 (713-840-7411)
60 Bloor St West 201, Toronto, Ontario M4W 388 (416-961-3131)

Apart from their stands at major airport and railway stations, the Tourism Department (*Turismo*) has offices in towns and cities throughout the country. These addresses are listed where applicable in the itineraries of each route.

LOOKOUT MAGAZINE is a glossy monthly published in English on the Costa del Sol which caters mainly to expatriate residents. Well-researched articles on travel plus topical pieces on festivals, restaurants and cultural events make it worthwhile reading, especially while on tour. Pick it up in newsstands on the Costa del Sol, the Costa Blanca or in Madrid and take advantage of advice from 'Old Spain hands'. Or contact Lookout, Puebla Lucia, 29640 Fuengirola (Málaga) tel. 460950.

Glossary

albergue	government-run wayside inn
alcázar	fortress or fortified palace
bodega	shop selling wine or where the wine is made
Meseta	the flat, central plateau
Moor	A North African Muslim
Morisco	Moors who were Christianised after the re-conquest

Mozarabic	Moorish-influenced Christian, ninth century
Mudéjar	Moorish-influenced architecture, 12th-16th century
parador	government-run hotel
Plateresque	finely carved, early Renaissance style of architecture (from *platero* : silversmith)
pueblo	village
ría	long, narrow inlet
venta	roadside inn

Metric Conversion Tables

All measurements are given in metric units. For readers more familiar with the imperial system, the accompanying tables are designed to facilitate quick conversion to imperial units. Bold figures in the central columns can be read as either metric or imperial: e.g. 1kg = 2.20lb or 1lb = 0.45kg.

mm		in	cm		in	m		yds
25.4	1	.039	2.54	1	0.39	0.91	1	1.09
50.8	2	.079	5.08	2	0.79	1.83	2	2.19
76.2	3	.118	7.62	3	1.18	2.74	3	3.28
101.6	4	.157	10.16	4	1.57	3.66	4	4.37
127.0	5	.197	12.70	5	1.97	4.57	5	5.47
152.4	6	.236	15.24	6	2.36	5.49	6	6.56
177.8	7	.276	17.78	7	2.76	6.40	7	7.66
203.2	8	.315	20.32	8	3.15	7.32	8	8.75
228.6	9	.354	22.86	9	3.54	8.23	9	9.84

g		oz	kg		lb	km		miles
28.35	1	.04	0.45	1	2.20	1.61	1	0.62
56.70	2	.07	0.91	2	4.41	3.22	2	1.24
85.05	3	.11	1.36	3	6.61	4.83	3	1.86
113.40	4	.14	1.81	4	8.82	6.44	4	2.48
141.75	5	.18	2.27	5	11.02	8.05	5	3.11
170.10	6	.21	2.72	6	13.23	9.65	6	3.73
198.45	7	.25	3.18	7	15.43	11.26	7	4.35
226.80	8	.28	3.63	8	17.64	12.87	8	4.97
255.15	9	.32	4.08	9	19.84	14.48	9	5.59

ha		acres	Metric to imperial conversion formulae	
0.40	1	2.47		multiply by
0.81	2	4.94	cm to inches	0.3937
1.21	3	7.41	m to feet	3.281
1.62	4	9.88	m to yards	1.094
2.02	5	12.36	km to miles	0.6214
2.43	6	14.83	km^2 to square miles	0.3861
2.83	7	17.30	ha to acres	2.471
3.24	8	19.77	g to ounces	0.03527
3.64	9	22.24	kg to pounds	2.205

1 ANDALUCÍA

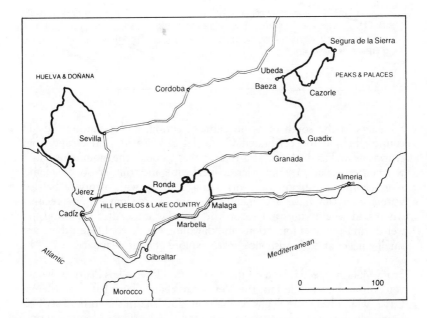

This is quintessential Romantic Spain where flowers and fountains spill onto tile-cooled courtyards and gypsy guitars string the warm nights. Dark-eyed girls sit in groups to clap the flamenco rhythms the same way their grandmothers did. Can the coastal highrise apartments crammed full of sunburnt grannies from Northern Europe really be within an hour's drive? They are, and the main road west from Málaga (the notorious N-340) has been nicknamed the Motorway Mortuary due to the number of tourists who have succumbed to the spell of sherry and sunshine and not kept their wits on the road. The sun shimmers off the whitewashed pueblos which cluster under Moorish castles on random crags, and I like to think that 'Anda Luz' (which can translate roughly as 'Walk, light') describes the extraordinary incandescence of the region's air and is not just a haphazard placename derived from the Arabic.

13

Hill Pueblos and Lake Country

3 days/410km/from Málaga

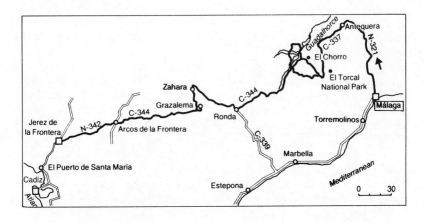

Summers in the south of Spain can be searing, and exploring the hill country behind the celebrated Costa del Sol provides an escape from crowds as well as the heat. This road snakes through the mountains and if you bother to pack a simple picnic (local wine and fruit, crusty bread and spicy *chorizo*, the ubiquitous pork sausage, along with plenty of bottled water), you can have a tremendous sense of freedom eating precisely when and where you want to on the first day out. After exploring the weird wind-sculpted formations and dawdling beside cool lakes, there are small villages and Moorish alcázars to explore at your own pace.

From Málaga, speed inland on the N-321 until Puerto Las Pedrizas, where you will find a wayside inn, the **Venta La Yedra**. Turn left. The **Menga Cave**, which has petroglyphs dating from 2500BC in the form of stylised human figures and solar symbols, is posted as a National Monument and can be found just beyond the great Bimbo Bread Factory. Entry fee is a mere 25 pesetas. Nearby, the **Viera Cave** is smaller and has a gallery of monoliths. Continue back along the road through Antequera.

ANTEQUERA pop: 41,000 Tourist Office: Coso Viejo (84 21 80). It is best to follow roadsigns directing you towards Seville to avoid getting lost in this busy town, known for its leather tanning industry. If you want to linger, the Renaissance style Najera Palace, housing the Municipal Museum (visiting hours 11–1 and 4.30–6.30) is worth a visit in the town centre. Efebo, an exquisite life-sized bronze statue in Spanish/Roman style which dates back two millennia, is the most unusual exhibit. In the same neighbourhood are the 16th-century San Sebastián Church and the Church of Carmen (open 10–1 and 3–7) noted for a chiaroscuro panel and its Mudéjar architecture. The Arc of the Giants (built by Moors in 1585) and the Church of Santa María La Mayor are nearby, on a rise

14

which provides fine views of the whitewashed houses and many of the 26 stone convents and churches. Santa María has become an art restoration centre, where stone masonry, woodwork and ironwork are taught, and the intricate and accurate results are on view. Ruins of the 16th-century Arab fortress, restored by Philip II, can also be toured. Prehistoric dolmen burial chambers on the outskirts, on the road back to Granada, need repair but are easily accessible.

On the edge of town, the state **parador** (84 02 61) also runs several hostals; **Manxanito** and **La Yedra** are preferred. The local specialities are *porra de antequera*, a thick piquant gazpacho garnished with ham and hardboiled eggs. Try *bienmasabe* for afters: concocted from almonds, lemon, sugar, cinnamon and rich egg yolk.

Leaving Antequera, turn left on the C-337. Continue on for 13km west, until reaching El Puerto de Boca del Asno (Pass of the Ass's Mouth), following the signs marked Albergue. **El Torcal de Antequera**, a national park, will be posted. The hiking trail indicated with yellow arrows takes about 1½ hours to complete, while the more taxing red trail takes 3. Wind- and rain-sculpted limestone, cunningly titled for those who need an aid to imagination and can speak Spanish, form a surreal background to wildlife ranging from shy green lizards to eagles and hawks. The most impressive of the rock formations has been dubbed 'the amphitheatre', and its tiers are just visible from the back below the refuge. Hikers are warned not to attempt the trail in sandals — not only is there apt to be loose sand which requires a bit of a scramble, but an occasional viper or scorpion lurks in a rock crevice. Sharp winds can also whip through the shadowy passages, so a sweater or light jacket is advisable. The yellow trail ends in a grand finale along a south-facing bluff which overlooks Villanueva de Concepción. A panorama stretching beyond the Costa del Sol to the Mediterranean can be enjoyed on a clear day.

From El Torcal, drive on to Alora, where the road forks. The left turn leads to the Moorish fortress guarding over the town; more historic turrets await farther on, so take the road on the far right towards the **El Chorro Gorge**. Climb gently through small holdings of almond and olive until the valley narrows and expansive citrus orchards, mainly Marife oranges, line the road. Hairpin turns around sheer granite cliffs begin to make for slow and cautious progress, especially when a coach comes lumbering unexpectedly at the next blind curve. Courage. Pull off just past the power station wherever there's room on the shoulder and look down, way down: over 200m of sheer rockface soar above the river, and the gorge which cuts it is a mere 10m across in places. Almost as amazing is a railway tunnel bored through the stone. Just a few kilometres down the road, the strange karstic outcroppings which twist and tower in El Torcal reappear, though here the government has planted hectares of pine to curtail the erosion of centuries. The landscape is less stark. Accommodation for non-campers is available high above the El Chorro station at **La Almona**, with self-catering apartments and cottages let out on a weekly basis by an English couple during the late March–late October season. (No phone.

Write Barbara Hands, La Almona, El Chorro, Málaga.)

Bobastro, an old Mozarab enclave, sits atop a small mountain just a few kilometres detour off the main road. Turn left onto a small paved road and follow it past the reservoir. An obscure sign points off to the pine trees: park here and walk about 400m down the slope. The gargantuan boulder blocking the path has been carved into an entire church, complete with delicate arches and a round window. Omar Ben Hafsum, the Christian convert who ruled Bobastro in the 9th century as an independent kingdom, freed from the caliphate in Córdoba, is entombed here. His castle, on the site of an earlier Roman settlement — Bobastrense —, was reputedly the most impregnable in all Andalucía, but today stands in ruins. Head back to the main road towards the Conde de Guadalhorce dam and turn right at the crossroads.

ICONA maintains a public park on the shores of a large lake, stocked with black bass and carp, where picnickers and campers are welcome. Past the park is a restaurant (**El Oasis**) with a fireplace and a view over the river. The road loops around the trio of lakes (the drinking water supply for Málaga) and there is much scope for hiking and fossil hunting in the countryside. Return to the crossroads and head straight for **ARDALES**, clustered beneath a Moorish fortress which, along with the castle at Turon, protected Ben Hafsum's kingdom. From here, adventurous drivers can proceed directly to the pretty walled village of **EL BURGO**, following the C-344 which testifies to the inaccessible roads that made these mountains the haunts of bandits and smugglers. One can also continue back first to **CARRATRACA**, an old spa town which still has a pink Victorian city hall which hints at the recent past when Lord Byron, Alexander Dumas and the Spanish nobility sported in the sulphur baths. From here, a steep road descends to **ALORA**, where the landscape finally levels out to tame wheatfields. From there, take the MA-403 and then the MA-404 up to El Burgo.

Follow the C-344, past the primitive *pinsapo* pines unique to this region and keep on the lookout for wild Iberian mountain goats, until reaching Ronda.

RONDA pop: 31,383 Tourist Office: Plaza del Mercado, 1. Well known to aficionados of the bullfight as the birthplace of the modern *corrida*, Ronda gained international renown after Rainer Maria Rilke, the German poet, stayed here and extolled the dramatic landscape. The town is cloven in half by the Guadalevin River, which runs some 160m below the Tajo, the steep promontory. The three-arched bridge (Puente Nuevo) is a good vantage point for the dizzying view of the ravine. Coachloads of tourists up for an outing from the Costa may be bothersome after you have had the hinterlands to yourself, but Ronda is worth sharing with rubbernecks. Aside from the historic bullring which dates from 1785 and is almost a shrine for classicists, most of the sites are not in the Mercadillo, but in La Ciudad, the old walled town. The Collegiate Church. Mondragón Palace (residence of the Catholic kings), Casa del Rey Moro (which has lofty views from the gardens over the old Roman bridge) and Moorish Baths all merit a visit. Wander down the narrow streets of the old town, especially the Carrera de Espinel with its unusual wrought iron balconies, and seek out the Marquess of Salvatierra's palace for a look at the 'savage couples' carved on the windows. **Don Miguel** (Villanueva, 4; 87 10 90) is a somewhat pricey restaurant with views over the Tajo and serves decent regional food, with roast lamb (*cordero*) a speciality. Inexpensive *tapas* bars close to the bullring have less atmosphere but are better value for money, with the bonus of smug satisfaction that comes from dining cheaply with the locals.

Leave Ronda on the C-339, winding past cliffs of dark pink and grey, and distant olive groves, until you spot a lone tower on a pinnacle, with tile-roofed white houses sheltering beneath. This is **ZAHARA** — 'flower' in Arabic. Turn left on the short, steep C-531 and find a place to park near the main square. This pueblo is best seen on foot. Grouse are hung in doorways, fattening up in their tight cages for someone's Sunday supper and their grunts make a doomed bass note to counter the trills of the pet canaries. Black grilled windows trail red and pink geraniums and the village church has an unusual steeple of blue and white tiles which stands out amongst all the ochre roofs. Only one tower remains of the original Roman fortress after fierce battles between Moors and Christians in the 15th century, and the Arab legacy can be seen in the door knockers: graceful hands of Fatima, clutching a round ball, still ward off the Evil Eye on many doorways. **Hostal Marqués de Zahara**, which has a typical open-air patio, is a pleasant place for coffee and can provide rooms for the night.

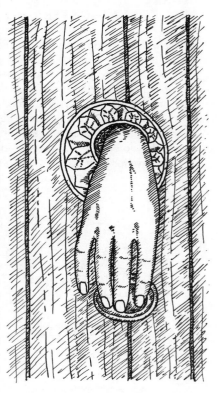

Door knocker in the form of the graceful hand of Fatima

Descend the hill and take the twisting road through the Puerto de las Palomas (pass of the doves), up to the Boyar Pass — soaring 110m, it has a sweeping panorama — and on to **GRAZALEMA**. This village is famed for fine wool blankets, and also for being one of the rainiest spots in southern Spain. With feet tucked beneath a heavy tablecloth, toasting around a central charcoal brazier in March, we watched hailstones bounce off the rooftiles like beads from a broken rosary. The bodega sells a smooth local wine, golden and slightly fortified, which takes the chill off the looming mountains. Local bakeries make 'cubiletes', an unusual light pastry with a melon filling. Nuestra Señora de la Aurora (Our Lady of the Dawn), an 18th-century church, has a splendid cupola and an Arab bridge spans the spring-fed stream. **Hostal Grazalema** (956 111342) right in the village is comfortable. When it does warm up in summer, there is an open-air community swimming pool which might give flatlanders vertigo with its staggering views of mountains.

The road to **EL BOSQUE** (C-344) provides distant views of oak and pine forests, with white pueblos and lakes glinting in the sun. Long-horned cattle sometimes challenge cars for roadspace, so take blind curves gingerly. If you long for more adventurous fare after the plain grilled meat served at most of Andalucía's eateries, try **Las Truchas** (72 30 86 x61; closed Nov) for trout. Best style is to have a thin slice of serrano ham tucked inside. Good rooms are available here. But more elegant accommodation can be had at the National Parador just outside Arcos de la Frontera (**Parador Casa del Corregidor**, 70 05 00).

ARCOS DE LA FRONTERA pop. 25,000, probably the best known of the *pueblos blancos*, has a commanding view of the Guadalete River valley, with its far-off olive groves, tidy vegetable plots and horses dozing in the heat. Park near the Plaza del Cabildo. The stunning churches of Santa María (15th century) and St Peter (16th- and 18th-century towers) seem perched precariously too near the cliffs, and the town's faithful are split into fiercely rival parishes. Hooded Nazarene penitents emerge from these ornate doors during Easter Holy Week, trailing behind heavy wooden floats which bear the treasured icons of the churches. These are carried by dozens of volunteers, stifling under heavy velvet drapery, invisible save for their grubby trainers and an occasional hand grasping for

Arcos de la Frontera

a paper cup. Though this ritual parade is enacted with fervour and much heavy incense each Easter Week (Semana Santa) throughout Spain, it can be particularly poignant in Arcos where it keeps a community scale. A young boy soprano sings a lament as Santa María passes below his grilled window and the boisterous crowd is hushed. Not so the next morning, when a bull is let loose in the narrow streets. It's a spectacle where people go to be seen as much as to watch, taunt, run, yell, laugh and cringe.

Arcos, like many Andalucian villages, has a medieval Arab quarter walled off from the newer overspill of dwellings. In this case, the maze of cobbled alleyways is towards the top of a grand spiked rock. Just outside the new town are some classic 18th-century *cortijos*, large farm estates with embellished archways leading onto an inner patio, often with intricate glazed tilework and a decorative fountain beside a more utilitarian well and watering trough.

*Priego de Córdoba —
a typical fountain of the region*

Beyond Arcos, the road becomes tame again and the 31km along the N-342 speed past. Soon, urban traffic surrounds the car, confirming arrival in **JEREZ DE LA FRONTERA** pop: 176,238 Tourist Office: Alameda de Christina (34 20 37). The population here increases exponentially at the end of May, when the international Feria del Caballo (Horse Fair) gets in full swing. Though the town has an alcázar and four churches of architectural merit (Gothic: Sta María La Real; Mudéjar: San Dionisio; Isabeline: San Miguel; Baroque: San Marco), most travellers seek out the five big bodegas for a sherry tasting tour. Sherry is an anglicising of the old placename, Xeres, which goes back to 1608, though the English shippers helped build up the industry here in the late 18th century. Only Sandeman requires prior arrangement — 24 hours — to see the processing of the fortified wine. Otherwise, except on Sundays, simply turn up on the morning, or try again after siesta. During the September Wine Harvest Festival, all aspects of the wine-making are on view and a flamenco fest adds to the exuberance.

Huelva and Coto Doñana

3 days/335km/from Seville

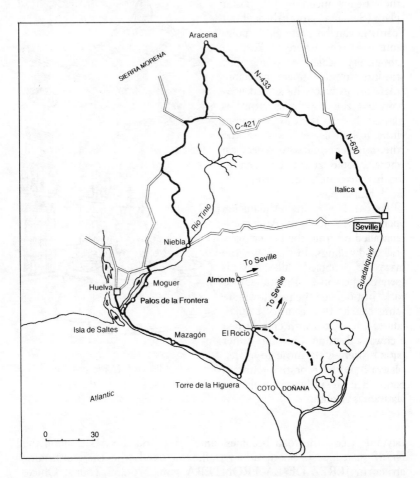

Columbus and his crew set out from Huelva province, but few people have bothered to make it a destination, despite the fact that it is not far from the river border with Portugal's Algarve. Here, it's time warp rather than time-share. New industries are strawberry and oyster farming, and there is some stirring to get ready for a salute to Columbus 500 years on. Nearby, the Doñana marshes form a grand ecological preserve, where thousands of migrating birds stop over on flights between Africa and Europe. They are also home to lynx, fox, badgers and, during the day, a handful of travellers and students of ecology. Northwards, the Rio Tinto copper and pyrite mines lay bare the bright viscera of Spain's geology, before cork and eucalyptus forests cloak it again on the approach to Aracena. A cavern here reveals pastel grottos that extend for a kilometre.

SEVILLE pop: 653,833 Tourist Office: Queipo de Llano, 9B or AmEx, Hernando Colon, 1. To southern Spain's Grand Dame, visitors are not the number one concern, though her elegant boulevards, sunwarmed plazas, and the way oranges dangle ripe from pavement trees like so many Christmas baubles have drawn admirers for centuries. Do take time to tour the Giralda Tower and massive Cathedral, see the Alcázar and walk about the old Santa Cruz quarter, peering in the patios and listening to the canaries and fountains. The Casa de Pilatos, with its extraordinary tilework, is worth a visit, and the Fine Arts Museum, in an old Merced convent, has a striking collection of paintings by Murillo and Zurbaran. The Indies Archives in the Archaeological Museum, open mornings only from 10–2, holds maps and ancient 'intelligence documents' which trace the discovery and conquest of the Americas. When the urban pace and crowds begin to grate, it is time to leave Seville for more rural destinations.

Take the Merida Road (N-630) north, 9km, and turn off just past Santiponce towards the ruins of **ITALICA**, the large Roman town where Emperor Hadrian was born. After viewing the amphitheatre, climb the hill, picking through the network of old streets, and see the mosaics at the very top. A clear vista way across the Guadalquivir Plain gives an odd sense of time and distance stretching. The quiet is broken only by insects and distant traffic. On the far side of the highway, excavation of the theatre is still in progress. Entry to the site is 100 pesetas, and it closes at dusk.

Branch off on the left highway towards Lisbon (N-433), and travel 81 quick km along a good road. The Sierra Morena along here is green with eucalyptus and cork oak, which has an odd look about the graceful limbs once the bark has been trimmed away for processing, almost as if the branches are draped in lady's long evening gloves. **ARACENA**, a pretty terraced town, is topped by what remains of a Knight Templars' castle. One tower is a convert; once a minaret, it still is carved in the Almohad style (seen at its peak of development in Seville's Giralda) but only on the north side. The Church of the Castillo dates from the 13th century and boasts a beautiful Baroque altarpiece. Beneath the castle are 'Marvellous Grottoes', which do actually live up to their billing, as if some resident magician remodelled the basement over the centuries to keep his spells up to scratch. Only in 1914, when they drained off the underground river that carved the cavern, did the full impact of the narrow caves with their tall multicoloured formations capture the popular imagination. The first chamber is dubbed '*El Pozo de la Nieve*' (Snow well), after the bright white of its stalagtites. Do not spurn what looks like a tourist trap restaurant here: **Casas** (Pozo de la Nieve, 36; 11 00 44) dishes up regional cooking with panache. The fresh goat cheese is especially good, as is the moist acorn-fed ham (*jamón jabugo*). This is regarded as a treat and a delicacy throughout Spain.

On the drive south, the dense pines stop sharply and the huge opencast mines of **RIO TINTO** stain the waters below, proving that their name is the obvious choice. Most of the copper comes from a 600m deep gouge, while silver, gold and copper are mined from a second cut and pyrites from a third. Bella Vista, a leafy English colony complete with club, is a holdover from the last century when English bankers, heading an international consortium, bought out the mines. Football was one of their lasting cultural contributions to the community. Take the secondary road through Campofrio, turning onto the C-421 at El Campillo. Join the main road briefly, turning off at Valverde, towards **NIEBLA**, where the River Tinto passes. Stout walls, over 15m thick, protect the old town which is approached through four gateways. A Moorish capital, Niebla held out nine months against a Christian siege that saw the first use of gunpowder on the Iberian peninsula. Ultimately, it fell in 1257.

Follow the main highway, turning across the bridge just pass Candón. Vines are everywhere. Besides traditional use in sherry, Zalema grapes are now fermented into a light white table wine for immediate use, an innovation by local vintners who are seeing many of the old vines ripped up and replaced by the cash crop of the 1980s, strawberries.

In **MOGUER**, a busy port where 16th-century conquistadors left the Old World behind for the New, the Gothic convent of Santa Clara is noteworthy. The church, where Columbus worshipped upon return from his first voyage, holds exquisite alabaster tombs of the convent's founders just under the niches. The high street is named for Spain's literary Nobel prizewinner, poet Juan Ramón Jiménez. His modest house is now a museum, open to the public.

Down the road, the historic port of **PALOS DE LA FRONTERA** is frankly a letdown. The harbour that saw Columbus — Cristóbal Colón in the Spanish world — and his three ships set out for parts unknown is now silted up, the river polluted. A new white monument outside San Jorge Church lists 35 voyagers who set sail from Palos, amongst them Hernán Cortés, conqueror of Mexico. The brickwork fountain, now restored but utterly dry, once filled water casks before the crews set off exploring. The woods nearby must have provided masts for the ships. At least Columbus' family home, no 38, still exists on the main street of Palos.

LA RÁBIDA Monastery still retains some of the atmosphere of those times when Columbus was dismissed as crazy rather than brave. Legend has it that he arrived by foot at the cross, pleading at the door for bread and water for his son. The Franciscans gave him refuge, and today will guide you around where the astronomer priest, Antonio de Marchena, and the Prior, Juan Pérez, listened to Columbus expound his theory of sailing west to reach the East. Their support was crucial in getting royal backing for the voyages, overriding charges of blasphemy and the usual commercial caution. A small museum contains replicas of the three sailing ships, maps and books. Across the modern bridge is **HUELVA**, the provincial capital.

HUELVA pop: 127,806 Tourist information: Plus Ultra, 10 (24 50 92). This industrial port city doesn't reveal its true age, as most of its buildings were flattened in 1755 by the same earthquake which damaged Lisbon. It overlooks the Isle of Saltes, caught in the confluence of the Tinto and Odiel Rivers, which is held to have been part of the Trojan Empire. Quite a number of scientists have sought Atlantis close by. The mineral riches certainly attracted Phoenicians, Romans and then the Moors, who were expelled in the 13th century. Three churches here date from the 16th century, but more striking, due to size and sheer oddity, is the 40m sculpture staring out to sea which the United States erected in 1929 to celebrate its discoverers. A petrochemical plant on the coast nearby is another reminder of just what Columbus helped unleash. There are a number of comfortable if characterless hotels in the city.

Best to proceed to the more remote **Parador** at **MAZAGÓN (Cristóbal Colón,** 37 60 00), just 24km east along the coast road near a small pine wood. Beaches along here, as port industry gets left behind, are broad, sandy, and mostly deserted. Continue along to **TORRE DE LA HIGUERA**, named for one of a series of Moorish lookout towers along the coast which kept watch for Barbary pirates after the Reconquest. **MATALASCAÑAS**, a highrise tourist complex here, is an eyesore on this almost virgin coast, but tasty seafood can be found at **El Ciervo Azúl** (Avda de Adelfas, 2; 43 00 68; shut all winter). The local favourite, cuttlefish, isn't ordered much by outsiders. The complex comes just to the edge of the protected shores of the **Coto Doñana** where winds push the sand dunes inland up to 6km, in peaked sets like breakers. The peaks build higher and more precarious until finally they are anchored by dune grass or umbrella pine. With extensive saltmarsh, dunes and thickets of umbrella pine, cork oak and scrub, Doñana is one of Europe's most important ecological preserves. To arrange a visit here, phone ahead to secure a place (43 04 32, 24hr answerphone). Then proceed inland up the Rocío road. At the first left turn, by a salty lagoon, is **EL ACEBUCHE**, an information centre for the national park. If it's Monday, you will need to drive up the 12km to the main entrance in El Rocío, called La Rocina. It is open daily, though it does shut down for a long siesta between 1.30 and 4 pm. Park entrance fee is 900 pesetas. Because the balance of nature on the dunes and saltmarshes is not up to supporting onslaughts of camera-toting tourists, there is a quota of 56 visitors at any one time, with two sessions daily. Landrovers and micro-buses set out from the centre (the park extends some 50,000 hectares) and there are observation posts to spy the shyer creatures. Great flocks of flamingo and spoonbill, birds of prey, geese, ducks, storks: up to 200,000 birds of 150 different species crowd the skies during peak migration times. Mammals range from lynx, boar and stag to weasels and the dormouse. Reptiles and amphibians abound, as do (ahem) insects. Mosquitoes easily outnumber the birds, so come prepared.

EL ROCÍO, the nearest settlement to the Park, is practically as quiet as the swamps unless you happen to arrive during Pentecost. For three days, throngs of Andalucíans — including 70 brotherhoods — converge on the town in pilgrimage to the Virgin of El Rocío. Some come in dotty 'carretas', like flamenco-style covered wagons, complete with flounces.

Others arrive on horseback or foot. Drums and flutes pace their plodding. Finally, after up to a million people have arrived on the final day, church bells peal and firecrackers explode as the carved image is carried from its hermitage on walkabout for 12 hours. This 'Romeria' fiesta has been going since the 13th century, when a shepherd supposedly found the image in a hollow tree, tried to carry it up to **ALMONTE**, the next village, but discovered that the Virgin preferred her chosen place of apparition when she reappeared there, unassisted. There she stays, and a traveller who stares at the impassive carved face behind the iron railings of the hermitage is hard-pressed to explain the almost pagan veneration. There are a number of quiet hotels in the village which cater for Park visitors.

Peaks and Palaces

4 days/485km/from Granada

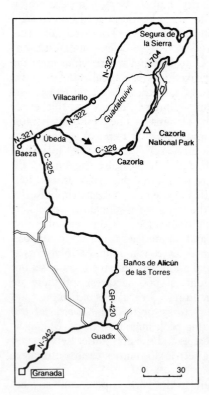

This road cuts through the centuries, scrambling one's sense of time as it reveals stark contrasts of scenery. Set out from the last stronghold of the Moors in the snow-capped Sierra Nevada, and go on past cave dwellings with all modern conveniences, driving north to take a leisurely 'cure' in hot springs. A stately Renaissance town of palaces and grand churches gives way to vast holdings of olive groves, where orderly rows of silvery trees stretch beyond the horizon, and only the hills distort the strict geometry laid on the chalky earth. Abruptly, cultivation halts and wilderness reigns in the mountains. The Cazorla Sierra is a preserve where eagles soar above hidden springs and the Great Guadalquivir River issues forth a mere trickle. Wild boar, deer and mountain goats roam at will, though there are hunters stalking parts of these peaks as well. Isolated castles guard domains long gone. And downrange, save for the computerised slot machines in the bars, the old towns could be locked into a distant past.

GRANADA pop: 262,182 Tourist Office: Casa de los Tiros, Pavaneros, 19. In haste to explore rural routes, don't give this city short shrift. Even midwinter, when the magnificent Generalife Gardens are less lush, the hillsides beyond the red walls of the Alhambra Palace are touched with almond blossom and the Sierra Nevada mountain range is as bright as a freshly whitewashed wall against the piercing blue sky. In fact, on a clear day it's worth a daytrip detour to drive up the Sierra Nevada road GR-420, the highest in Europe (only 66km return) and head for Solynieve, a slick ski resort. From here, ride the cable car to the Veleta peak. The view sweeps down to the coast, across the straits of Gibraltar to the very tips of the Rif Mountains in North Africa. Rulers in the Alhambra used to send 'neveros' to the sierra and await saddlebags packed with pure snow even at the height of summer. Mixed with crushed grenadine (pomegranate) or oranges from the pleasure gardens, the snow provided some of the first sorbet in Europe. The rustic meals of roast chicken or *choto* (tender young kid) in the mountain inns are a far cry from such bygone luxury, but a visit to the Alhambra Palace back in Granada can summon it up. Decorative arts — plaster and stucco stalagtites of mind-boggling intricacy — reached an apex here, and the Lion Court, for example, has a symmetry rarely equalled. Allow at least half a day for even a cursory look at the Alhambra and Generalife, and don't miss the Palace of Carlos V. Do be prepared to dodge scores of carnation-hawking, palmreading gypsies. Best way to avoid a curse is to indulge the first woman who approaches and then wear the carnation in a conspicuous place: proof that you've already been had.

Take time to explore the Cathedral quarter, including the Capilla Real (royal chapel). The Carthusian Monastery, Churches of San Juan de Dios and San Jeronimo, and the Moorish Baths, all merit a visit. One of the best views back to the Alhambra is from the San Nicolás terrace on the Albaicín Hill (access through the Cuesta del Chapiz). This was the final Arab retreat when Christians came to reconquer in 1492. The **Parador Nacional de San Francisco** (22 14 93) holds the 33 most sought after tourist rooms in all Spain, and only luck, or careful advance planning, can secure a reservation. **Los Angeles** (Cuesta Escoriaza, 17; 22 14 24) is an unpretentious but comfortable hotel and has good views towards the mountains, clean bathrooms, and easy access back to the road, avoiding the worst of fierce city centre traffic.

Leaving Granada, however reluctantly, follow the signs towards Murcia (the N-342). After the Puerto La Mora, the green plain becomes a dun-coloured plateau on the approach to **PURULLENA**, where there is a well-established colony of troglodytes. All preconceptions about 'cave men' are quashed; these subterranean homes are cool, clean, and many sport television aerials. Rocks around the entrances are whitewashed, as are the distinctive conical chimneys. The true centre of cavedwelling is just down the road in **GUADIX**, where almost half the citizens live in a warren of individually crafted caves. The town, whose roots go back into prehistory, first shot to prominence during Roman and Visigoth times.

Though it has finally grown beyond the boundaries of successive walls (Las Murallas), Guadix does not sprawl. Its urban caves, hollowed out of the soft tufa stone, have supported a vital community — now numbering over 6,000 — since the Reconquest of the Catholic Kings, which literally sent the Arab population underground. At the far end of the Santiago Road, the kitchen chimneys and elaborated entrances to the caves emerge level to the paths, shaded occasionally by dusty fig trees. Most are oriented towards the east or south, for maximum light. Each cave has a single wooden outside door, while interior rooms are simply curtained, to aid ventilation. The floors are mostly of paving stones or quarry tiles, though a few more humble caves have earthen floors. The cavedwellers are quite used to visitors wanting a look around, and some will oblige for a small gratuity. A pleasant amber light filters through the caves, and even the back rooms are far from murky. But what a contrast to the sundazzled balcony on the palace of the Marquess of Cortés and Graena, or to the intricate Baroque façade on the Cathedral. *Tocinos del cielo* (translation: bacons from the sky!) is the local speciality, an unusual cinnamon-scented egg custard, heavy enough to slice.

Proceed towards the village of Benalúa de Guadix, then up a secondary road to **BAÑOS DE ALICÚN DE LAS TORRES**. Two outdoor thermal pools are open all year round, protected by the hills of Mencal. The waters have been declared a public utility since 1869. The pools, revamped in 1985, are vast. Mudbaths and massages can be arranged. The **Hostal Residencia Reina Isabel** (69 40 22) is quite comfortable. Such an indulgence for driver's fatigue! The road follows north along the Fardes River, up to the Villanueva de las Torres, where luscious local peaches are sold from roadside stands in high summer. Fork left towards

The Gaudix caves, Andalucía

Dehesas de Guadix and Estación de Cabra (goat station), and take the rugged road through Cabra de Sto. Cristo. Join up with the C-325 there, and drive north to Úbeda.

ÚBEDA pop: 30,100 Tourist Office: Plaza de los Caidos, 2 (75 08 97). A large portion of the citizenry in Úbeda seem to be clergy, but that is fitting enough in a town where the main square keeps a perfectly preserved Renaissance elegance. The narrow streets of the remainder seem dull by comparison, except where they overlook the surrounding landscape. The **Parador Condestable Davolos** (75 03 45) is impressive and usually has rooms available, perhaps because this corner of Jaén province is still relatively undiscovered by tourists. Just left from the parador is the El Salvador Church, built for family worship by Francisco de los Cobos, secretary of state to Carlos V and the Holy Roman Empire. On the right is the Casa de las Cadenas (House of Chains), built by the same noble family, this time for the nephew, secretary to Felipe II. This square, Plaza Vázquez de Molina, is named for him. Directly across from the parador is the Santa María Church, built atop the former mosque. The Casa de los Salvajes, with reliefs of a couple clad in animal skins and girded with bramble belts, recalls a similar window carving in Ronda. Just outside the old city walls, on Calle Valencia, potters make the distinctive green-glazed local ceramics. Tightly woven baskets and mats of esparto grass are still exported as they were in the 12th century when the Moors ruled supreme. But the major industry here is pressing olive oil, as the ancient olive groves that cover the hillsides attest. The virgin olive oil — now sold locally as Oro de la Loma — has been famous for millennia and sharp Italian dealers have bought it cheaply and resold it as their own. Olive oil snobs should stock up before leaving town.

Drive through the groves on the N-322 to Torreperogil, where you turn towards the mountains. Continue through Peal de Becerro, an unexciting village, and turn left on the C-328 towards **CAZORLA**.

Gateway to the wilderness area, Cazorla is an unselfconsciously pretty village, with steep streets running in all directions. Mountain crags 2,000m above somehow beckon rather than loom. Five convents jostle for space with simple houses of white stucco or stone. The river cuts the village in half, so most alleyways dead-end with no warning. Beware a *callejón*, for it means a street with no exit. Two turkeys chortled at my predicament when I was forced to reverse up a 30° slope or stay forever wedged beside a white wall. Best to park in the Santa María Plaza, near the ruins of the old church. My visit coincided with All Saints Day, and the shops were selling marzipan *brazos del santo*, slightly macabre sweets with a lemon curd filling meant to be the marrow in the bone of the saint's arm. More usual dishes are *ajo blanco*, white garlic in cream, *gachamiga*, a wheaty porridge garnished with hot peppers and bacon, as well as roast game, especially rabbit and venison in season. This is apt to be fresh and not hung in accordance to English taste, so adjust the taste-buds. Two hostals right in town are inexpensive and clean, and a

National Parador, El Adelantado (72 10 75) is found outside town, clearly marked on its own road in the midst of the Sierra. Unlike most paradors, this is not in an historic dwelling and the ambience is more like a lodge for avid hunters and fishermen.

Camping is encouraged in the National Park between the Cañada de las Fuentes and the Tranco Dam, with sites set out beside pre-chopped firewood. (This prevents eager woodsmen from felling green trees, the government gamekeepers explain.) Herons and otters prowl the streams for fat trout, while the skies are patrolled by eagles, hawks and the rare bearded vulture — lammergeyer — whose wingspan can be 3m across. Stags, mountain goats and huge wild boar inhabit the glens and the rocky outcrops. The isolated 80km × 30km zone was set aside as a wilderness preserve in February 1986, yet if one keeps to the main route, a roadside bar is never far away. Guides can be arranged for hiking in the farthest reaches, but most hikers on their own could find their way to the spring which eventually becomes Spain's most famous river, the Guadalquivir. As it grows and is tamed into reservoirs (one islet in the midst of a lake holds the remains of Bujaraiza Castle), the J-704 road stays steadfastly beside it. Go through Tranco, turn right and continue to **HORNOS**. From two lookout points in this village, one sheltered from the elements, there are particularly fine views: the length of the river valley with the limestone mountains reflected in the lakes. Cobbled streets lined with carved wooden doors that sport fine brass knockers lead to a pleasant town square (Plaza Mayor). Descend to the road and backtrack to the fork, where a right turn leads to **SEGURA DE LA SIERRA**, with its castle on a high crest. Here the wilderness recedes, for Segura's roots go far back in time. Silver and iron mines, exploited by Romans and Phoenicians, are said to be close by. Visigoths ruled here until the Moors ousted them in the 8th century, extending the emirate of Córdoba. The town was burned to the ground by Napoleon's troops, but the Arab fortress, if anything over-restored today, still stands. A bullring (with square corners) is partly carved from rock and lies at its base. It still sees service during October, when the village celebrates its fiesta.

ORCERA, the next town, was once known for its woodsmen and lumberjacks. Its 16th-century church reflects former glory and riches. During September, bulls are let loose in the narrow sloping streets as they are in **VILLACARILLO**, a larger town on the N-322, heading back to civilisation. The entire mountain range towers over hills dotted with endless olives and from the car it appears as if a backdrop painted by an obsessive pointillist was commissioned for this road, which seems to fly past after the tight curves of the Sierra. Watch for potholes. By-pass Úbeda and veer off on the N-321, to **BAEZA**, whose monuments are just as proudly preserved.

BAEZA pop: 14,799 Tourist Office: Plaza de los Leones, Casa de Populo. This deceptively peaceful town, with ornate palaces, mansions and a university, all built of toffee-coloured stone that catches the light, was an important capital under the Moors and, after recapture in 1227, it was in the front line of the Christian Reconquest. With the peace that followed came prosperity and Baeza developed into an intellectual centre: a printing press was set up in 1551, followed by a university. Learning still goes on in the ancient classrooms, now a high school, and the celebrated Spanish poet, Antonio Machado, taught French grammar there from 1912 to 1919. Students at the Seminary, in Plaza Santa María, would traditionally inscribe their names and graduation date in bull's blood on the left wall, so today it holds four centuries of curious graffiti. Romanesque arches, Gothic vaulting and Plateresque windows occur throughout the town and modern businesses don't detract from them: it requires some searching to find a cold beer (*cerveza*) without its being spelled out, but there are bars and cafés aplenty. Either ask or follow a thirsty-looking local. The cathedral is splendid, and its archives can be perused. The Jabalquinto Palace, Church of Santa Cruz, Town Hall and Jaén Gate are all rated as architectural treasures. Even the former slaughterhouse, in use from 1550 to 1962, is impressive with its imperial coat of arms. The **Hotel**

A whitewashed Pueblo Blanco, detail

Juanito (Avda Arca del Agua; 74 00 40) is small and friendly, and a **restaurant** of the same name (Paseo del Acre del Agua; 71 00 40) provides hearty regional meals.

2 THE BALEARIC ISLES

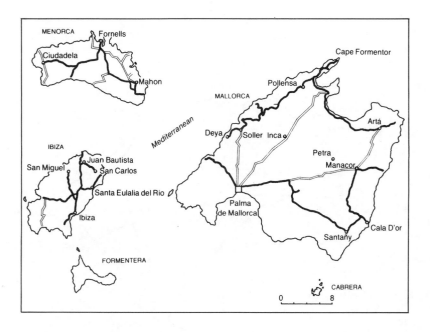

Majorca, Minorca, Ibiza, Cabrera and Formentera ... the quintet of Balearic Islands off the coast near Valencia have continued to be a key traveller destination since the Bronze Age, often visited by Phoenicians and figuring as a major stop on the hippie trail of the 1970s. The striking scenery and pleasant Mediterranean climate make it obvious why. Today, the airport at Mallorca (Majorca) logs as many international flights as Europe's busiest capitals, with charter flights bringing in crowds who push the beautiful people off the beaches and back aboard their yachts. With their reputation as a cheap destination for group tours to the sunshine and discos, it might seem terribly defeating to comb the islands for rural pleasures. Yet the 'beaten path' was trodden for good reason, and beyond the beaches are wooded mountains, herb-scented meadows, old monasteries, walled villages with labyrinthine streets, and quiet coves without a whiff of suntan oil about them. In a place where the locals dine on pig's knees

31

and starlings, the rural traditions are still vibrant.

Car ferry connections are most frequent to Palma de Mallorca, 9 hours from Barcelona or Valencia and 11 hours from Alicante. Barcelona also is 9 hours by boat from Mahón, Minorca's capital, or Ibiza. Alicante and Valencia are both 7 hours by boat from Ibiza. Inter-island connections are sporadic. For travellers in a hurry, reasonably priced late-night charter flights are on offer to all these cities.

Majorca Meander

2½ days/470km/from Palma de Mallorca

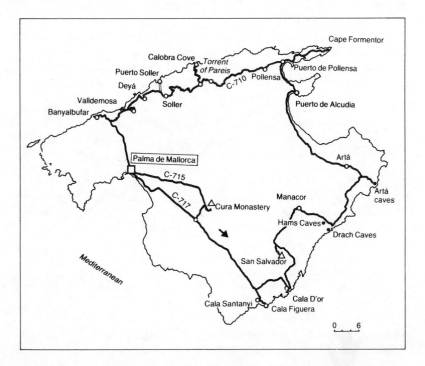

Highlands, monasteries, caves and coastlines ... all wound together by roads which climb and dip, sometimes spectacularly. The route passes by windmills, artesian wells, clumps of prickly pear, and groves of lemon, orange and ancient olives, gnarled into fanciful shapes that rival the con-cretions in the caves on the eastern coast.

PALMA DE MALLORCA pop: 304,442 Tourist Office: Avda Jaime III, 10 (21 22 16). Palma has got to be one of the most underrated places in Spain. Although more visitors pass through here than any other town in the nation, few stay. Seen from the harbour, it is striking: the huge cathedral (Renaissance portal, 15th century) makes it clear to any would-be marauders that this city has God on its side. And looking down on the highrise hotels is Bellver Castle, with pine-covered slopes falling steeply away on the west. Elegant old mansions in delicate Italian style mingle with the classic Majorcan houses of the 18th century, with their court-yards framed by thick marble columns, and stone steps accented with wrought iron tracery. The Genoese commercial exchange (*Lonja*) in Guillermo Sagrera's sober fortress-like building has military pretences, but inside are perfect proportions. The Royal Chapel boasts an enormous iron canopy over the altar cast by Antonio Gaudí. Churches and palaces are everywhere, and the mixed history of Palma, with its farflung trading partners in Africa and north Europe, is captured in stone. Even the Spanish Pueblo, with replicas of landmark houses from all regions of Spain, is not nearly as contrived as it sounds. Despite the costumed crafts-men at work and the roving folkloric dancers, it doesn't feel like Disney-land. A lively flea market springs up on Sundays. There are any number of restaurants, but **Violet** (Zanglada, 2; 22 17 92) deserves a splurge. The food is seasonal and inventive, served in an authentically refurbished small palace. No shortage of hotels and hostals in any price range.

Leave Palma by the east motorway (the airport signs will point the way at first) and follow the C-717 towards Lluchmajor, there turning and climb-ing to **RANDA**. The road spirals up the mountain, leading to the **Cura Monastery** (17th century). The library has manuscripts by Ramón Llul, one of the earliest missionary monk/scholars, who studied foreign languages in order to make converts through persuasion rather than the sword. Don't miss the west terrace, where the view extends from the city of Palma, to the harbour, the mountains, and even the northernmost tip of the island, Cape Formentor.

Backtrack down to the C-717 and head for the coast, speeding through Lluchmajor and Campos. Beyond Santanyi (Santány) are two coves: **Cala Santanyi** has the better beach, but **Cala Figuera**, with pines down to the waterside and a fishing fleet, is more picturesque. On return to the town of Santanyi, take the right fork and drive in the shadow of Puig Gros 9km towards Calonge. Here, turn off to **CALA D'OR**, a resort which is not yet overrun. A creek spills into a cove here, and the water is exceptionally clear. The sandy bottom is as golden as Palma's cathedral stone, and big boulders ring the inlet, which is also fringed by woods. After indulgence in sun and sea, return by the ridge road. Drive about 10km, then branch off to the left and take the tortuous curves up to the **Sanctuary of San Salvador**, 490m above. Founded in the 14th century, the monastery was rebuilt in the 18th. Pilgrims still come to venerate the statue of madonna and child behind the Baroque altarpiece. A splendid panorama of the mountain ridges to the east.

It's best to descend to the coast road, though drivers whose passengers have strong stomachs might opt for the mountain road snaking through **MANACOR** where they can reward themselves with a look around the 16th-century town hall, a Renaissance church and a small archaeological museum. **Fonda March** (Valencia, 7; 55 00 02) dishes up good fried seafood. From here, the road straightens out and the **Drach Caves** are 13km ahead. The coast road is almost as twisty, but glimpses of sea and small coves around every bend make it fun driving. Do be prepared for the occasional tour bus: the caves are a major excursion for more adventurous groups. Hour-long guided tours of the caves (cost 200 pesetas) may make you feel one of the herd, but the four chambers, with ceilings aglitter with thousands of sharp stalagtites, are majestically reflected in still pools. The tour ends with a short boat ride. Nearby, the **Hams Caves**, following the course of an underground river, are less impressive, much smaller, though the entrance fee is higher. Give them a miss. Follow the road through **PORTO CRISTO**, a self-conscious fishing village which profits from waves of tourists to the caves, and head towards Son Severa. Turn right here and follow the signs towards the **Caves of Arta**, along a breathtaking corniche road on the northern cape of Canyamel Bay. Gaping 35m above the sea, the mouth of the cave opens onto chambers with massive pillars inside. The ceiling is marked from hand-held torches used by last century's visitors. One chamber has been done up as 'Dante's Inferno'. Entrance fee is 150 pesetas.

Very narrow roads lead up to **CAPDEPERA**, where ruins of a 14th-century fortress guard the hillside. Within the ramparts is a restored chapel. The old sentry path overlooks the approach from the sea and small coves beneath. Palm frond baskets with a vaguely Polynesian air are hawked by the locals.

Back along the main C-715 road, drive 8km towards a lofty rock bearing a medieval castle and San Salvador Church. This is **ARTÁ** Along the road, just past the stone walls that divide the fields, are conical heaps of stone called *talayots*. These remnants of the Bronze Age sometimes covered funerary chambers, and five bronze warrior figurines, on display in the Artá Museum (Plaza de España, 4), were recovered from a *talayot* near Capdepera. Detouring just 2km inland, at **Ses Paisses**, an overgrown prehistoric site preserves a weird mural depicting a cyclops, and there are several excavated *talayots* nearby.

Head past the rice fields, brilliant green, towards **PUERTO DE ALCUDIA**. Boat trips to Barcelona or Minorca leave from this pine-bordered bay, and in the autumn dry season, when the wooded hills can suddenly blaze, sea planes bellydip into the wide bay and scoop up water to douse the fire. **ALCUDIA**, 2km up the road, still has its 14th-century walls. A Roman colony lived just south of the ramparts, where the church is, and a ruined theatre can still be seen.

Going past the Pollensa Bay, most of the wide beaches are hidden by lowrise tourist villas. The water is shallow, warm and very calm and has been sought out by novice waterskiers, windsurfers and sailors. **PUERTO DE POLLENSA**, with its yacht moorings, is a good spot for people watching, but intrepid travellers will be unable to resist the Cape. Go gingerly along the steep road, rising in hairpin turns through dry scrub. **Es Colomer Belvedere** is worth a stop, with a viewing table that looks out over a sheer drop. Park on the verge and take the stepped path alongside the precipice. After this, the route should inspire less vertigo. Continue until the road dips into a valley of oaks and pines and approaches a sheltered beach looking out on an islet: Formentor Beach. The **Hotel Formentor** (53 13 00) has 5-star luxury and its bright gardens contrast with the wildness all round. After the fraught journey, a little comfort seems deserved, so enjoy the sybaritic indulgence of beachside drinks. Prices match the ambience. Thriftier service is available at the opposite end of the crescent beach, at **Miguel** (Cala Pi; 66 13 09), though it is closed Mondays off-season and December through February. Once fortified for the drive, head through the tunnel and along the jagged crest out to the lighthouse at the extreme tip of **Cape**

*The coast of Mallorca —
Cape Formentor*

Formentor the most northerly point on the island. A dramatic 200m drop where the wall of grey rock hits the sea is awe inspiring.

Follow the road back along the mountain spine and continue inland to **POLLENSA**, with its squat houses of red stone. To the west is a cypress-bordered hill with impressive statues of the Crucifixion, while the Puig rises 320m in the east. The village boasts three old churches, two museums and a Roman bridge. Several good hotels are open in season (Apr–Oct) and the **Illa D'or** (Paseo Colon, 265; 53 11 00) offers rooms all year round.

A scenic journey overshadowed by the Tomir Ridge leads to a pass which overlooks the broad Pollensa Bay, before rising to the **Monastery of Our Lady of Lluch**. The 'Moraneta', a Gothic carved Virgin of dark wood, is smaller than the 14th-century alabaster statue of Sta. María, but it is to her that the pilgrims supplicate. The white statue is in the museum, alongside bronze figures found on the island, and not in the shrine. The monastery closes briefly for lunch, and entry fee is 100 pesetas. Simple shelters for the pilgrims line the road outside the monastery, though unused now.

Proceed down to Gorg Blau (Blue Gorge), where the road forks right to the **Calobra Cove** and the **Torrent of Pareis**. Accustomed now to the twisting curves of the road, drivers should still look out for rogue tour buses. Pass through oak forests and olive groves on the steep descent, ending up in a stark rockscape on the approach to **LA CALOBRA**. The Pareis River cuts through to the sea nearby, and a hike through two underground passages brings you to the white shingle beach, dotted with campers' tents, where the freshwater mingles with the sea. Concerts are held in summer and the acoustics off the cliffsides are quite special. Water is clear and fairly calm, though the pebbles require tough feet. Beachgoers seem to be mostly locals. A small hotel, **La Calobra** (51 70 16), offers rooms except in February and March. There are a number of seafood restaurants with open-air service.

The climb back up the narrow road is dominated by the mass of Puig Major, tallest peak on the island and a forbidding enough site for a military installation. Leave the course of the Pareis River, go through the long tunnel and branch left towards **FORNALUTX**. Continue straight through this village of steep cobbled streets to the smaller pueblo of **BINIARAIX**. On the outskirts are dozens of walled gardens, using ancient 'piedra seca' construction which depends on the careful stacking of the stones; no mortar keeps them in place. Olives, vines and grains are the main crops, and pink plumes of pampas grass wave sedately in the breezes. A grand 16th-century church is surrounded by ancient stone houses which date from the founding of the village, whose Arab name translates as 'Sons of the Cripple'. The sole café, which doubles as a tobacconists, is the meeting place for the poets, painters and occasional poseurs who seek out the untainted atmosphere of this small hamlet. Francisco Bernareggi, an Argentine painter friend of Picasso, was one of the founders of the small art colony here at the beginning of this century. There are no inns or restaurants.

The winding road to Soller looks out on the steep Alfabia Sierra before levelling out to a basin of orange and olive groves which surround the town. At the end of September, a bicycle race thoroughly slows progress on the roads as very tired cyclists wobble two or three abreast along the curves, cheered along by throngs of fans. In May, battles between Moors and Christians are enacted here in full costume. The main square is attractive and two churches and the 18th-century hospital merit a visit. Compared to the resort cum submarine base at the circular bay in **PUERTO DE SOLLER**, connected by a quaint Edwardian railway line, **SOLLER** is quiet. Simple restaurants and cafeterias are inexpensive and there are several unpretentious hostals.

Take the C-710 past Lluc-Alcari to **DEYA**, home of the late poet, Robert Graves. Red stone houses on hillsides wooded with oaks and conifers give it a mountain feel, while blossoming almond trees midst olive groves reassert the Mediterranean climate. Far below a steep path leads to a creek and a sliver of beach. A surprising number of expensive hotels have sprung up around the village.

Son Marroig, farther along the coast road, is an old mansion, former residence of Archduke Ludwig Salvator. His collections of archaeological finds, furniture, and Majorcan art are displayed alongside his own volumes on the islands. The Foradada, looking like an unfinished Henry Moore sculpture tossed into the sea, can be seen from the covered balcony. Entrance fee is 75 pesetas; closes at 2 pm for a 1½hr lunchbreak.

The road becomes dizzying, with 400m drops down the cliffsides. Stop at the lookout (mirador) for a broad vista before continuing inland.

Where the road forks, turn left towards **VALLDEMOSA**, where a Car-thusian monastery is set among terraces of olive and almonds. Long brown seedpods dangle like scabbards from the branches of carob trees and horse chestnuts bristle with conkers. The curious tiered bulb shape of the monastery's blue dome is repeated inside on chandeliers and again in the local glassware. A formal garden allows for meditative strolls through cypress, oleander and red rose bushes. After the monks left this monastery in 1835, rooms were let out to visitors, the most famous pair being com-poser Frederic Chopin and George Sand. Though the couple was spurned during the winter of 1838–9 for loose morals (her) and carrying tuber-culosis (him), they are remembered fondly a century and a half later. Tour groups are led through their holiday cells, and a fresh rose is placed daily on Chopin's Pleyel piano. Down the corridor, an old pharmacy is still stocked with Catalán apothecary jars and phials of blue-tinged Majorcan glass, along with some ancient pharmaceutical instruments. Odd drugs — 'Nail pairings from the Great Beast', for instance — are labelled. With a monk acting as chemist, the place was in use as late as 1912. The church and sacristy are open to the public.

While large numbers of tourists whisk through Valldemosa in a morn-ing, it is worth nosing around the narrow streets. The birthplace of Santa Catalina Tomás (Thomas), a 16th-century saint venerated as 'the Pearl of Majorca', is open, and she is feted on 28 July with a home-town pro-cession and fiesta. There is a pleasant hostal near the post office (**Ca's Manuel**) and an impressive restaurant which serves Majorcan food: **Ca'n Pedro** (Archiduque Luis Salvador; 61 21 70). Less dear are the seafood restaurants at the port, **PORT DE VALLDEMOSA**, which require some searching out. Just outside town, turn right off the C-710 and follow the narrow road, plummeting through piney slopes, until it arrives at a pebbly beach protected by a breakwater. Dive from the rocks into clear green water and spare tender feet. If the fishing boats are any measure, the catch is fresh.

Clinging to tight curves, climb back up to the C-710, and turn right. The main road will be wider, but nearly as winding and the sea glints far below. Continue to **BANYALBUFAR**, where the hills are terraced almost down to the water's edge and support a tangle of grape or tomato vines. The sweetish wine from the local bodegas has a hint of bright red, but no trace of tomato flavour. Fine meals are served at the **Maryvent** (971 71 24 45), perched high up on the cliffs.

Backtrack to the turn-off for **La Granja**, an old mansion on the road to Esporlas. From here, it's a fairly straightforward run on the downslopes through Son Berga to complete the circuit back to Palma.

Ibiza Idyll

2 days/109km/from San Antonio Abad

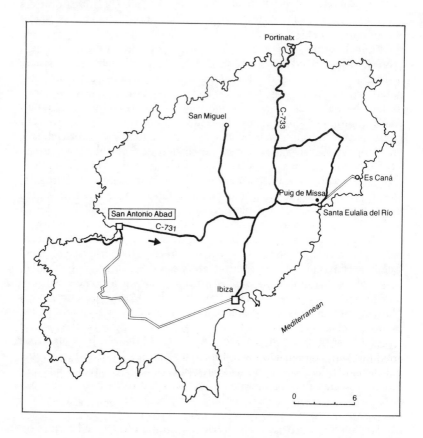

Roads between the limestone hills on the 'White Island' go basically point to point, so touring requires a lot of backtracking. But since the entire island is only 40km long, drivers make good time even if lost! Looking at the bays and coves, it's difficult not to long for a boat, the perfect way to explore the coastline. Yet motoring between the villages and the distinctive churches, cool and dark within blazingly white walls, opens up an insular countryside ignored by tourists who don't bother to leave the beaches.

Explore the upper part of **SAN ANTONIO ABAD**, with its 17th-century parochial church, and the yachtsmen posturing in the bay seem distant indeed. Still, the sails of their pleasurecraft complete the scene of this beautiful bay, with highrise towers outlining the curve against soft green hills like a pocket-sized Rio de Janeiro. Intrepid swimmers can take a dirt track 5km southwest to **CALABASSA**. Sea rocks here are smooth, perfect for basking. Water is so calm that bathers dive off the boulders and even swim between them. Perfect snorkelling conditions. Campgrounds are nearby in **PORT D'ES TORRENT**, or there is a large assortment of hotels in San Antonio, though many are shut in the low winter season (Nov–Feb).

Take the only main road (C-731) inland to **SAN RAFAEL**, and turn left on the far edge of town. On the approach to C'an Roig, turn left again, eventually following the course of the Santa Eulalia River. **SAN MIGUEL** is 12km along this road. A large fortress-church, built in the 14th century but later restored, hovers over the village, ready to fend off Barbary pirates. The 4km distance from the sea was thought sufficient warning time, and the signal bells still peal. The houses are typical; Ibiza's distinctive clusters of cubes, whitewashed countless times by the women. Their blinding white is broken up by triangles of blue sky outlined by the chimneys. Flat roofs, slightly tilted so that any water will be easily collected, are not used as terraces as they would be in North Africa. Plenty of small fountains, minuscule vegetable gardens and tubs of oleanders appear in odd corners, and the sole use of brick (whitewashed, of course) is to fashion the domed ovens. Many of the homes are without electricity or telephone. This contrasts with life down the road in **PUERTO SAN MIGUEL**, also known as **BALANZAT**. The place is tourist-ridden with several grand hotels and accompanying discotheques.

Retrace the route past Santa Gertrudis, turning left before C'an Roig and following signs to Sta. Eulalia del Río. Just before the petrol station, turn left and climb the hill to **PUIG DE MISSA**. This tiny fortified town probably survived onslaughts of invaders because the populace easily fitted inside the sanctuary of the church. The traditional peasant building style is quite intact and reflects the island's Carthaginian origins, merging with later waves of Romans, Arabs and Christians. Pines and junipers dot the hills closest to the sea, and the river valley becomes green with market gardens. **SANTA EULALIA DEL RÍO**, though it has its share of big hotels, seems less resorty than some other island towns, with its two impressive parish churches. More recent relics are at the hippy market, established now nearly 20 years, right on the long beach at **ES CANÁ**, 6km farther along. To visit Ibiza's prettiest beach, head off for San Carlos and veer left. Another sharp left turn at the fork brings you to the fortified town of **BALAFI**. Turn right onto the C-733 and head straight on past the mine near San Juan Bautista, finally winding through almond trees and oaks, with the cove of Xarraca beckoning below. At **CALA PORTINATX** creeks spill out onto sandy beaches where fragrant pines and tall cliffs provide shelter and privacy.

After a romp on the beach take the C-733 directly back to the capital, 44km in all. From the road, note the old walls that split the city into two distinct parts, the 13th-century Cathedral dominating the upper town.

IBIZA pop: 25,489 Tourist Offices: Vara del Rey, 13 or Via Romana, 8. It's easy to dismiss this as a commercial if colourful tourist trap if you confine yourself to the shopping streets near the port. Don't. The Dalt Vila of

Eivissa (Ibiza's old town) still has a medieval feel to it. From the bastion next to the cathedral the stunning view spans the town and harbour. The Archaeological Museum exhibits Punic (Carthaginian) art and Egyptian amulets, all found on the island. Entrance fee of 100 pesetas also covers a visit to the Phoenician/Carthaginian necropolis with underground vaults hollowed from the rock and some 2,000 tombs. Sa Penya, the fishermen's quarter, has cubic peasant houses like spotless tumbling dice. At times they completely block the alleyways or nudge each other to the cliff edge. It is built on a narrow spit of land by the harbour's entrance. A detour out by the airport to **Las Salinas** is interesting. The salt processing has continued since the Carthaginian traders' era, and 50,000 tons are still exported annually.

Boat excursions to the neighbouring island, **FORMENTERA**, can be arranged from Ibiza harbour and make for an enjoyable day trip. Schedules are erratic. The island, 7km to the south, is small and flat with just one sizeable town. Most visitors remain flat out, too, baking on the nudist beaches. Cereal, almonds, figs and a few vines are grown on the plains, and several old windmills are still in working order.

Minorca

1 full day/118km/from Ciudadela

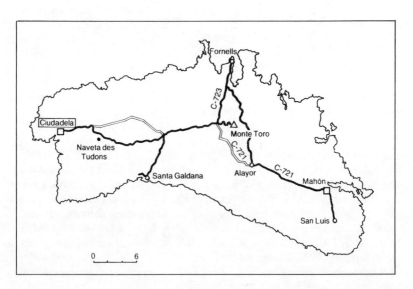

Flatter, greener, often a bit misty, Minorca (Menorca) has stronger British ties than the other Balearic Isles and it somehow seems fitting. Sheep graze in abundance. Peasant houses are tiled and walled bright white and the air echoes with a soft island dialect of Spanish. Echoes of a more

distant past occur in over 200 Bronze Age stone cones (*talayots*), frequently found near the roadside.

CIUDADELA, the former capital, has been known since Phoenician
times and is impressively fortified against sieges. When the boat from
Palma docks in the harbour, it feels as if the town is prepared for any
minor threat from the sea. Aristocratic family mansions, dating from the
time of Alfonso III and still belonging to the same select few names, give a
weighty presence of established wealth to the narrow arcaded streets. Not
far from the main square, Plaza España, is the stronghold of the Gothic
cathedral, built atop a small mosque in the 15th century, and still the seat
of a Bishop. The town hall is Moorish, built in a former Alcázar, and there
is a small archaeological museum in the seminary near the 18th-century
palace. Borne Plaza, once the citadel's parade ground, livens up on 24
June, just after the Summer Solstice, when San Joan (St John) comes to
town, barefoot but covered in furs, inviting all and sundry to celebrate his
fiesta. As they have done since the 14th century, celebrants dress in
riding boots, short vests and ancient hats, and watch skilled horsemen
perform tight manoeuvres in the square. Heading the motley procession is
a Maltese Cross, held aloft, which links this rite to other island celebrations in the Mediterranean. The excitement is infectious and it's clear
that this is no ritual revived by an overeager tourist board, but simply how
the town always has, and is likely always to, welcome Midsummer.

Leave on the main inland road, C-721. The third turning to the right
(about 5km along) is marked **Naveta Des Tudons**. Approaches to the
megalithic monuments all over the island are usually along uneven stony
paths. Remember to shut the gates behind you. This naveta is probably
the best known of the tombs, shaped like an upturned boat, and is
thought to be dedicated to the goddess Isis, sacred to sailors and explorers. Return to the secondary road, turn right at the crossroads and continue inland, passing by two more tombs, **Torrellafuda** and **Torre-
trenoada**. Near the riverbeds, approach **PAS D'EN REVULL**, where
the landscape takes a curious turn to the stark and sculpted. At the first
fork, bear right on a noticeably better road, past the small settlement of
Santa Ponsa, and on down to **SANTA GALDANA**, where bare cliffs
soar above a sandy beach. The bay is calm and clear, and small pines grow
near the shore. A swim is almost irresistible. Go back up the road about
7km until it intersects with the C-721. Bear right, passing Ferrerías, and
head for **MERCADAL**, 8km farther. You are likely to pass shepherds on
the road, and the salty local cheese made from ewes' milk, plus some
sweet dried figs, are good snacks to buy from the village shops. Follow the
signs up a spiralling road which makes 3½km stretch forever to the
Sanctuary of Monte Toro perched on the highest point of Minorca. The
17th-century church provides the best panorama of the island, and you
can make out the split personality of the two shores. Northwards you see
the ragged inlets, to the south the straight-cut drop of the cliffs. Mahón,
the capital, suns itself in the southeast.

Wind back down the road and head north from Mercadel to

FERNELLS, on the C-723. A tower marks the entrance to the inlet, which is crowded with fishing boats laden down with lobster pots. This is the best spot on the island to try fresh crayfish with mayonnaise — originally a local sauce (from Mahón). *Caldereta de langosta* is the house speciality at **Es Pla** (Pasaje d'Es Pla; 37 51 55), with its seaside terrace. There is a long beach as well as the port. Two largish hotels are open in season, April through October.

Coming back from the peninsula, turn left, and after 2km, left again through San Juan. The road meanders, following the more rugged terrain of the grazing lands, and descends onto **ALAYOR**. Here, aside from a couple of shoe factories, the citizens busy themselves by continually whitewashing their houses: even the tiled roofs are brilliant. This is quite a contrast to the capital, 12km east, where tidy English houses complete with sash windows look seawards.

MAHÓN pop: 21,800 Tourist Office: Plaza Generalissimo, 13, reflects its domination by the British during most of the 18th century with these bay-view bungalows, plus the Georgetown base. Admiral Nelson himself spent a month on Golden Farm, in the San Antonio quarter on the bay's north side, where he completed the final draft of his autobiography. Many of the city monuments dating back to Roman occupation have been lost in skirmishes, but the small archaeological museum, housed in the Archive Palace on Conquista Plaza, has artifacts from the Carthaginian era and the Bronze Age. Pretty churches abound in the crowded streets, and the enormous pipe organ inside Iglesia de Santa María is quite impressive for such a small island. Worth searching out, the ex-convent Sant Antoni, now a Gothic monument, is preserved at the centre of this same church. Mahón has plenty of seafood restaurants, plus hotels and hostals in all price ranges.

Just 4km south, the French settlement **SAN LUÍS**, with a geometric layout of a new town, is a reminder of the seven years that the French took hold of this strategic Mediterranean port during the 18th century. On the road back, practically facing the airport, the **Trepuco** site preserves the largest ceremonial altar (*taula*) yet discovered in the Megalithic burial grounds that riddle Minorca.

3 CANTABRIA AND THE BASQUE LANDS

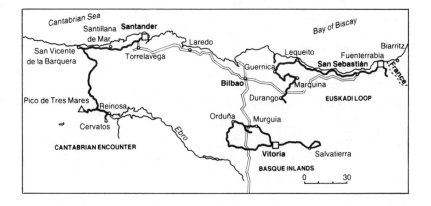

Though sometimes damp, Cantabria and the Basque country to the east are full of odd customs and unexpected scenes which make independent touring here an adventure. History is etched on cave walls and caught in the medieval streets of some of the interior villages. Church architecture runs the gamut from sober Visigothic temples to flamboyant Baroque, with a surprising tantric-type carving of voluptuous sinners at play in one rural church. While the sea is important, stone also looms mighty in Basque culture, whether built upon, dragged, hefted or hurled. Exquisite and inventive cuisine would be reason enough to visit these green provinces. The coast, the bright rivers gushing through mountains, and most of all the sturdy people with ready laughter, make it extremely pleasant.

Cantabrian Encounter

2 days/200km/from Santander

Besides a rugged coastline sweet-
ened with a few broad beaches of
pink sand, Cantabria boasts steep
valleys and rain-doused mountains.
Not only are the seafood and river
crabs good, but dairy products are
superb. No surprise, considering
that there are some 350,000 head
of cattle in a province of some half
a million residents. With the
variety of scenery this region offers,
no visitor will allow damp weather
to douse his sense of discovery.

SANTANDER pop: 180,328
Tourist Office: Plaza de Verlarde,
1. A full 24 hours ferry cruise from
Plymouth across the Bay of Biscay
brings drivers to dock at Santander. It's a green coast which
greets them and some may well
shake their heads wondering just what became of the sunny
Spain they held out hopes for during a rough crossing. The buildings around the port are a bit scruffy, but aren't typical of Cantabria's
main city. Much of it was damaged in a tornado and fire in 1941 which
miraculously took no lives. Quite a bit is World War II era reconstruction.
One swank part of town, the Sardinero, affects an almost Monte Carlo
elegance with its casino and beaches. A summer haunt for the royals in
the past century, it has pleasant gardens and promenades. The summer
university sessions for foreign students bring out the youthful intelli-
gentsia. The Cathedral is worth a visit, with a 12th-century crypt still
intact, as is the Magdalena Palace. Of the four museums, the Menéndez y
Pelayo Library is the most impressive (closed weekends). The philosopher's modest house opposite shows how his fabulous book collection
ate up most of his income. A Fine Arts Museum (11–1; 5–8; closed
Sundays) features mostly contemporary Spanish painters, and a Prehistory Museum displays the finds from the area's caves. Still a mystery
are remarkably carved batons, the finest one fashioned from an antler.
There is a wide range of hotels and eating places.

Go west on the N-611, turning off on the coast road C-6316, to reach
SANTILLANA DEL MAR. Filled with graceful mansions dating from
Spain's empire, it is not a typical one-street dairy village. Originally, it
grew up around a monastery which holds the relics of the martyr St.

Juliana. Despite the coachloads of
tourists who have descended on
the place since Sartre dubbed it
Spain's prettiest village in his
novel, *Nausea*, it manages to retain
a rather countrified majesty. Mansions with iron or wooden sun balconies, most with noble crests
carved in the stone façades, nestle
between palaces and churches left
as reminders of Santillana's prestige as a pilgrimage place in the
Middle Ages. The Collegiate
Church, with its elliptical cupola
and richly carved capitals, dates
from the 12th and 13th centuries
and was the seat of much power.
Not far off, on the Plaza of Ramón
Pelayo, the 15th-century Borja-
Barreda Tower sets the tone of
understated elegance with its
pointed arch doorway and a

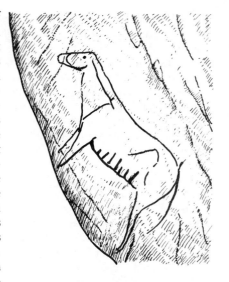

Typical cave drawing

Renaissance patio. A display inside is devoted to regional seafaring
history. It is a pleasure to linger in the village at sundown, when the
tourists have moved on and the unpretentious villagers lead their livestock back from pasture. Many cattle are the ground-floor tenants of the
grand stone houses. Fresh milk is sold by the glass in the village streets.
On the lovely main plaza, one palace has been refurbished as a state
parador (**Parador Nacional Gil Blas**, Plaza de Ramón Pelayo, 8; 81 80
00).

Cattle of an older sort — 12,000 BC — are on show at the nearby
Altamira Caves, but unless you have booked months in advance to view
the famous ochre bison, you won't be among the party of 10 whisked in
for a ¼hr look at these masterful cave drawings. Moisture, compounded by
the breath of so many visitors, led to erosion problems, especially on the
ceiling where the best drawings are. A museum on the site shows a video
which outlasts the tour of the real thing (9–1, 4–6; closed Sun pm) —
some small consolation. Another cave has been rigged with lights for
visitors to see the natural formations. Write Centro de Investigaciones de
Altamira, Santillana del Mar, Santander, to try and secure a place on a
tour-party.

COMILLAS, 19km west on the coast road, is odd. Long a seaside
retreat for the aristocracy, the Barcelona crowd commissioned a few
modernist touches before the turn of the century to put a distinctive
stamp on the town. Gaudí's El Capricho is a bizarre rendering of a
Catalan/Moorish fantasy with punchy patterns in the brick and tiles and a
tower like a chess piece. Only prospective buyers may tour (with an estate
agent), otherwise it is closed to the public. Next door, the Marquis de

Comillas hired Gaudi's colleague Joan Martorell to design a sprawling summer palace and chapel, now a museum and public garden. A huge neo-Gothic Jesuit Seminary, by Domenech i Montaner, is a third remnant from this era. The beach below town is handy, but Playa de Oyambre is longer and worth the extra walk. In season (generally May–September), there are comfortable hotels here. The tourist office (La Aldea, 2) lists private houses that let rooms for the night. **Colasa** (Antonio López, 11; 72 00 01) is a traditional restaurant which dishes up big servings of seafood and mountain cooking, with home-baked tarts for afters.

Just 10km west is **SAN VICENTE DE LA BARQUERA**, which high tide cuts off from the mainland save for a skinny isthmus. Once the tide ebbs again, the locals come out to rake the sandbeds for a harvest of cockles and clams or to net shrimp. Simple bars that line the town's high street provide ample opportunity to sample the fresh *mariscos* in myriad preparations. Turn inland on the N-634, then take a right onto the C-625 and follow it up into the highlands. Once past Fresneda, turn left towards Correpoco where the small road halts at **BÁRCENA MAYOR**. With arcaded streets and the smell of fresh wood, this small village of wood-workers could almost be in the Middle Ages. **Río Argoza** is the place to eat good mountain stew — *Cocido de Montaña* for around 750 pesetas. 'Los Tojos' — the so-called gorse bushes in the foothills of the local mountain range — are the big local attraction. Birch and beech trees grow along the slender streams that weave through the region.

Cantabrian fishing village

REINOSA seems very metropolitan in comparison, though the population is under 14,000. While quite close to the mountains, the town has surrounding flatlands planted with grain. Heavy industry is growing, but Reinosa hopes to become a sports centre with its access to a large reservoir lake and a ski station. Many of the travellers passing through in the summer are cattle, who arrive from scorching Castile and Extremadura penned up in cattle trains. When they are released, the town is sensibly boarded up while the bellowing beasts are led through the streets up to the rain-washed meadows beyond town. The last Sunday in September sees the Dia del Campóo, the biggest gathering of Cantabrian folk dancers and musicians anywhere. One traditional stringed instrument, the *rabel*, must be made only of wood cut in full moonlight if it is to have the true mournful sound. A reasonable meal can be had at **Vejo** (Avda Cantabria, 15; 75 17 00) with delicious *setas*, flat wild mushrooms, the star item on the menu. *Pantortillas* (puff pastries with butter and anise) are another local speciality. The most comfortable hotels are on the highways leading out of town.

CERVATOS, 7km south on the N-611, is worth a detour for the 12th-century Collegiate Church. The carving is remarkably detailed, with an Eastern flavour in the rendering of the vines and a fierce frieze of lions, back to back. Unmistakably erotic figures decorate the corbels and the nether side of the capitals supporting the south apse window. Spain's other X-rated church, over in Yermo, also is 12th-century Cantabrian. The standard explanation is that the explicit carvings were planned to warn worshippers off the temptations of the flesh!

Back in Reinosa, for a romantic daytrip take the road posted to the Alto Campóo ski resort. **FONTIBRE** is a pleasant stop. Signs lead the way (along footpaths) to the **source of the Ebro** River, the most important on the Iberian peninsula, which starts out here in a green pool beneath a few poplars and mossy rocks in an ash wood.

Return to the C-628, heading past Espinilla, and keep on it to the end. Park and climb to the summit of the **Tres Mares Peak** with ease, by chairlift (9–5 summer hrs; 150 pesetas). From this height it's possible to see rivers that flow into three different seas, all starting out from this particular mountain in the Pena Labra Sierra. The Hijar links up with the Ebro and pushes out a delta into the Mediterranean. The Pisuergo joins the Duero west to the Atlantic. And the Nansa flows straight into the Cantabrian Sea. From the crest, with rivers flowing in all directions beneath, it seems like the top of the world. Lakes and distant mountains crowd the horizon. The misted Valle de Pas ahead is reputed to be the home of the last direct descendants from the original Iberians, fierce isolationists known as *pasiegos* who are respected and feared by most other Spaniards. A short hike on the way down to the Mirador de la Fuente del Chivo gives a second eagle's eye view, this time straight over the Nansa River. The alternative is to ride straight back down to the car and a dreary anti-climax. To avoid this on return to industrial Reinosa, book at the **Vejo** (Av Cantabria, 15; 75 17 00) with a bright garden and comfortable rooms.

Euskadi Loop

2 days/175km/from Fuenterrabía (French border)

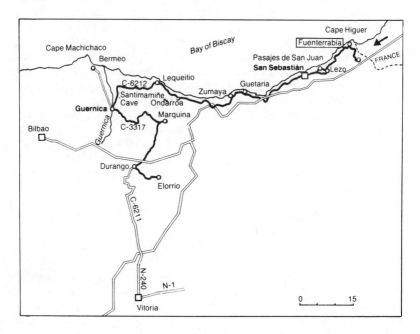

Many visitors are apt to feel apprehensive at first when touring through countryside where the placenames have figured in news articles about political terrorism. But unless you are a civil guardsman or perhaps a French industrialist, you won't be a target. ETA (the Basque separatist movement) has largely avoided random violence to civilians, but the separatists have burnt cars with French plates. Government targets (French as well as Spanish) are ETA's primary aim. This said, the Basques themselves are enormously friendly and their green coast and mountainous hinterland present an unusual Spain. Aside from outdoing each other in new ways to eat seafood, the Basques like contests of strength. With a pair of oxen, dragging 3-ton boulders for a distance is a favourite. So is tossing poles. Yet there are competitions for brute intellect as well, when *bersolaris*, Basque poets, challenge each other in verse.

Crossing a border usually puts a traveller's expectations in check. But once past nondescript Irún, **FUENTERRABÍA** offers up castles in Spain, clean beaches, a picturesque fishing fleet and good dose of history. The old stronghold with its ramparts has fended off attacks in its time, mainly from the neighbouring French, and the port town still celebrates outlasting a two-month French siege in 1638 with a big fiesta each 8 September, dedicated to the Virgen Guadalupe for her divine deliverance. Hundreds of sword-brandishing men and boys parade all day long.

Brightly decorated fishermen's houses

The main gate through the ramparts, the Puerta de Santa María, is inscribed with twin angels venerating Guadalupe. Many of the houses are emblazoned with noble coats of arms while the popular quarter is bright with fresh paint and blooms on the balconies. Knobbly tamarind trees line the promenades by the marina, and the narrow main street, with its rows of iron balconies, makes a pleasant stroll. Santa María Church, a massive Gothic structure, was the scene of the proxy wedding between the French King Louis XIV and the Spanish Infanta María Teresa. The most impressive castle, supposedly founded by Sancho the Great, Navarre's 10th-century king, has been dubbed after Carlos V, because he visited. Now that it is a state **parador** (El Emperador; Plaza de Armas de Castillo; 64 21 40) it sees plenty more visitors. This parador has no dining facilities, and with the wealth of good Basque cooking available in town, it's just as well.

If possible, try to drive on the Jaizkibel Road west into the sunset. A sweeping view back across the French coast and the Bidassoa can be seen just past the Guadalupe Chapel and the 16th-century pirate's castle. Climbing through pines and yellow gorse, the road reaches the Jaizkibel Hostal at the base of a peak, with a lookout point and map. Nearby, the **Hotel Provincial de Jaizkibel** (64 11 00) on the cliffs overlooking the Atlantic is isolated and romantic. The dining room has decent food, even by obsessive Basque standards.

The descent allows views either of the mountain crests or inlets of the Spanish coast as you round the bends. **PASAJES**, a collective of three codfishing villages around a sheltered bay, is known for record catches. Pasajes Ancho, at the back, is a port-of-call for African-bound ships.

PASAJES DE SAN JUAN, literally a one-street village, has tall houses with wooden balconies and arches. The poet Victor Hugo lived at number 59, with its harbour view, in 1843. Park by the factory at the village entrance, and walk at least to the pretty main square, Plaza de Santiago. The footpath to the lighthouse goes by ancient fortifications.

Continue on the coast road until you reach the beautiful scalloped bay of San Sebastián, framed by Mount Urgell, with its castle, and the leafy Isla de Santa Clara.

SAN SEBASTIÁN (DONOSTIA) pop: 175,576 Tourist Offices: C. Andia, 13 or Victoria Eugenie Theatre on the river for municipal maps. An elegant resort town which takes dining out very seriously, San Sebastián dates mostly from the last century, as sundry plunderers and pillagers have burned it to the ground a dozen times in its long history. Wellington was the most recent victor. La Concha, the main beach, is a wide arch of sand around a bay filled in summer with kayaks, sailboats and surfers. Aside from the beaches and the casino, visit the churches Santa María del Coro, San Vicente, and the former Dominican monastery San Telmo, now a museum of Basque culture, though the painting section boasts three El Grecos (open 10–1.30; 3.30–5.30). Give the Aquarium a miss.

It is nearly impossible to have a bad meal here, though inexpensive ones require some searching. Three restaurants are regarded as gourmet shrines: **Akelarre** (Barrio Igueldo; 21 20 52) has the most ambience, with sea views to enhance the exquisite seafood. Closed Sunday nights and Mondays, and all October. **Arzak** (Alto de Miracruz, 2; 28 55 93) in the same calibre, also shuts Sunday nights and Mondays. **Nicolasa** (Aldemar, 4; 42 17 62) completes the triumvirate and is dark all day Sunday plus Monday nights. Hotels are in all categories, though the bargains tend to be jammed with students.

Keeping to the coast, **GUETARIA**, with a mouse-shaped islet in the bay, is a fishing village with considerable charm. Native son Sebastián de Elcano earned himself an enormous monument for his feat of being the first to sail around the world, completing Magellan's voyage. Toast him with a glass of local txakoli wine, smooth golden stuff which one barman insists 'tastes like Dom Perignon left uncorked in the fridge overnight'. San Salvador Church, from the 15th century, has an exceptional altar and a ship model. There are also two pleasant beaches. **Hotel San Prudencia** (83 24 11) is a short walk from the beach. Eating places are near the port: **Asador Kalpe**, or the **Kaia** upstairs, are recommended.

Don't cut inland after Zumaya. Keep to the winding pot-holed coast road in the wake of vans burdened with surfboards. **MOTRICO**, set back on a slender inlet, was once a whaling port and still has one harpooned on its official crest. Many of the houses are up to six storeys high, built of characteristic grey stone and adorned by crystal galleries to catch the sun. Steep streets dead-end at the river port, and the porch of the ancient *Lonja* (fish auction house) bridges over the access road to the pier.

Saturraran is a quiet beach nearby, bordering on the neighbouring province, Vizcaya. At **ONDARROA**, a provincial customs house still stands next to an old stone footbridge. Santa María, the decadent Gothic church with its gargoyles and other excesses, is beside the port. Narrow six- and seven-storey houses are built up on all sides, and though the green hills and pine slopes above the town are beautiful, the entire focus is seawards. This is a fishing town, with boats that still go out on the high sea and sailor families whose ancestors would sail the Spanish Main.

LEQUEITIO, farther west, is snug beneath the Cantabrian hills, with its two exposed beaches farther out of town. The fish dinners here are simple and quite cheap. Try **Zapiraia** (Igualdequi, 3).

Turning inland, take the C-6212. Just before Guernica turn left, following signposts to **Santimamiñe**. A cave here (closed Mon; open 10.30–7 weekdays; Sun, 11–12.30 only) has some important ochre drawings and proof of nearly 30,000 years of continuous habitation. The ceiling group of horses and bison is the most refined drawing, but the natural bright orange limestone formations along the gallery are pretty astounding in themselves.

GUERNICA, 5km south, shines all rebuilt at the end of the Oca estuary. The ancient oak tree, symbol of Basque liberty, which survived the air-strafing of 1937 unscathed, still stands by the parliament. The trunk of the original oak where the lords of Biscay would promise to uphold Basque privileges is under a protective pavilion; the seedling — barely a century old — spreads its branches. Apart from the tree and the Casa Junta, there is little to see. Basque nationalists are demanding that Picasso's stark mural be moved here from the Prado Museum in Madrid, to little avail. If it's a week-end, watching the Basque national sport at the new *pelota* court is quite an experience. The most popular style here is with the scooped baskets, very rapid.

Head east on a secondary road which winds through the hills towards **MARQUINA**, where most of the world's *pelota* champions hail from. Stop by the Artibay River at the **San Miguel de Arretxinaga** hermitage for a look at an extraordinary altar. A statue of Saint Michael is framed by three outsize boulders that some believers claim were dropped into place as shooting stars. The place still puzzles historians and archaeologists. **DURANGO**, despite its wrangler name and industrial outskirts, preserves a lovely Baroque quarter behind a gateway, Portal de Santa Ana. San Pedro Church, 17th century, is noteworthy for its large west portal. In one of the outer neighbourhoods stands the Kurutziaga Cross, a 19th-century monumental carving. **Juego de Bolos** (San Agustinalde, 2; 68 10 99) is a clean place to stay overnight.

Just 9km east is **ELORRIO**, which retains a medieval air about it with its hoard of stone crucifixes from the 15th and 16th centuries, displayed in pretty squares among the stone houses and fountains. At the east entrance of the village, one unusual cross has a spiral base. At the opposite side of the village, another is carved with a crowd scene. The Basque Church of Our Lady of the Holy Conception has heavy pillars and star vaulting, plus a beautifully rendered altarpiece.

From Elorrio, it's a not quite two hours' drive back to San Sebastián and its exquisite restaurants, especially if you get on the motorway. Vitoria, the Basque capital, is a little closer, though it will take longer along the more mountainous roads with white farmhouses standing on the slopes, which level out to a grain-covered plateau.

Basque Inlands
2 days/145km/from Salvatierra

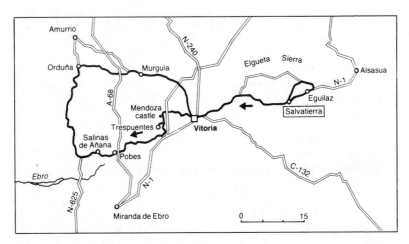

Easy touring around Vitoria, the pleasant Basque provincial capital and a centre for wonderful chocolate truffles. Quick drives between Roman ruins and ancient dolmens, ornate old churches and medieval streets, allow plenty of time for eating the fine Basque cuisine; the rivers nearby provide a few new creatures for the pot. If your timing is lucky, folk-dancing or music may brighten a local festival. Sword-dances — men only — are not uncommon.

SALVATIERRA-AGURAIN, on the main road east from Pamplona or southwest from San Sebastián, sets the mood for this short trip. Recognised by Alfonso the Wise in 1256, Salvatierra preserves its noble main street, lined with Renaissance or Baroque mansions displaying intricate family coats of arms below balconies laden with flowers. In fact, the street layout in the old centre coincides exactly with the 13th-century town map on display in the town hall. The Zadorra River flows by and the old town is hemmed in by mountains to the north and the south. Summer solstice and the Day of St John the Baptist in Midsummer (24 June) puts the quiet village into manic motion. The day before, youngsters chop down a black poplar and set up rustic stands around the main plaza. Evening vespers are performed outdoors and singers and dancers, accompanied by flutes and drums, take to the streets until dawn. The next day, the white-clad musicians with their red berets escort the city elders on horseback to **ARRIZALA**, the next village. Mass is heard there, refreshment shared, and then everyone troops back to continue the celebration. Should you come when the village is not celebrating with eat and drink in the open, try **Merino** (Plaza de San Juan, 3; 30 00 52). Right on the main square, it dishes up good stews and sauces every day but Christmas.

EGUILAZ, 5km east, displays Aizkomendi, an enormous dolmen — a Celtic burial monument of upended stones — at the village entrance. Discovered a century and a half ago, it was transferred stone by stone to its present site so that more people could wonder at it. In neighbouring Arrizala, a smaller dolmen is nicknamed Sorginetxe (Witch's rock) in a mock explanation of how it came to be engineered. Head back on the N-I towards Vitoria, but take the first left turn for a stop at **GACEO**. The church here boasts some odd but well-executed Romanesque frescoes in the chancel. The north wall shows Hell in the shape of a whale's gullet. Turn left to get back on the N-I, where the **Parador Argomaniz** (28 22 00), converted from the old Palacio de los Lassos, has a fine kitchen and some rooms with lovely views. Even the provincial capital, Vitoria, has nothing which betters it.

VITORIA (GASTEIZ) pop: 192,773 Tourist Office: C.E. Dato, 16. Once past the grim industrial outer ring, visitors to Vitoria will be surprised. An old inner core around St Mary's cathedral rises up in tiers of mansions, the concentric streets connected with stone stairs named for medieval trades. The spiritual centre is just beyond the old cathedral at the Plaza de la Virgen Blanca, where a venerated statue presides over the niche at the 14th-century San Miguel Church. Local custom in August is for all onlookers to light up a cigar as she makes her annual descent from the belfry. Correría, the liveliest street in the quarter, has a handsome 15th-century building at no. 151, the Portalón, still in commercial use as a restaurant. A half-timbered building farther down this same street houses the archaeology museum (closed Mon. Open 10–2; 5–7 weekdays; 11–2 Sun). Roman finds and artifacts from local dolmens are the most extensive displays. On the other side of Florida Park and the neo-Gothic cathedral stands the Provincial Museum. Its painting collection spans from Flemish masters (*Flamenco*, it's called here) to Miró and Picasso, and all are exhibited in a contemporary mansion which has plenty of natural light coming from bright gardens. See also a quirky museum devoted just to playing cards (an important city product) and a Museum of Arms, which features Wellington's trouncing of Joseph Bonaparte in the Battle of Vitoria. (The placename is a reworking of the Basque *Beturia* — for the rise it was built on — and doesn't refer to victory at all.) If you linger in Vitoria, eat in the old quarter, but stay overnight in the new part of town.

Follow the Calle Tomás de Zumárraga west out of Vitoria for 10km, until you reach **Mendoza Castle**. (Closed Mon; open 11–2; 5–7, except Sun pm.) Climb up into one of the four stout towers for a long view over the plateau. Perhaps overly restored, the castle displays photos of all the heraldic crests used by provincial families. The Mendoza crest itself, both the Castile and León branches, it boldly emblazoned on an old pillory in the village, above some rusted iron hooks.

TRESPUENTES is at the end of the next right turning, beside the Zadorra River. An impressive Roman bridge with 13 arches leads across the river to the mound on the edge of Irún, where other Roman relics have been unearthed. Most are on display back in Vitoria.

Return to the N-I for just 1½km, and bear right towards **POBES**. On the approach to **SALINAS DE AÑANA**, parched saltpans ripple the slopes beside the village and give the landscape the look of a budget Star Trek set. The Romans first leached salt from the waters of the Muera, and the tradition continues today. The parish church in this remote village has a treasured Flemish painting of the Annunciation.

After intersecting with the N-625, turn right. The road climbs to the Orduña Pass, with a vista over the verdant hollow where **ORDUÑA** village crouches, with the distant Basque mountains beyond. Pull over to the lookout point to savour the view. The second week of May transforms this quiet village into a non-stop celebration, with amateur bullfights, concerts, Basque feats of strength, folkdances, singing and general merry-making for seven nights straight. A Midsummer cattle fair every 22-23 June also draws crowds from all over the province, though it usually doesn't reach the same pitch as the *ochomayo*. When not being feted in May, the Virgen de la Antigua can be seen in her sanctuary. Two churches also are worth a visit: Santa María, just east from the main square, has a masterful Flemish altarpiece in its third chapel, protected by Plateresque grillwork. San Juan el Viejo dates from the 17th century. Should the sightseeing work up your appetite, **Llarena** (Urdanegui, 6; 589 39 99) serves traditional Basque food at popular prices. Closed Thursday nights. The quickest return to Vitoria is through Murguía, where the road widens.

4 CATALONIA AND ARAGÓN

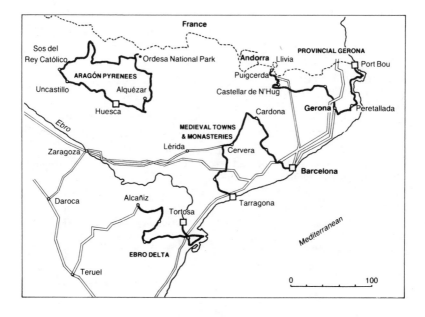

Catalonia, wedged into Spain's northeast corner with the Pyrenees keeping it just this side of France, has long had a heady, liberal feel to it, tempered with an underlying pragmatism. From the time it was reconquered by Charlemagne's son, Louis, it's kept a separate identity from the rest of Spain, and has been embroiled in continual uprisings: intellectual, political and industrial. Innovative artists such as Salvador Dalí and Joan Miró were nurtured there. Antonio Gaudí was let loose to build curvilinear cathedrals and pleasure parks. But Catalonia is known for urbanity: Barcelona, the most dynamic city in post-Franco Spain, hogs the spotlight. The Costa Brava, where unchecked tourist development still has not completely blighted the beauty of the rugged coast, strains for attention. Yet the countryside need not be eclipsed: the delta of the Ebro River has a special charm, while the monasteries on the flanks of coastal mountains have unmatched majesty. Burnt-out volcanoes open their craters to the rain. And in the high valleys of the Pyrenees, secluded villages go about daily habits in timeworn fashion. One curious custom: the *casteller* societies or *Xiquets*, in which men and boys stack themselves up into human towers, all in time to groaning *grolla* tunes.

Aragón's links to Catalonia go back to the 12th century when the merger created a Mediterranean empire and power base respected in all Europe. (Catherine of Aragón hailed from this rugged country round the Pyrenees.) The last monarch managed another union — this one with Isabella of Castile — which forged the kingdom of Spain. A counterpart to the Catalan *sardana* is the vigorous Aragonese dance, the *jota*. After decades of suppression, both folkdances are proudly performed today, not as quaint spectacles sponsored by the tourist board, but for solidarity and fun.

Provincial Gerona

3 days/235km/from Port Bou

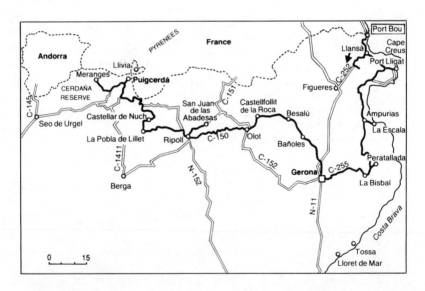

This route loops inland before the worst excesses of the Costa Brava, but still takes in the rugged headlands plunging into the sea which brought the tourists here in the first place. Walled medieval villages, ancient monasteries with almost omniscient views, and even older settlements still under excavation are found in a rural landscape of cork oaks and vine-yards, giving way to wooded slopes. Roadsigns can be confusing. Although officially bilingual, Catalonia (Catalunya) is assertively regionalistic and frequently omits placenames in the more familiar Spanish, which means that map references may not always jibe. Luckily, Catalan often

Cutting cork

has a recognisable similarity to the Spanish: Girona as opposed to Gerona. But don't assume it's a dialect. Proud of their own literary traditions, Catalans take great offence if the language that was so stifled under Franco's regime isn't given full status.

Driving down the Mediterranean coast of France, after Perpignan (whose train station Salvador Dalí maintains is the centre of universal forces!), a driver can enter Spain close to **PORT BOU**, and follow the coast road through **COLERA**, notable mostly for its name, which tends to discourage passers through from drinking the water. The San Quirze Monastery, though not nearly as impressive as what's in store, merits a look. At the fork in the road, turn inland to **LLANSA (LLANÇA)**, a tidy town whose college students all commute by train to Figueras. If the shops are open, pick up a picnic of crusty bread, fresh fruit, a cooked butifarra sausage and cheap local champagne. Loop around 10km to **VILAJUIGA**, then continue up the winding track to the monastery **Sant Pere De Roda**. The last 10 minutes must be made on foot, but bring you to a crest 670m above the sea. There is another possibility: an unpaved track signmarked as a right turn off the Llança/Selva road, close to a development of vacation houses. A splendid view takes in all of Cape Creus, sweeping north to Cerbère in France. The Benedictine builings have stood over a millenium, though abandoned for a couple of centuries, and only the church is in reasonable repair. There is Córdoban influence in the strapwork and carving of the capitals. A slow but thorough restoration is underway now that the monastery has been classed a National Monument, and remains of a temple to Venus Pirenaica lay beneath the foundations. Legend has it that the head of St Peter, on loan from Rome, vanished along with other relics hidden in a grotto here. A crumbling tower rises even higher than the monastery, reached by a watchpath that is built along the defensive walls. From these heights, the Trasmontana winds whisk about you and the mountain seems to drop away.

On return to Llança, turn right and head for **SELVA DE MAR**, just 4km from **EL PORT DE LA SELVA**. It was moved inland many years back for defence against Barbary pirates, who would sail into the protected harbour then pillage at will. Even today, Selva is practically invisible from the port. The town has narrow stone streets and several bodegas, where local wine is pressed from the sweet purple grapes that grow near the olive groves. The village women still wash their laundry in fresh stream water, which they also take home in jars rather than drink from the tap. The beaches just beyond Port de la Selva are bordered by flat stones that catch the tidepools when the sea is low and make a series of saltwater ponds to explore. Water is colder than on the other side of the cape owing to the prevailing currents, but it doesn't deter the hardier swimmers.

The well-paved road across the cape to **CADAQUÉS** whizzes 21km around rocky hillsides of wild thyme and rosemary, oak and olive. There is a pleasant venta and picnic tables along the way. What was once a plain fishing village has been discovered by arty types who'd like the weird genius of Salvador Dalí by osmosis. His home above the creek in neighbouring **PORT LLIGAT** is set off by giant eggs on the white wall, though the invalid artist no longer resides there. Adding to the general absurdity are a number of German skindiving clubs which patrol the rocks around the cove with all the latest spearfishing gear. Within its ramparts, Cadaqués has curving streets and a lovely parish church that faces the sea. A museum now occupies the hotel on the main square where Picasso, Miró and Buñuel would stay on their visits to Dalí. Though interesting, it seems tacky rather than over-the-top and lacks the touch of Dalí's own display in Figueras, his hometown.

Follow the left fork down the slow slope towards **CASTELLÓ DE AMPURIAS (CASTELLÓ D'EMPÚRIES)**, where the Albres hills smooth out and meet the fertile Emporda plain. The 13th-century Church of Santa María, with a Catalan tower beside it, is this town's centrepiece, and its exquisitely carved alabastar altarpiece is noteworthy. Stroll amidst the Gothic houses in the walled neighbourhood. Just on the highway, near the Castelló Nou development, an 18th-century *masia* has been renovated as a restaurant, the **All i oli** (25 03 00), which serves hearty Catalan cuisine with Ampurdan wines and can provide rooms for the night.

On the outskirts of town turn left and follow the secondary road to **L'ESCALA**, on the far side of the Gulf of Rosas. Two promontories protect the bay, which is noticeably warmer and calmer than the inlets farther north yet not overdeveloped by Costa standards. **Ampurias (Empúries)**, an excavated Greek settlement 2km farther on, layers a millennium's artifacts on a restricted site and is rich in altars and statues. The adjoining Roman town across the road is still not fully excavated, but obviously will be quite large. Several mosaics have been uncovered. So much history is concentrated in this spot: **SANT MARTI D'EMPÚRIES**, presently an unpretentious village which benefits from the odd outing by antiquities hounds, was a Phoenician settlement six centuries before Christ. The Greeks 'new town' flourished, becoming a Bishopric complete with Basilica before legions of Romans invaded, followed in the 8th century AD by the Moors, who were in turn driven out by the Christian forces. Entry fee is 150 pesetas, and everything shuts two hours for lunch, reopening at 4 pm.

PERATALLADA, a medieval town with ramparts softened by flowers, stands in the midst of a plain scattered with cork oaks, which provide the long stoppers for the *cava*, Catalonian champagne. Feudal power emanates from the stout stone walls of the castle, complete with a sort of moat, which have stood on the huge sandstone crag at least since 1065. The neighbouring palace reflects a succession of architectural eras, from the 14th century onwards. Most of the houses close by are Gothic. The deep trenches cut in the rocks to double the village's fortification no doubt gave rise to its name: from Petra Tallada, or Cut Rock.

Proceed back to the main road, through **LA BISBAL**, with its impressive Palace of the Bishops, and on 29km to Gerona, the provincial capital.

GERONA (GIRONA) pop: 87,648 Tourist Office: Ciutadans, 12, near Plaza de Vi. Poised at the strategic confluence of the Ter and Onar Rivers, Gerona was beset by siege after siege, with ramparts continually repaired and rebuilt by Iberians, Romans and the medieval Catholics. In 1809, the city kept 35,000 of Napoleon's forces at bay for seven months, before all supplies were spent. The citizens' battalions, including one all-female resistance band, are commemorated by a plaque in the main square. The walls still stand on the west and north limits of the old city on the hillside, while the modern industrial growth has spread beneath it alongside the river. Best views of the old quarter are from ancient foot-bridges crossing the Onar. The sunless alleys retain much of the Middle Ages atmosphere, and the Calle Força — a twisting high street that follows the route of the old Roman road — was the boundary for a distin-guished Jewish quarter in the 13th century which gave rise to an important mystic cult of Cabalists. Its old school, Isaac el Sec, still stands on Sant Llorenc and plans are underway to refound it. The Cathedral, atop 90 steps, is outstanding, and its single aisle, a radical architectural departure in the 15th century, creates exceptional spaciousness and light.

Take time to view the Treasury, which boasts a Tapestry of Creation replete with 11th-century sea monsters plus the *Codigo del Beatus*, dated 975, which has illuminated miniatures in unusual Mozarabic style to illustrate the Apocalypse. The Sobreportes Gate stands close by the temple to St Felix, the spire of which was partly lopped off by lightning. This event is relived every October when fireworks rain down during the fiesta for the city's patron, St Narcis, who was martyred here. The Arab baths, Collegiate Church and Romanesque church of San Pedro Galligans also merit a visit, if time allows. The best food in the region is, oddly enough, south on the airport road, exit A17, at **La Pequeña** (Riudellots de la Selva; 47 71 32). A rustic setting for traditional Catalan food, it is sought out by the locals. Closed on Tuesdays. **Hostal Bellmirall** (Calle Bellmirall, 3; 20 40 09), near the cathedral is a pleasant and inex-pensive inn. There are a number of comfortable if colourless 3-star hotels, most on the edges of town.

Head north of Gerona, climbing the Garrotxa Mountains for around 16km until reaching **BAÑOLES (BANYOLES)**, beside a natural lake. Carp fishermen and a few windsurfers have discovered the village, but the Benedictine monastery, San Esteban, dating from the 9th century, is surprisingly unvisited as are the two stone churches in the central plaza. The regional archaeological museum, in the Gothic Pia Almoina, features a Neanderthal jawbone. A road circles the bright blue lake, passing by the 12th-century church at **PORQUERAS** with its carved arch, and looping back to the main road after 4km. Turn left here onto the C-150.

Approaching **BESALÚ**, the landscape takes a turn and becomes even greener, due to rich volcanic soil. The village is an anachronism — a per-fectly preserved medieval stronghold with a 12th-century fortified stone bridge angled over the Fluviá River. Known to the Celts, it was later settled by the Iberians, Romans and Muslims before the Catholic Recon-quest. As a measure of its potency, it even ruled an autonomous country for a couple of centuries before being taken over by the House of Barcelona in 1020. On the farther side of the bridge, with its eight mis-matched arches, a Jewish quarter thrived. A rare Romanesque Mikwah (a synagogue's place of ritual ablution) was uncovered there recently, one of only three in Europe and the sole Spanish example, now restored. Sant Pere Monastery, with lion carvings, the old Cathedral of Santa María, Sant Vincenc, and the arcaded Plaza Mayor all are fine examples of 12th-century Gothic architecture. While conscious of its extraordinary heritage, Besalú is basically a village of cattle farmers with a small textile industry: Catalan red cloth caps.

The road to Olot passes through a landscape which once smouldered like the morning after Guy Fawkes, with the cones of some 40 extinct volcanoes in the region. Most craters are obscured by greenery, though Sant Pau has bleak lava beds. While none of the volcanoes is active, several cones do burp up occasional puffs of fresh air, called '*els butadors*'. The woods are more varied here, with a particularly pretty beech grove. Big basalt outcrops loom up, and the **Castellfollit de la Roca** clinging to the top of one of the highest escarpments, looks most precarious.

OLOT, in the midst of this dramatic scenery, has nurtured an art colony since its School of Fine Arts opened in the 18th century. Wood-carving, especially of polychromatic sacred figurines for the church, is an important industry here, though the region is mostly devoted to cattle and sheep. The collection in the regional museum includes an El Greco, plus gold and silver filigree work on ornaments from the 15th and 19th centuries. While both the cloister of Carmen and Church of San Esteban are noteworthy, the modern Sola Morales house is an innovative and striking contrast to all the sober stonework from centuries past. Fiestas are hard to miss in Olot, with two big cattle fairs competing in the calendar with folk festivals and religious processions. The second Sunday in July sees 5,000 dancers converge on the town to interpret 50 varieties of *sardana*, the Catalan circle dance with linked hands. And every 18 October, since the king granted favours in 1314, the town has celebrated Sant Lluc. Alongside folksong and dance competitions, the townspeople dish up what must be the biggest bargain in all of Catalonia: the *cena de duro* (tuppence supper). A donation of 5 pesetas buys a plate of rice, bread plus a glass of wine and a very fine time indeed.

Leaving town on the secondary road towards **SAN JUAN DE LAS ABADESAS (SANT JOAN DE LES ABADESSES)**, look back for a painterly view of the alley with its lush green volcanic cones. The Ter River is full of trout, and a restored 12th-century bridge crosses it into San Juan, named for its collegiate church. Las Brujas (the witches), its most revered treasure, is a 15th-century wooden carving whose figures have a somehow menacing presence.

Just west is **RIPOLL**, a town whose fame spread through Europe for its friars and its firearms. The library of the monastery **Santa María de Ripoll** was vast, and the place became a centre of ideas and learning under the Benedictines, who did not discount treatises from so-called heathens. First founded by the Visigoth Recaredo in 589, it was rebuilt beginning in 879 to rectify damage caused by the Moors. Count Wilfred the Shaggy, who mandated the first reconstruction, is buried here. The monastery is a hotchpotch of styles, often enlarged and remodelled, and severely damaged by fire in 1835. One impressive relic of the 12th century is the

West Portal, known as the Ripoll Bible, recounting most of the Bible in carved stone images, with a few gargoyles for good measure. It is rather worn, unfortunately. Next to the monastery, the Folklore Museum displays many samples of the prized guns, going back to the 16th century, which Ripoll exported. The remainder of the town is lacklustre. If you must stay overnight, try **Solana de Ter** (70 10 62) outside town on the Barcelona road.

Otherwise, leave town on the N-152, and turn left at Campdevano. Continue on this winding road for 24km, until La Pobla de Lillet, where a country road cuts right, up the slopes. This leads past a simple but elegant Romanesque church, Sant Vicenc de Rus, and crosses a medieval bridge close by the cascade, Salt de la Farga. Keep going, past the impressive Fonts del Llobregat, where Barcelona's big river surges forth, carving the limestone beneath it. It is very cold water, the spring mingling with snow-melt off the Pyrenees. **CASTELLAR DE NUCH**, just above the springs, has a glorious past reflected in the number of Romanesque monuments. The parish church, with a lovely bell tower, was drastically remodelled in the 18th century, but still holds traces of its 12th-century origins in the nave and the ironwork on the great door. Most of the village's prime plots of land are reserved for cultivating potatoes, cereal and animal fodder, while the two-storey houses are clustered on the steep hills. Each August, on the final Sunday, the village hosts an international sheepdog contest with fierce competition and celebration.

Leave Castellar climbing northwards and turn left at the fork onto the N-152, which passes high on the mountain, way above the steep wooded slopes that loom over the narrow valleys. There is rarely a straight stretch in this serpentine road. Arrival at **PUIGCERDÁ** brings civilisation of sorts in a ski-oriented Pyrenees bordertown. Balconied houses overlook old streets and a pretty lake north of town rents boats to paddle amongst the swans. Terrific meals can be had in **MERANGES**, a village just off the scenic road southeast of town, with views over the Cerdaña Valley. Turn right just past **GER**, and follow the road until it peters out before the National Reserve. **C'an Borrell** (Regreso, 3; 88 00 33) rents out rooms as well as serving up regional treats such as leek flan, rabbits with turnips, and imaginative game dishes. Closed Mondays and from January through Easter. A number of reasonable hostals and comfortable hotels are available back in Puigcerdá. This is a good pause before setting out on the mountain roads to explore the national parks nearby, notably **Aigües Tortes**. This deserves an anticipatory rest, as the wilderness often becomes too rough for family cars and demands exploration by landrover, horseback or on foot or skis.

Medieval Towns and Monasteries

3 days/375km/from Tarragona

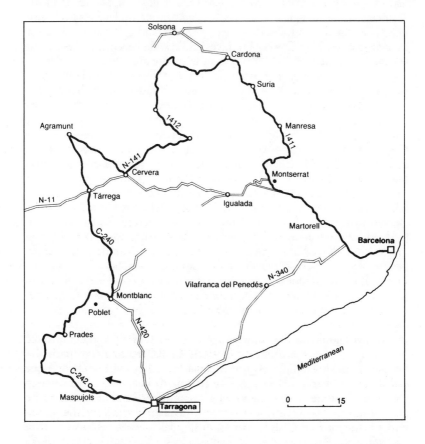

The counts of Barcelona put their distinctive stamp over the entire provincial region of Tarragona, Lérida and Barcelona. Feudal walled cities crop up in the wooded landscape and amidst terraces of grapevines, destined to become champagne, and cork oak forests for their packaging. Wealthy patrons would show their savvy by competing to endow spectacular architectural experiments in monasteries, thereby gaining power, beauty and possibly rewards in the hereafter. Their efforts are as magnificent as ever. Still, the landscape surpasses these buildings: mountains of pure salt, jagged ranges topped with spires, green hills beside bright rivers. And flowers everywhere.

TARRAGONA pop: 111,689 Tourist Office: Rambla Navoa, 46. As one of Spain's first major settlements (the massive walls date from early in the first millennium BC), Tarragona rivals Mérida for archaeological merit and is much visited by scholars of antiquity. The Romans built it into an important foreign capital, traditionally the birthplace of Pontius Pilate. After the invasions by Visigoths and then Moors, it became the seat of the Christian Church in Spain until Toledo supplanted it in the 11th century. Today, it is a prosperous city of wine traders. Its lively sea-front is so popular with vacationing Spaniards that hotel rooms are sparse in high season. With flowered terraces and a wide beach, it is one of the few places on the Costa Dorada with atmosphere and style. Some Roman or medieval buildings rise from their bulky Iberian foundations like clumsily grafted trees. Visit the 12th-century cathedral, built over the Temple of Jupiter, which houses an immense altarpiece dedicated to St Thecla, city patron. The cloister, with its tapestries and statuary, is very impressive. But best is the Archaeology Museum: Roman mosaics — a Medusa head is unnerving; an erotic oil lamp, plus masks, sculpture and trinkets are all taken from the local area. Closed Mondays and Sunday evenings, as well as for siesta on weekdays. Entry fee: 100 pesetas. The Paseo Arqueológico through gardens along the base of the city walls reveals 2,000 years of history, starting with enormous Cyclopean blocks marked in places with Iberian symbols, and topped by Roman and then medieval refortifications. The outer ring was added by the English during the War of the Spanish Succession. Also closed Mondays. Entry: 25 pesetas. Hotels in all categories offer rooms on Tarragona, though it's wise to book in summer. Seafood is a speciality, and the El Serallo *tapas* bars can provide a tasty and cheap alternative to the restaurants. Foodies wanting a treat might try **Sol Ric** (Vía Augusta, 227).

Leave Tarragona on the motorway towards Reus and exit onto the N-420. The second turn-off, through Maspujols, sets you on the C-342, twisting through the hills. At the Albarca Pass, turn right and climb the ear-popping road to **PRADES**. The rich earth near the village is deep red, and the stones of the medieval walls and Gothic buildings echo the same tones. A tall Gothic cross greets travellers who enter the village beneath the main arched doorway and step back centuries into La Plaza de Sant Roc. The parish church leans against the 13th-century walls to form this square, and through an arch just the other side, a narrow alley leads past the wrought iron balconies of the old houses and opens onto the Plaza Mayor. Here, surrounded by arcades for shade and shelter, a round Renaissance fountain with eight water jets dominate the central Plaza Mayor. A small bridge crosses the ancient moat.

Leaving town, follow the signs towards the fabled Cistercian monastery of **Santa María de Poblet**, some 20km northeast. **ESPLUGO DE FRANCOLI**, still medieval in appearance, is the gateway to the monastery, reached after a gentle hike for ¾ hour ... making one feel like a true pilgrim. The church's power politics were played out in Poblet, founded by Berenguer to mark the Reconquest of Catalonia from the Moors. It became the final retreat for most of the Kings of Aragón. Their tombs are remarkably restored, as are the cloister, chapter house, refectory and kitchen. An enormous wine cellar is nearly as big as the library. Gilded bronze doors lead into this architectural haven, and it's difficult to believe that all the restoration has taken place since 1935; the Napoleonic Wars gave an excuse for the locals to wreak revenge for corruption in holy places; the great library was shredded and burned while buildings and monuments shattered. Hour-long tours are given daily (closed 12.30-3). Entry: 125 pesetas.

Head north and turn right on the N-246, towards **MONTBLANC**, 8km away. The fortified gates are so narrow that the highway has had to by-pass this former ducal village, leaving it in relative peace. The massive 12th-century ramparts loom and many of the 34 towers still stretch towards the Cabra Mountain Range on the horizon. The Gothic Church of Santa María, unfinished behind its Baroque doorway, is the hulking presence on the hill and worth a look. The Hospital of Santa Magdalena has an exquisite patio, and wandering among the Gothic houses to reach the Plaza Mayor and a quiet coffee under the arches is a pleasure. One of the houses on this main square, by playing up the relief on its façade with unorthodox pastel paint, contrasts with the sober town hall and Desclergue Palace. Accepting the unordinary is routine for this village: Moriscos (officially Christianised Moors) built an advanced system of underground irrigation tunnels in the region, bringing agricultural riches that the rulers could not technically understand but used to great advantage. Just outside the great walls is a Franciscan monastery. Its 14th-century church served as a wine warehouse until quite recently. Perhaps this is a reflection of mixed regard for its most famous monk, a sort of Morisco in reverse. Anselm Turmeda, a distinguished medieval Catalan friary-scholar, left here to convert to Islam and today is worshipped as a Sufi saint in North Africa.

To reach **AGRAMUNT**, take the C-240 just north of the ramparts, and drive on past Tarrega. The fields are green with vegetables along this 55km stretch, thanks to efficient irrigation from the Urgell Canal. An early 13th-century church is the pride of this village (note geometrical motifs around the covings of the portal), and the 18th-century town hall is also impressive. The road south passes by three castles within 20km before coming to **CERVERA**, overlooking a river valley from its site on the hill and apparently oblivious that the main highway to Barcelona tunnels underneath it. A grand octagonal tower belfry stands beside the Santa María Church, and the round Sant Pere el Gros (St Peter the Big), dating from the 11th century, is thought to have been a temple for initiating pilgrims or a funerary chapel. Santo Domingo merits a visit just for its cloister. A century as a university town has given Cervera an air quite distinct from the medieval towns around it. The multi-storey houses seem a little forlorn since the big Bourbon university relocated to Barcelona in 1841, but the old campus is sometimes used as a cultural centre. Five Baroque sculpted heads and torsos support the town hall balcony and their pained expressions must have amused any crowd hearing out long speeches down below. Deep passages under the old walls reveal irregular arches and crude support beams fashioned from entire logs, complete with bark. Figures of arched black cats and moon faces on the lintels are the focus of popular legends about witches' covens plotting beneath the walls.

Leave town on the north branch of the road, N-141, as far as Calaf. Here, bear left on the 1412, and then loop right again at Toro. After passing through wooded hills, turn right at the fork. Soon **CARDONA** begins to dominate the landscape, even though approached from the rear. A citadel and castle loom 120m above the entire feudal village, and today have been converted in part to a state parador, next to the Lombard style Collegiate Church with its impressive vaulting. During the War of the Spanish Succession, Philip V withstood a French assault from these ramparts, his last stronghold. Below, the houses seem almost stunted even though most stand four or five storeys in the hilly streets, each window shaded with a green Persian blind. The parish church in the village boasts a lovely polygonal apse and narrow Gothic windows. On the outskirts is the curious *Sali*, or Salt Mountain, some 80m high and 5km round, glinting white in the sun. Natural grottoes within the mound are open to the public, and potassium deposits nearby have been exploited for over 50 years. The **Parador Duques de Cardona** (869 12 75) is an ancient beauty, worth a splurge just for the views over the river valley or the sparkling mount of salt. It prides itself on the regional cooking of its restaurant: rabbit with snails is a speciality, and *crema quemada* (burnt cream) as dessert is surprisingly tasty.

Exit south, through Suria, and continue hugging the riverbed until reaching **MANRESA**. Here, intrepid lovers of religious architecture can view an impressive Jesuit residence — Santa Cueva de San Ignacio — plus the cloister of the San Ignacio Church. See also the Seo de Santa María de la Aurora, with noteworthy Gothic portal and crypt. But be aware that an entire monastery awaits in yonder hills. The old bridge (13th century) contrasts quite subtly with the so-called new bridge (14th century). In August and September, the bullring comes alive for fervent local aficionados. A meal worth seeking out — though the restaurant is open only on weekends — can be had in Sant Cristofal (Castelbell i Vilar) at the **C'an Japet** (835 70 06), heading south on the 1411, and turning off to the left. After lunch here, return to the 1411 and follow the signs to the Monastery. These are for pilgrims as well as for tourists. At **SANTA CECILIA**, you leave the secular plain behind. Well, almost.

Despite having to cope with hordes of daytrippers up from the Costa Brava as well as hundreds of legitimate pilgrims coming to light a candle to *La Moreneta* (the Black Madonna), no visitor to this region should miss **MONTSERRAT**. It is not just another monastery. The mountain range has a mystical appearance of steep cliffs and weird pinnacles as if a coral reef had been conjured above the domes and terraces of the deep red sierra. Wagner set his opera, *Parsifal*, here and it seems plausible that the Grail would be uncovered in this other-worldly setting. In fair weather, eager alpinists loop their bright ropes on every outcrop. This, combined with the cable cars, tour buses, honeymooning couples and overpriced snacks may put you off the place, regardless of the majesty beneath this carnival. Persevere. Listening to the *Escolanía* boys' choir at morning mass, salve or vespers — one of Europe's oldest choral groups, founded in the 13th century — reaffirms that you are in Catalonia's most holy shrine. Only here could the Catalans under Franco worship or exchange vows in their own language. Montserrat (Montse for short) is a popular Spanish girl's name, summoning up beauty, reverance and romance.

Benedictine monks created the monastery in the 11th century, on the ruins of an 8th-century hermitage which had been overrun by the Moors. With increased influence, the place grew to become an independent abbey and grand building works were commissioned by powerful patrons; Pope Julius II of Renaissance Italy was a former abbot. After the French sacked the sanctuary in 1812, only one side of the Gothic cloister remained. Most of the rest is now ornate 19th-century reconstruction. The museum, with paintings by Caravaggio, Brueghel, Zurbarán, El Greco and many more, also holds curious archaeological treasures from Mesopotamia, Palestine, Egypt and Cyprus. But the buildings are hard pressed to rival the surrounding countryside, and the ruined hermitages amidst the crags and grottoes are great fun to explore. The more distant ones are linked by a sort of ski-lift and, incongruous though it may seem to stalk the haunts of religious hermits in this manner, the funiculars and cable cars provide incredible views. From the highest hermitage, Sant Jeroni, follow the short path to the summit. From here, a panorama takes in Montserrat, the distant Pyrenees and, if the clouds are high, across the Mediterranean to the peaks of Mallorca. The monks try to distill this vision in a potent herb liqueur, *aromas de Montserrat*, and a sip is almost obligatory before descending the mountain. Campsites near the monastery are sometimes overcrowded, and a **youth hostel** (835 00 35) in 10th-century chambers below the cable car station is a good alternative. The order administers two hotels, **Abat Cisneros** and **Hostal El Monastir** (both 835 02 01), and reservations are well advised.

From the monastery, Barcelona is just 60km away. You could coast behind the lines of tourist coaches making for the N-II. At **MARTORELL** stop to see the Gothic bridge before hopping on the motorway into the city.

BARCELONA pop: 3,096,748 Tourist Office: Gran Vía de les Corts Catalanes, 10. At last, out of the Middle Ages and into a metropolis. Night life. Style. Sleaze. As the leading city in post-Franco Spain, Barcelona merits a thorough visit. It is the antithesis of rural Spain, although many of its residents have just recently arrived from the countryside for city opportunities. Trek around to see the idiosyncratic buildings of Antoni Gaudí (the unfinished Church of La Sagrada Familia, Güell Park, two apartment blocks on Passeig de Gracia — Casa Batlló (at 43) and Casa Milá (at 92)). But do spare some time to see the newest architecture. The Olympic velodrome, readying for 1992, is sleekly futuristic while the Plaza de Sants, an urban space by the main railway station, eases the concrete with amusing fountains and detail. New Wave art galleries, such as Metronom, Metras, Plensa and Colomar, will make an impact after viewing so many traditional paintings out in the provinces.

Still, grand museums and palaces abound: Federico Marés Museum houses an extensive collection of polychrome wooden statues, and the

Museum of the City traces the history from Phoenician founders through to the 19th century. Both of these are in the Gothic quarter, near the Cathedral. Up on the terraces of Montjuïc, with views across the city and harbour, there is an amusement park in the grounds of the old fort plus more museums ... most closed Mondays. Catalan art rates the largest exhibition, but museums of Ceramics and Archaeology have innovative displays. The Joan Miró Foundation has several hundred paintings by the prolific artist as well as 3,000 drawings. A holdover from the 1929 fair is the *Pueblo Español*, which collects different styles of popular architecture into plazas and squares (the motley result recalls certain southern Californian suburbs, except for the regional craftsmen at work). The Martime Museum is exceptional, and a wander around the large port can be fun. The Picasso Museum, in the 14th-century Aguilar Palace, displays mostly etchings, drawings and engravings alongside some early paintings. Allow time for a stroll along the Ramblas, watching all the stylish people eyeing one another. For a grand view over the city, mountains and sea, drive (or catch the cablecar) up to Tibidabo, and look out from Pedralbes Palace. The odd name of the 530m hill supposedly comes from a corruption of Satan's words tempting Christ ... 'All this I will give to you' (*Haec omnia tibi dabo*). Hotels and restaurants galore, in all price ranges. Be aware that hours can be extremely late: some clubs don't even open until 3am!

Aragón Pyrenees

4 days/420km/from Huesca

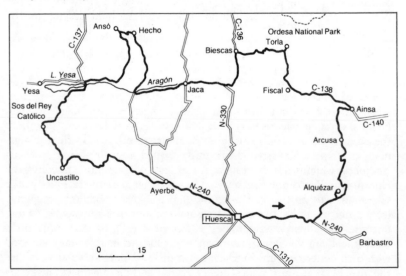

It's difficult to choose between the magnificent wild scenery of the Spanish Pyrenees: Aigües-Tortes in Lérida, the Valle D'Aran in Catalonia or Ordesa Park just east in Aragón. Each has its proponents and different appeal. Ordesa, north of Huesca, is less visited and more rugged. Animals outnumber the hikers. Don't attempt a visit outside the May–September season, because the weather is unpredictable and a clear pass could be snowbound before departure. Many villages nearby are little changed after centuries, though the people are open to new ideas. Farther south, monumental villages look as if they remain in the Middle Ages.

HUESCA pop: 44,372 Tourist Office: Coco Alto, 23. Long the capital of Upper Aragón, Huesca has grown fat with fertility (rich farmland surrounds it). None the less, it hides some treasures. The church of San Pedro el Viejo holds the tombs of two kings of Aragón, and has even recycled a marble tombstone from the 2nd century. Though restored, the cloister of this former 11th-century monastery contains some exemplary Romanesque sculpture. Quite convincing monsters lurk on the capitals. The old university, which incorporates some of the royal palace buildings in its grounds, houses the Provincial Museum and its painting collection. Most interesting is the gallery beneath, the *Sala de la Campana* (Bell Room), where Ramiro II supposedly staged his massacre, beheading the rebel nobles he'd asked to counsel him on the casting of a giant bell. A grisly painting in the town hall (across from the cathedral) depicts the event. With its octagonal tower and Mudéjar gallery, the Late Gothic cathedral is unusual. Its 16th-century alabaster altarpiece is exquisite. Though not a real tourist town, Huesca has plenty of mid-range hotels. **Hostal Aragónesa** (Pl de Lizana, 15; 22 06 50) is a good one near the old centre. Much of the upper part of the town still bears scars from the Civil War during which the Republicans failed to take hold despite an 18-month siege.

Take the N-240 east out of Huesca. After about 25km, past Angües, look out for a left turn onto a secondary road which leads to Abiego. (If you reach Lascellas you've missed it and will need to about-face.) Bear right at Abiego and follow the roadsigns to **ALQUÉZAR**. Inside double walls behind two deep canyons, the 300 villagers here seem well guarded against the intrusions of the 20th century. The only gate is surveyed by three towers, one joined to the Collegiate Church. To visit it, find the alleyway marked *Teléfonos*, which leads eventually to the entrance. The north side of the cloister survives from the early 12th-century construction when the Christians modified a Moorish castle into this fortress/church. From the lofty position, look down over the Río Vera and its streams which carve out the green bordered channels. Narrow streets all atilt maintain a Gothic feel, and the popular architecture, with arched doorways bordered with brick and tiny arched windows outlined in contrasting paint, echoes the lines of the main plaza's shady arcades. Beautiful chimneys are a hallmark of Upper Aragón, where the harsh winters demand a hearth fire.

Once out of the village (there's just the one exit), proceed up the narrow road past Arcusa until you reach the former medieval capital,

AINSA. This lovely walled town has neat cornfields in the lowlands beyond the modern buildings which skirt the ramparts, and is a lively centre for the surrounding villages in the Pyrenees. Rough stone houses cluster in the old quarter up the hill. The double row of Romanesque arches in the central plaza are thick and shelter against the strong mountain winds. Roofing sometimes replaces the usual terracotta tiles with wooden shingles. Once an Arab stronghold, Ainsa obliterated much of the Moorish legacy when Garcia Jiménez founded his independent kingdom, Sobrarbe. Quite a bit of the old realm is now up north in Ordesa National Park.

Driving up the C-138 towards Fiscal, watch the river beside the road. Peculiar shark-fin shapes jut threateningly from the water. They are rocks. Up ahead, Torla can soon be seen dwarfed against the rising green of the valley. **TORLA** is the jumping-off point for exploring this wilderness. Plenty of accommodation can be found in the old stone village, and a mountain view is virtually guaranteed. Campgrounds are the cheapest option but **Vinamala** (Nueva Plaza, 1; 48 61 56) is open all year round. Picnics can be bought from the local shops, though there is a fair selection of restaurants and bars.

Ordesa, proclaimed a national park back in 1918, is breathtaking. Vertical rockfaces striped blue grey or brick red tower over the valley floor. The Arazas River, tumbling past the poplars and beeches in the basin, jumps with trout stalked by sleek river otters. Evergreens crowd the lower slopes, some ancient fir trees topping 24m. Spring snowmelt transforms the cliffs with waterfalls and cascades, and chamois leap about the upper peaks. Summer brings edelweiss, and hikers pass by clumps of heather, broom and sweet briar. At the beginning of the park road, a belvedere looks out over a general view, allowing you to savour what's ahead. Further on, a second lookout views the Tamborrotera Falls, almost 61m high. Paths are signposted from the information centre, the restaurant, and from some of the cosy refuges that seem to crop up just when you want a rest. You needn't be a mountaineer, but a stout pair of walking shoes and a rucksack packed with a windcheater and drinks is a good idea. The Soasso Circle Route, about six hours long, takes in all the prettiest falls plus the steep gorge. Experienced climbers can tackle the 300m high rock faces, and the Three Sisters (Tres Sorores), a trio of mountains over 3,000m high, challenge alpinists. The air seems almost perilously pure for average city lungs.

Passing back through Torla, take the C-140 to Biescas, where you bear left and follow the signs to Jaca. This is a good road, but in holiday season it can be quite crowded with Spanish skiers. Patience. On the approach to Jaca, the Gállego River valley widens, carving away the limestone banks.

JACA pop: 13,771 Tourist Office: Paseo Calvo Sotelo (36 00 98). The tourist office gives information about the whole region, not just this ancient garrison town, and its detailed maps of the Pyrenees trails and peaks are invaluable. Jaca, with the oldest Romanesque cathedral in all Spain, has long borne the excitement of a wayfarers' stop. The pilgrims to

Santiago de Compostela who took the Aragónese road would set out from here. The old cathedral influenced religious architecture all along the pilgrimage trail. Every May, a fiesta honours the courage of Jaca's women and girls who drove off an attempted Moorish reconquest in the 8th century. Even back then it was a well-established settlement, having hosted the Roman consul Marco Poncio Caton in 195BC. It's worth stocking up at Jaca's bakery, one of the few places where traditional Upper Aragonese pastries, renowned among sweet-toothed pilgrims, are still made. Hungry skiers crowd the better restaurants which serve hearty game dishes and roast lamb.

Outside Jaca, along the N-240, take the first turning to the right until the narrow road halts in **HECHO**. The secluded village gets into its stride in July and August, when its symposium of Modern Sculpture and Painting takes to the hills and startling shapes appear in odd places. Just 10km west, in the next valley, the villagers of **ANSO** aren't so forward-looking. Some of the older women still wear the traditional embroidered dress and quite a few speak an old dialect limited to this remote valley. Some of the homes are daubed with weird glyphs claimed to harken back to the *agote* population. These were isolated bands of outcasts, owing to being lepers, albinos or mystic heretics . . . historians dither. An ethnographic display in Plaza de San Pedro doesn't solve the mystery. **Posada Magoria** (37 00 49) is a newish hotel which boasts a good if unlikely vegetarian restaurant.

Back down to the main road, bear right towards the big Yesa Reservoir. The vegetation gets patchy and the earth becomes tinged an unearthly blue. Don't suspect the playful artists from Hecho of fooling with the landscape; these mounds of tertiary sediment were heaped up centuries ago. Turn left just before the artificial lake, and head for **SOS DEL REY CATÓLICO**, birthplace of King Ferdinand.

The largest of the *Cinco Villas de Aragón* (Five Aragón Towns) distinguished by Felipe V for their loyalty during the War of the Spanish Succession, Sos maintains a solemn medieval air. Narrow cobbled streets lead off from the Palacio de Sada (Ferdinand's former nursery, now quite deteriorated), and the arched windows and fine grillwork on the old mansions retain the illusion that this is still the Middle Ages. The Romanesque Church of San Esteban (note 16th-century carved stalls) has some fine 14th-century murals by its crypt.

Press on 22km farther to **UNCASTILLO**, another one of the select five fortress towns on the frontier with Navarre, but smaller and less visited. The protective walls are still there, and three towers stretch skywards above the tile roofs of the village. Many of the houses have windows bordered with a whitewashed strip, right on top of the ancient stone, just as far as an arm holding a brush can reach from inside. San Martín, the Romanesque church, sports pinnacle turrets on its belfry. But the intricate carving on its south portal, well preserved from the elements, sets this apart as an exemplary Romanesque doorway. The ruins of the Gothic palace stand high on a promontory next to a squared-off tower.

Heading east from Uncastillo, cut over the hills through the **Sierra**

Mayor pass on to **Ayerbe**, right on the main road. After stopping in there for a look at the Marques' Gothic palace, take the first left turn-off past town, and climb the formidable 7km to **Loarre Castle**. The road has as many hairpin turns as stones. Yet overlooking the plain of Aragón from the round towers up on this rocky point gives a sense of peace rather than power. Now carefully restored, this great 11th-century military castle was built by Sancho Ramirez to blend into the surroundings. The three big towers are outstanding, and the Romanesque chapel within the fortress is impressive. Allow time for exploration and dreams. Backtracking through Ayerbe, Huesca lies just under 30km away on a fast road, the N-240.

Ebro Delta

3 days/285km/from Tortosa

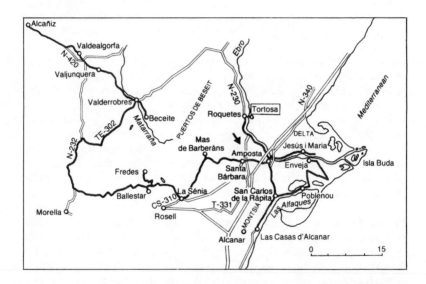

The Ebro River makes one last hurrah, up in the heights of the Beseit Range (where rare wild Iberian mountain goats have been sighted swimming across its tributaries), before fanning out into a wide delta at the very base of Catalonia. Life here is placid, with eel fishermen and rice farmers plodding through their chores. Progress is measured by the river itself, which pushes out 10m, farther into the Mediterranean each year. Seafood is simple and good, and artisans create pottery and woven esparto (grass) with traditional care rather than churning it out for the tourist markets.

TORTOSA pop: 47,000 Tourist Office: Plaza d'Espanya. A line of cypresses is a windbreak for orange and peach orchards on the terraces above town, and beyond them the rows of olive trees are laid out on chalky soil as tidily as a military cemetery. This is fitting, for Tortosa was the scene of the fierce Battle of the Ebro, in which over 150,000 lives were lost in brutal trench-warfare. A memorial rises from the river itself to mark the site of this last Republican offensive in 1938. The 14th-century Cathedral, crowded by surrounding buildings so that the full frontal effect is lost, has several fine chapels, notably the Baroque chapel of the city's patroness, Our Lady of the Ribbon. Her relic, a stylised belt, is surrounded by inlays of local jasper and marble. The Bishop's palace features an enormous flight of steps that dominates one side of the patio. And San Luis College, founded for Moorish converts by Carlos V, has an even more attractive patio. Much of Tortosa's strategic advantage has been lost with the advance of the delta, but in Roman times it guarded the only river bridge and was the first bastion against sea-invaders. La Zuda, a former Templar citadel, rises above the town for a wide panorama which extends across the rooftops to the plains and the sierra. It became the residence of the Count of Barcelona, Ramón Berenguer IV, who wrested it from the Arabs. Now it has been remade into a luxury parador: **Parador Nacional Castillo de la Zuda** (44 44 50), probably the sole reason to spend the night in this town. Mediterranean cuisine in the dining room is better than standard. Try the *romesco de pescado*, fish in wine sauce with ground hazelnuts and garlic.

Cross the river to Roquetes, and pick up the N-230 along the banks of the Ebro south to **AMPOSTA**. A lively market takes place here every Tuesday. Turn right here and drive down to **SAN CARLOS DE LA RÁPITA**, an extraordinary fishing village which has a half-moon plaza and a Bourbon flavour to its elegant 17th-century buildings. Las Alfaques, a huge natural harbour, was never fully developed according to Carlos III's schemes, but is just beginning to catch up, now that offshore petroleum has been located. **Fernandel** (Highway N-340, km 163) is a sea-view restaurant with pricey meals that exceed expectations. Shellfish is a speciality along with savoury fish soup (closed Mon and 20 Jan–20 Feb). Several adequate hotels are available in season down by the beach. To reach the lookout point of Sacrada Corazón, take the narrow road past the town cemetery and follow the signposts. From up here, you can see where the delta opens up into two principal channels, and canals cross the marshes like silver ribbons, with great flocks of migrating seabirds shadowing them. Over 200 different species stop over here, including a colony of flamingos. Behind, in the Montsia Range, Moorish castles stand in ruin. There seems to be little sign of the *Ribbath*, La Rápita, the Sufi monastery that gave its name to the town and must have whirled away in Dervish haste before the Reconquest campaigns.

A short detour 14km down to the beachfront at **CASAS D'ALCANAR** presents a broad strand with a view of the lighthouse out on Bania peninsula plus a simple restaurant, **El Pescador** (Cadiz, 4; 73 70 93). The proprietor, Angelines, is known as a wizard of the frying pan for being able to find the precise point to fry each of the sundry sorts of Mediterranean fish brought in by the local fleet. Backtracking to San Carlos de la Rápita, turn right and go to **POBLENOU DEL DELTA** (it abandoned its old name, Villa Franco, when the dictator died and rechristened itself 'our town' in the formerly forbidden Catalan). Eel fishermen are out in force here checking their fixed *pantenes*, gadgets which they use to trap the adolescent eels on their way back from the Sargasso Sea, ready to spend adulthood in freshwater. These succulent *anguilas* are grilled fresh and also dried for export. Lampreys, those blood-suckers of the sea, are also caught. Just beyond the plain 1940s style town, cross the l'Encanyissada between two lagoons. A right turn leads to the **Playa des Eucalyptus** with camping sites and strolling food vendors in season. A dirt track to the left leads across swampy land (beward of quicksand) over to the Alfaques peninsula with its pines and marshes. A small two-car ferry crosses from **SANT JAUME D'ENVEJA** to **DELT EBRE**, operating only in daylight as it is very low tech, with no running lights. Delt Ebre is a reception centre for the natural park on this northern half of the delta, and has a list of vacation houses and private homes renting out rooms in the area. Don't forego a hike to the top of **Montell de les Verges**, on a small promontory, which has a wide vista out to the rice fields, the isolated island of **Buda** and the web of riverlets heading to sea. **LA CAVA** has a couple of decent places to eat, and then the riverbank road leads through **JESÚS I MARÍA**, across a bridge and back to **AMPOSTA**.

Take the local road east through Santa Bárbara and through the olives up to Mas de Barberáns in the foothills of the Beseit range. Skirt along the mountains down to **LA SÉNIA**, where there is some overnight accommodation, and turn right. Switchback up the mountains, remembering that though at times the crags on top are hidden by mist they are still there. The river along here forms deep green pools and then carves itself a narrow gorge to hide in. Until 25 years ago, when dams were put in, the Ebro — the biggest Iberian river — was an important trade route, with flat coal barges lumbering to the coast. The hamlets up here now are quite isolated, some with fewer than four families, but are linked as a community. All were founded at the time of the Santa María monastery with funding from powerful feudal gentlemen who kept their special rights well into the 19th century. Only when the Carlist Wars gripped this region, the Maeztrago, did they lose their privileges. Much later, in the 1970s, the monastery was restored by nuns and now houses the only Carthusian convent in all Spain, the **Convent of Benifasar**.

The road winds up past Fredes and continues near the *Tossal de los Tres Reyes*, a peak which legend says was the scene for some of the first summit conferences, when the monarchs of Aragón and Catalonia would discuss differences with the Moorish king of Valencia and work out compromises away from the pressures of court. Whatever the truth of it, the three regions touch each other close by and that alone might have given rise to the name. If the weather is fine and dry in full summer, the network of rough forest roads leads over to **BECEITE**, whose town hall was reproduced in 1929 for Barcelona's Spanish Village at the Inter-

Flamingos in the Ebro Delta

national Exhibition, and beyond to **Valderrobres**. The forest is sparse and bent by the wind and the twisting Parrisal Ravine leads to a dilapidated 19th-century refuge, Mas de la Lluvia. Wildlife, particularly Iberian mountain goats protected by this national preserve, now far out-number visitors. Passes are likely to be blocked in midwinter. Should you feel more confident sticking to marked roads, retrace your route down past the convent and turn right towards Ballestar. The local road is rough and is still unpaved between Castell de Cabres and Herbeset. Join the N-232 at the pass of Torre Miró and head north as far as Monroyo. There, turn right onto the TE-302 past the hermitage of the Virgen de la Vega and on to **VALDERROBRES**.

On the south side of a bleached hill, Valderrobres was singled out by the Archbishops of Zaragoza as a second residence, though the powerful fortress-castle which dominates the town didn't stop its founder, García Fernandez de Heredia, from being assassinated in the early 15th century. Cross the Matarrana River over a Gothic bridge to enter through the old gate which still has traces where boiling oil was poured down on intru-ders. The medieval quarter is very rustic, with steep streets cut by stone stairs and plaster crumbling around wooden lintels and whitewashed rocks. The Renaissance town hall, with its grand municipal coat of arms and wrought iron balconies, reigns over a few noble mansions gathered around the main square. The Gothic Church of Santa María stands out with its lovely rose window and polygonal bell tower, but its deeply carved west doorway is the real treasure. The church is linked to the palace through a gallery for the archbishops' protection. A climb up to the palace, which is rather too luxurious to be called a fortress, is rewarded by a vista over the deep khaki-coloured rooftiles of the village and back to the Puertos de Beceite, green with the traces of the Ebro river. Valderrobres is the centre for the *chapureau*, a blend of Catalan and Aragonese culture, which has a distinct language of its own. The fierce General Cabrera, known as the Tiger of the Maeztrago, set up his base in town during the Carlist Wars, from which his guerrillas would foray south into Castellón.

Follow the TE-300 along the riverbank, past Valjunquera, until it intersects with the N-232. Branch off on a short detour to the village of **Valdealgorfa**, where artisans still make the traditional mountain coats peculiar to this region. Traces of Bronze Age settlements at **Charco de Agua Amarga** (Bitter Water Creek) are close by. The road loops around to join the N-232 which leads on to **ALCAÑIZ**, about 15km ahead.

On a hillock covered with tall buildings of mustard-coloured stone, Alcañiz surveys groves of olives and almonds which grow in the yellow earth of its sunken valley, ringed by the river Guadalope and distant hills. Most of the roofs of the four-storey houses are anchored down with a rim of rocks because of gusty winds. The town claims to be the prehistoric capital of Aragón, supported by the rich archaeological finds in nearby Cabeza del Cascarujo, El Palao, Val de Vallerias and Masada del Ram. Its recent history began with a primitive community of Moorish converts to Christianity (Mozarabs) which accounts for the town's Arab name, that translates as 'churches'. Reconquest came relatively early, in 1119, and the surviving castle dates from that era when the Knights of Calatrava had the upper hand. Alcañiz' main square has been compared to Tuscany owing to its graceful proportions and Renaissance buildings. But intricate Mudéjar arabesques in brick on the far side mark it as distinctly Spanish. Aside from the Collegiate Church, with lofty towers softened by curves and a surprising Baroque portal, the *Lonja* or auction house, with a series of late Gothic arches, distinguishes the Plaza de España. Don't miss the Chorros Fountain, with six dozen water jets and almost as many legends. The national parador chain has commandeered part of the castle for lodgings. (King Charles V did the same for himself as a temporary residence.) **Parador La Concordia** (Castillo de Calatravos; 83 04 00) has just 12 rooms and the dining room highlights the local Aragonese mountain cuisine, with grilled ribs *costillas de ternasco*, or marinated rabbit *conejo escabechado*, recommended. Almond paste sweetmeats, *almendeados*, make a good after-dinner treat, and make sure to try the extraordinary local olive oil on salad. **Meseguer** (Avda del Maeztrago, 9; 83 10 02. Closed Sun nights and 14–30 Sept) is another good choice, with earthy cooking at popular prices.

Modern civilisation is close at hand, no matter that Alcañiz seems caught in a Golden Renaissance glow. To reach **ZARAGOZA**, cross the desert of Calanda on the N-232, and continue 104km. Alternatively, **LÉRIDA** is almost equidistant along the lake route up the C-231 to Fraga, then north on the motorway N-11 into the city. Mudéjar architecture fans will want to head south on the N-420 to **TERUEL**, 162km away.

5 EXTREMADURA

This is a stark region which people have been leaving for centuries: first the explorers and conquerors of the New World, who did come back to retire at home with their takings and, lately, the peasant farmers who either seek fortune in a Spanish metropolis or send money home from a stint working abroad. Traditionally, Extremadura was a buffer zone between the kings of León and the Moors. There is a lonely grandeur in the vast sweeps of grain, past single trees, the distant mountains, the cherry and chestnut trees abloom in the river valleys. Storks nest atop towers and turrets in every village. Winters are mild here, except in the mountainous north, but the distance from sea breezes makes summer something to suffer through. Luis Buñuel turned his lens on the dismal poverty of the northern zone, focusing attention on the plight of villages far from any modern convenience. Improvement is on the way, but Las Hurdes, remote from good

roads, power lines, and even running water in some cases, is almost a land unto its own. Spaniards who come to Extremadura often bring their guns: the hunting is legendary. In some parts they hunt wild boar under the moon while mounted on horseback, with a specialised lance as the weapon of choice.

Upper Extremadura

3 days/325km/from Guadalupe

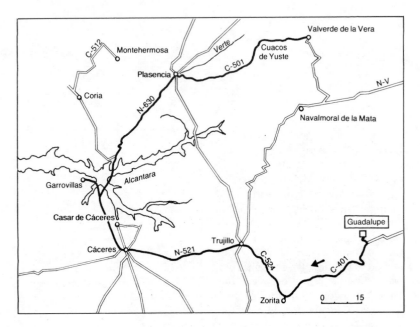

This land is harsh, but holds a certain power which made adventurers and an emperor choose to come back and retire here after seeing most of the world. One of the most revered of the so-called black madonnas, the Virgin of Guadalupe, was found in the stark hinterland centuries ago and has acquired a most fanciful shrine with the endowments of followers, many half a planet away. The past riches of Trujillo and Cáceres are hinted at by the splendour of their mansions and main plazas. North, past a rich river valley, the La Vera villages are peculiarly rustic, with balconies hung with tobacco and red peppers drying in the sun.

Within a morning's drive from Toledo, over the San Vincente Pass, and just off the C-401, **GUADALUPE** is above all a shrine, with a small village gathered rather incidentally at its base. Besides peddling souvenirs of the venerated virgin, the villagers smelt copper. The steep roofs of the whitewashed houses keep the place from looking like a classic white pueblo from Andalucía and all is subordinate to the deep red monastery with its high turrets and fortifications.

Since the 14th century, an unprepossessing oak figurine has had a fervent cult of worshippers, and fear of her power supposedly has kept the Moroccans at bay since 1340. When the conquistadors from this region brought the cult to New World Catholic missions, the Virgin of Guadalupe gained a wide following in the New World. Even today, she is

Storks nest in Trujillo and Cáceres

patron of Mexico. The first Indian converts were brought back to her shrine for baptism, and Columbus named a West Indies island after the virgin. Now, she has evolved into the emblem of 'Hispanidad', the unity among Spanish-speaking people the world over. Documents authorising Columbus' first voyage were signed here, and the date of his landfall — 12 October — is celebrated wildly here as the 'Day of Hispanidad'. Pilgrims come from afar. Inside the monastery, with its many styles of architecture, the light is dim and the little virgin on her revolving enamelled throne is nearly obscured by all the gifts of veneration. Chains left as votive offerings by freed slave converts can be seen among delicate filigree of silver and gold, rich embroidery work and illuminated manuscripts. Probably the most striking of the buildings is the Mudéjar Cloister with arches rising over a fountain. Nearby, the sacristy holds eight Zurbarán paintings. If you don't feel a trifle sacrilegious drinking in a Gothic cloister, try staying in **Hospedería Real Monasterio** (36 70 00), an inn set off in a wing of the monastery. With generations of pilgrims to put up, the village does provide inexpensive hostals near the plaza, and one palace has been converted to a state parador: **Parador Zurbarán** (Marques de la Romana, 10; 36 70 75).

Descending back to the C-401, bear right towards the Llano pass. The land is very dry, and wild boar wander around these hills. After about 40km, turn right at Zorita and continue on to **TRUJILLO**.

Entering town past terraces of nondescript post-war dwellings, you fear there's been some mistake. Keep climbing. When the streets narrow, it's time to park the car in the big lot near the Plaza Mayor. Unusual with wide steps linking its variety of levels, the main square is especially dramatic at night. Overlooking all is an enormous bronze statue of a conquistador astride his horse, both man and beast wearing helmets. This is Trujillo's most famous native son, Francisco Pizarro, the conqueror of Peru. A twin of the statue is in Lima. One rumourmonger claims that the American sculptors Runse and Harriman set out to portray Hernán Cortés for Mexico City but

Statue of Pizarro, Trujillo

government officials there refused to glorify the man who destroyed the Aztecs. Cleverly, the sculptors switched its identity and donated it to Trujillo in 1927. Shortly after, Lima commissioned its own copy and the sculptors were not left out of pocket. Whatever the case, the conquistadors built many a monument for themselves, as a look around the 16th- and 17th-century mansions near the old quarter will affirm. The Pizarro boys (five brothers — all former swineherds — went on the expedition) were not the only local explorers. Ordessa, who opened up the Amazon for the Europeans, also hails from Trujillo, while Balboa, Cortés, De Soto and De Valdivia (founder of Chile's capital) were all born in the province ... as were many of the footsoldiers under them. Much of the hoard of New World gold and silver had to sustain the phenomenal cost of Spanish wars, but some managed to filter back to this community. The Orellana Pizarro Palace, with its lovely upper gallery, was funded by Peruvian silver. So was the Marquess de la Conquista's Palace, home of brother Hernando, who married the conquistador's half-Inca niece. Note the family crest, the busts of the two couples, and the corner window, all amid the rows of grilled windows. The Gothic Church of Santa María is the most impressive one, with Ferdinand and Isabella's seats still in place beneath the rose window where the monarchs would attend mass during their infrequent visits. From the belfry, a view sweeps over rooftops to the arches of the Plaza Mayor and square towers of the castle on its granite ledge. The Virgin of Victory, an apt patron for Trujillo, is still on guard above the castle keep.

The N-521 exit towards Cáceres is clearly marked, for this regional capital, about an hour's drive, is the only sizeable town around.

CÁCERES pop: 71,852 Tourist Office: Plaza del General Mola, 33. The new town, with its university, sprawls westwards, but the old quarter of sober mansions, each with its coat of arms, is stately behind the ancient Roman/Moorish walls. This city of warriors formed the military Order of Knights of St James, back in 1170, and protected the pilgrims on their road to Santiago de Compostela while the Moors were still ambushing. On the orders of Queen Isabel, to forestall trouble, all but one of the fortified towers on these households were cut down in 1477. Casa de las Cigüeñas (the storks' house), over in the old Moorish centre, was the only exception. The Plaza de Santa María, graced with a Gothic church, is the hub of this quarter with gold-toned ochre façades ringing round it. The Bishop's palace is decorated with medallions of the Old and New World, and it's curious to see just what was known of our planet at that time. One street runs down from the palace through the Arco Cristo, an original Roman gate still basically intact. The hulking Torre Bujaco is mostly Roman, though the gate next to it — Arco de la Estrella — is an 18th-century flourish. An odd brick-topped tower marks the Toledo-Moctezuma Mansion, now a building society, which was built with the Aztec dowry of Montezuma's daughter. She married local boy Juan Cano, one of Cortés' underlings, and ultimately fled to Mexico. The Church of San Mateo, built on top of the old mosque, is also worth a visit, as is the city museum in the Moorish Casa de las Veletas. The Casa del Mono (monkey house) holds the fine arts collection.

After all this time, Cáceres really knows how to host a fiesta. Each 23 April, to toast the patron St George, the city fathers put a dragon to blazes in a main square bonfire while fireworks blast from the ramparts. It sets many a stork aflutter. The local livestock fairs (sheep and pigs) are held at the end of May and during September with just as much verve. Some of the best regional food is served at **El Figón de Eustaquio** (Plaza de San Juan, 12; 23 31 47). The air cured ham is a speciality (*jamón de pata negra*). Try to see some of the city after dark, when the lighting plays on the old stone.

The north exit from Cáceres puts you on the N-630, a highway that's wider and better paved than most of these roads. After 26km, before passing the Tajo River, turn right and head for **GARROVILLAS**.

This little town is famed for having the most convincing professional mourners in all Spain, and the bleak scenery here may explain why. A Templar convent and the 15th-century Church of San Pedro merit a stop, but the Plaza Mayor is the real prize. Just two whitewashed storeys, the lower one with arches supporting a gallery above, have been built with each pillar slightly askew, so that the effect is like entering a child's lopsided drawing. The town castle, built by the Moors with old Roman stone, is named Alconetar, Arabic for 'of the two bridges'. Part of the ruined arches of a Roman bridge, flooded over by the dam, have been hauled out for show by the main highway. On the outskirts of town, in the scrub where flocks graze, prehistoric burial chambers — the Garrote dolmens, can be visited.

Follow the road back to the highway and turn towards Plasencia, 55km north. The country is open and rolling, with the Montfrague National Park on the right. Cherry and chestnut trees grow in abundance on the approach to the Jerte River.

PLASENCIA pop: 32,178 Tourist Office: Trujillo, 17. As its name implies, a pleasant enough town with many Renaissance and medieval buildings preserved. Two cathedrals, both unfinished, were joined to make the present one. A wall separates them today, and the older one is known as the Parish Church of Santa María. Finely wrought iron balconies line most of the old mansions around the Plaza Mayor and the Mirabel Palace (open to the public). Most of the hotels in town are colourless, but **Alfonso VIII** (Alfonso VIII, 34; 41 02 50) is a good bet.

Take the C-501 east from town and head towards the hills. The powerful Charles V chose this unlikely corner of Spain to nurse his gout in retirement and, even 400 years later, it seems serenely green enough to soothe even the angst of a world-weary ruler. **CUACOS**, like most of the valley villages, grows tobacco as a cash crop. The brown leaves, alongside clusters of red peppers, frequently hang to dry from the wooden balconies of the houses. A left turning here leads up to **Yuste Monastery**, where the old Habsburg lived out his last days. His chambers have been kept as he left them, arranged so he might hear mass held in the chapel without stirring from his deathbed. The dining hall, Gothic church and two cloisters have been restored after sacking by French troops in the early 1800s.

Farther up the valley, **JARANDILLA DE LA VERA** boasts a feudal castle which has lately been refurbished as a parador (**Parador Carlos V**, Ctra de Plasencia; 56 01 17). Charles V himself stayed there, guest of the Count of Oropesa, while he waited three months for his retirement apartments to be done up. There are less expensive inns off the pretty village square with views over the Vera plain, planted with tawny tobacco plants. The woods nearby are curious, mixing chestnut and oak trees with the more Mediterranean figs, olives and oranges. Small streams jump with trout. And in the villages, water sounds continuously from the simple stone fountains on every plaza.

One of the prettiest villages is **VALVERDE DE LA VERA**, farther up the C-501. It, too, has narrow twisting streets and the half-timbered houses, each with an alpine-style balcony pointing south or west. It seems strange that so few houses have chimneys, but the kitchens on the top floor have a row of hanging hams that need the smoke; the remainder is dispersed through the roof tiles. There are vestiges of a castle, which used to double as the village cemetery, and a 15th-century parish church. The main square has a carved stone fountain as the centrepiece, while wooden lintels are propped up by granite columns to form the arcade. A glass of the dark red local wine helps wash down another local speciality, beef jerky (*tasoja*). **VILLANUEVA DE LA VERA**, down the road, has a more elegant Plaza Mayor, but there are not so many very old houses.

It is difficult to leave this untroubled valley, but there are two ways back to the fastlane. The most pleasant is to follow the C-501 over the Gredos Mountains to **ÁVILA** (just over 100km). Otherwise, cut south over the river on the local roads and follow signposts to the mighty N-V, which can whisk you over to **MÉRIDA**, which showcases classic Roman antiquities and has comfortable hotels in all price ranges.

Las Hurdes

3 days/265km/from Placensia

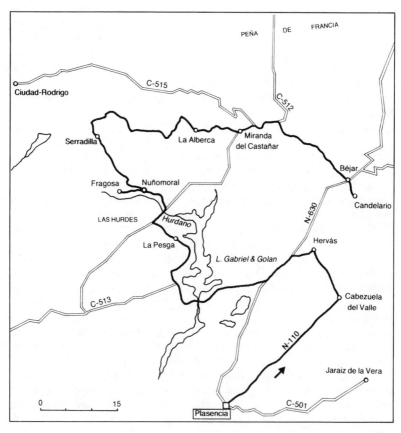

Pine, slate and a tangle of heather and briar characterise the landscape around Las Hurdes, in northernmost Extremadura. This tour also takes in a couple of villages across the border in Salamanca province, but all share the sense that time has left them behind: houses are crooked half-timbered affairs with the livestock downstairs for warmth and convenience. A sense of remoteness still pervades, though new schools, dams and sponsored cultivation of cereals and olives have improved the area. Roads still have a way to go. Moved by a numbing poverty that seemed almost surreal, Luis Buñuel filmed 'Land Without Bread' against the desolation of Las Batuecas back in 1932. Today, it is almost as isolated and still very rural. Folktales used to condemn the area for demonic bestiality, so many city Spaniards will do a double-take if you mention it as a holiday choice, dismissing it as the back of beyond.

From **PLASENCIA**, head north on the N-110, following along the river, passing neat cherry orchards. Turn left at Cabezuela del Valle, and head for **HERVÁS**. Under the protection of the Templar Knights, a large Jewish community prospered here and it is still well preserved around the ruins of the synagogue. Leaving town, turn left, then left again, joining the N-630 highway briefly. Turn off on the local C-513 to round the bottom of the reservoir Gabriel & Galan. You can climb to explore the deserted castle on the hill, **Granadilla**. From there, continue along the reservoir shore, through La Pesga, and turn right on the C-512. The windsurfers on the reservoir will seem an incongruous contrast to what lies ahead.

Turn left on the country road by the River Hurdano, and pick any of the picturesque villages to stop in. People may gawk at your foreign licence plates, for few visitors venture here. If you happen to be blonde, you may find your hair being stroked. **NUÑOMORAL** and **FRAGOSA** are welcoming, and beyond Fragosa, off the paved road, lies **EL GASCO**. Here, beneath the **Miacera Gorge**, a waterfall tumbles 55m. Do keep in mind, while trekking about, that wild boars roam free in these parts. **HUETRE** seems the most remote of all, although it does lie closer to the road, because of the villagers' traditional dress. You may be asked to buy ewes' milk cheese, fresh eggs, honey and, in early spring, boys will peddle armfuls of tiny narcissus they've plucked from the hillsides. If you offer large bills to be changed, you're apt to cause a commotion which will involve several people's pockets. It may be wisest to stick with exact change!

Looping up into Salamanca Province, the roads do not noticeably improve, but they are better marked. Bear right at Serradilla, go through the Paso de Lobos (Wolves' Pass) and bear right again through the twisting terrain. Besides heather and pine, the slate mountains grow *jara*, a sticky-leaved bush with streaked white flowers that can produce a remarkable honey. White apiaries are scattered amongst the wildflowers, and most beekeepers and village shops sell jars of nut-like pollen grains, beloved by marathon runners, as well as the pure honey.

LA ALBERCA lies at the base of the Francia Mountains, and in summer is distinctly greener than the villages just past. Kitchen gardens grow fruit trees and tall beans in the shade of old oaks and chestnuts. With narrow cobbled streets and ramshackle wooden structures listing

Chorritos Street, La Alberca

over their stone bases, La Alberca has a rustic air from another century. Sheep, goats and cattle are driven through the streets to pasture. The 18th-century church, with a coloured granite pulpit carved with the Twelve Apostles, is odd. On the stone wall outside is an unusual trinity: an old lantern flanked by two skulls reminds stay-at-homes of their mortality. The Plaza Mayor, with a carved stone crucifix over a small fountain, is a sun-trap. Beneath the stone pillars that support wooden-trimmed balconies, it's a pleasure to sip a coffee or a cup of wine. Often, the villagers gather here dressed in traditional finery: elaborately embroidered dresses for the women and white gaiters and black waistcoats for the men, with their shirts clapsed at the collar with a golden buckle. Easter Monday is a local holiday, but celebrations hit their height during

Skulls and lanterns outside a church, La Alberca

Assumption, 15 August, when the community not only holds folkdances, but performs the *Loa*, a mystery play which recounts the Virgin's victory over the Devil. It can be quite startling to see a tour bus lumbering into this little village, but though La Alberca is basically unspoilt, it is no secret. When lowlanders seek relief from searing weather midsummer, rooms here can be scarce. **Las Batuecas** (Fuente Canal; 43 70 30) near the town's entrance is pleasant and has a passable restaurant.

MIRANDA DEL CASTAÑAR, 15km farther along, is smaller, and the wooden balconies that teeter over the narrow streets bloom with flowers. The backdrop of the mountains can be quite spectacular. From here, get onto the C-515 towards **BÉJAR**, the largest town in the district. The mountain behind Béjar is frosted with snow most of the year and the air temperature seems to drop as you approach it. After the time warp of the villages in the Sierra, Béjar may seem daringly metropolitan. For calm and elegance, stroll in the 16th-century gardens of El Borque, or visit the Dukes' Palace, its comtemporary. There is a quartet of churches worth visiting; 13th-century San Juan has an unusual altarpiece and choirstalls. **Hotel Colón** (Colón, 42; 40 06 50) is comfortable, with a decent restaurant, or you may want to try the venta **Tres Coronas** out on the Salamanca Road. Should the sound of traffic be too much too soon, **CANDELARIO** is a mere 6km away.

Here, water runs down the middle of three stony streets in a sort of sluice, which means that drivers cannot blithely cruise around hunting for the Plaza Mayor. The houses have a traditional outer half-door at the entrances, raised up on one side. A local gent said this was to prevent cattle from wandering in, but it must also help keep the toddlers from taking unintentional dips in the canal. The older part of the village is at the top — mostly three-storey stone houses, with wooden balconies to catch the sun or the mountain view. The village gets slightly more modern towards the high street where you encounter a solid Gothic parish church. There are a couple of inexpensive inns here, though not open all year round. **Hostal Cristi** (Plaza Béjar, 1; 40 29 76) is the town's best. Some of the restaurants also let rooms. Mountain ham or sausage of wild boar are widely recognised specialities. A painting in the Prado (Ramón Bayeu's *El Choricero José Rico, de Calendario*) has advertised it for decades.

After backtracking to Béjar, it's a fast journey of 72km to the monumental university town of **SALAMANCA**, or a slightly longer journey to **ÁVILA**.

6 GALICIA AND ASTURIAS

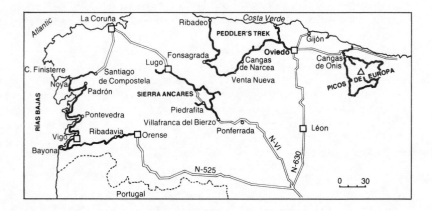

This green chunk of Iberia which juts out over Portugal breaks all the standard preconceptions of Spain. Certainly, castanets can be found here, only they click along to the sound of bagpipes and an energetic Celtic jig rather than a gypsy flamenco. The heavy mists, the bright green fields broken by stone walls, even the look of some of the people, bring Ireland to mind. Irish lacemaking, introduced by 16th-century immigrants, is still an important handicraft. And Catholicism is deep rooted: the ancient pilgrimage site, Santiago de Compostela, brought Spain's first wave of travellers here. Don't be put off by the sound of Costa del Muerte (Coast of Death), which still sees shipwrecks each year. The beaches along the *rías*, where the sea cuts inland in fjords, are in season some of the loveliest and least crowded in Spain. Wild horses run loose in the coastal highlands and in Asturias, the neighbouring region. With rugged mountains, mines and a mining tradition, Asturias is more like Wales. Some autonomists still want to revive Bable, the original language here. Pride runs deep, and the Reconquest which took over 5 centuries to penetrate south to Andalucía was started here by a bunch of tough Visigoths.

Rías Bajas

3 days/360km/from Orense

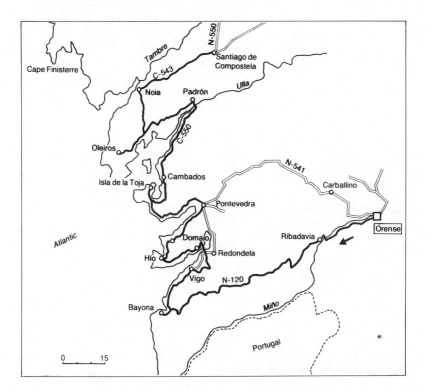

Surprisingly unknown to foreign visitors, the green northwest coast has deep inlets where the sea cuts in to mix with sweetwater rivers. Flat rocks for sunning and sandy beaches with privacy make the short season most enjoyable, even if the water can be a bit brisk. Traditional farming methods using oxcarts and hayricks are juxtaposed with some trendy crops like kiwi fruit and camellias in the villages along the coast. Lovely moss-tinged granite crosses in every settlement are reminders that the old Pilgrim's Way ends at Santiago de Compostela, as does this tour.

ORENSE pop: 96,085 Tourist Office: Curros Enriquez, 1, Torre de Orense. Legend has it that this city was named for gold (*oro*) in its river valley, but its best-known treasure is its therapeutic waters, Las Burgas hotsprings, which were famous in pre-Roman times. On a cool day, the steam rises from the thermal fountain near the town hall. A graceful Roman bridge, refurbished in 1499, crosses the Mino River and gives the city its distinct look. Though the 12–13th-century cathedral is impressive, especially the bright triple-arched west portico, it is essentially another cockleshell copy of the pilgrim's goal at Santiago de Compostela.

Inside, a wood and cloth crucifix with a real beard and headful of human hair has too much of a taxidermist's touch for comfort. Traditionally, it was found floating off Finisterra and is attributed to Nicodemus. The cloister museum displays early Galician books as well as a remarkable chess set carved of rock crystal in the 10th century. In the Palacio Episcopal, facing the Plaza Mayor, the Fine Arts Museum displays more religious statues and carvings while the Archaeological Museum traces back local history beyond the Visigoths. Hotels in the city are quite lacking in character, but the restaurants make up for them. Gallego cuisine rivals Basque cooking in the Spanish pantheon, with supreme seafood. Turnip greens — *gredos* — are another star ingredient, and even in the big towns

A woman carrying gredos *(turnip greens)*

you may see housewives toting them home from the market on their heads. It's worth splashing out at **San Miguel** (San Miguel, 12-14; 22 12 45) for very fresh fish exquisitely prepared in classic Gallego style, washed down with well-chosen wines.

Straight down the N-120 at a quick clip past the vineyards and apple trees soon gets you to **RIBADAVIA**, 20km on. The medieval Sarmonte Castle surveys the town and its houses hanging over the river. While there are a good number of sober palaces with crests carved in the stone, plus a trio of churches (Santo Domingo dates from the 14th century), a wander through the old streets is the most pleasant way to discover Ribadavia's charms. A Jewish section, founded in the 13th century, seems little changed today, with granite supports of unsteady wooden balconies all daubed with pale weathered paint. When John of Gaunt attacked the town, the initial resistance by this Jewish quarter earned savage reprisals. Later, despite accord with Lancaster, Pedro Madrugo torched the town and reputedly tried to feed the ear of a Jew to his best falcon, who refused to taste it. Prosperity came with the Ribeira wine trade, and the Viniculture Fair at the end of April has long been a major celebration. The Virgin's Birthday, on 8 September, sees huge skyrockets booming over the old tiled roofs, colours reflecting in the river. For a view over it all, climb up the San Gines.

Continue on the N-120, as it begins to twist like a grapevine, and head for the coast. Avoid the motorway when the highway divides, and get on any of the network of country roads which thread through the hills to the south coast. It's here that wild horses roam, except during the annual *rapa des bestas*, when local cowboys stage a round-up during May or June, trim the mane and tail in a ritual way, then after a couple of races set them all loose again. Turn right at the coast road, the C-550. At first all is very flat and much scrubbier than the hills. **BAYONA (BAIONA)** just to the north has a vast bay but is protected from the Atlantic's wrath by large promontories, wooded with pine and eucalyptus. It was here in 1493 that the *Pinta* sailed in with news of a New World. This was soon followed by all the booty of the Spanish Main. Battlements up on Monte Real oversaw the trade, and warned off ever more daring corsairs. On a clear day, the view from here extends out to the Estelas Islands, the horizon, and south to Cape Silleiro. It's fun to come at sunset and try to spy the elusive Green Flash, the fleeting after-image which appears as the red sun vanishes into the sea. The castellated fort, formerly a Governor's Residence, is now a state **Parador**, the **Conde de Gondamar** (35 50 00). With its pool and park setting, close by a children's playground and tennis courts, it caters for families. Recent development of the sand beaches is disappointing, but **PANXÓN** is a scenic fishing village watched over by a neo-Byzantine church. **VIGO**, a major port and industrial city of 25,724 inhabitants, is surprisingly attractive with stepped gardens which look out over the Cies Islands. Rural it certainly is not. Take the airport road and turn off after 3.5km, following the signs to the zoo. Park in front of the zoo and a short hike through the pines reveals the **Mirador la Madroa**, with a panorama over the city and the inlet.

Take advantage of the fast by-pass to save the extra kilometres of the curve, but turn off again on the coast road to **DOMAIO**, where the channel narrows and darkens with purple mussel beds. Stop at **HÍO** for a look at a very intricately carved calvary, before you go through the pines to explore the beaches. **BUEU**, a fishing village, is a good base for this. At the farthest reach of this *ría* is Pontevedra.

PONTEVEDRA pop: 65,137 Tourist Office: Benito Corbal, 47. Known as 'Old Bridge' even in medieval times, this provincial capital claims links with classic Greece, its legendary founder being Teucer, the nephew of Ajax. Now its pleasant arcaded streets are filled with old stone crosses, fountains and bright blooms against the granite buildings. *Solanas*, glass-fronted galleries facing the sun, are especially pretty on the Plaza Teucro, not far from a fine old cross carved with the temptation of Eve. Since the top of the *ría* silted up in the 18th century, Pontevedra has lost the port city bustle which drew a vibrant mix of explorers, sailors, traders and merchants, centuries ago. The old quarter is compact, gathered around the Plaza Orense. An 18th-century Baroque church, built in the shape of a cockleshell, is dedicated to the Virgin Pilgrim, the town patron. One of the last stops on the road from Portugal, the city has a fine collection of jet carvings from Compostela, displayed in the Provincial Museum alongside Celtic gold and some ancient if ugly sculpture (closed Sun afternoons). The museum is in a double mansion, connected by an archway, on the attractive Plaza de Lena, which rivals the Plaza del Teucro and Plaza de la Herrería for the beauty of the centrepiece stone crosses. Santa María la Mayor, a lovely Plateresque church built by the mariners' guild in the fishermen's quarter during the late 15th century, is caught in a web of narrow alleys and gardens. One local *pazo*, a Gallego country manor house with elegant lines broken only by a carved crest, has been revamped as a **parador: Casa del Barón** (Maceda, 85 58 00). The interior is elegant, with a particularly fine stairway. The city does offer comfortable lodgings at cheaper prices, and with fresh *empanadas* (a light Gallego pasty filled with tangy fish or meat) on sale everywhere, eating out need not eat into your budget. **Doña Antonia** (Suportales de la Herrería, 9 primero; 84 72 74) offers imaginative fish dishes in a gracious atmosphere, and her desserts are famous even in Madrid! (closed Sun).

COMBARRO, north on the trusty C-550, is a small atmospheric fishing village with some fine *hórreos* near its calm waters. These weird structures, raised on stone stilts and often topped with crosses, keep the grain or fruit dry and free from rats. Narrow slits provide ventilation, and some are so ornate that it's no surprise that many a foreign pilgrim mistook them for human shelters. Usually built of wood on stone supports, there are a number of all-granite ones. With small white houses on narrow streets and ancient granite crosses looking down on painted fishing boats and the silhouettes of the Ons islands, Combarro has a gentle calm. The coast road continues north, zig-zagging between sand dunes, citrus trees, corn fields, pines, and a parade of unassuming villages, with upended oars and nets drying in the sun. **ISLA DE LA TOJA (A TOXA)**, connected to the sandspit by a bridge, is known for curative salts. Though the stream is dried up, the pine covered island is a quiet contrast to the **RÍA AROUSA** ahead, the most developed and largest of them all, complete with casinos and poseurs. But do stop at **CAMBADOS** and visit the Plaza Fifinanes on the north side of town, with its square-towered *pazos* and graceful 17th-century church in an elegant square.

Carrying on the coastal road, **PADRÓN**, at the inner recesses of the inlet, claims to be where the stone boat which supposedly brought St James to Spain was washed ashore. At Santiago, the

An example of a hórreo

parish church beside the bridge, the old mooring stone is kept beneath the altarcloth, and doubters must flick on the lightswitch to view this proof. The town's other claim to fame is its miniature green peppers.

If it's a clear day (most likely, in the summer months), stay on the coast road for 40km, until reaching Puebla del Caramiñal. Turn here and drive 10km to the summit of Mount Barbanza (the Gallegos claim that Noah's ark landed here). A magnificent view from the **Mirador de la Curota** encompasses all four inlets of the Rías Bajas, and if the clouds are high, all the way up to Finisterra and over to the vines by the Mino River. Also atop the mountain an enormous dolmen, at **ANXEITOS**, marks a Celtic burial site with eight upright rocks balancing a huge flat boulder. From here, cut through to Oleiros and pick up the C-550 to continue along the wooded north bank of the *ría*. Some fine beaches will beckon if you want to take a dip. Caution is advised, though: the Celts would immerse themselves nine times to ensure fertility. **NOIA (NOYA)** is a proud village right in the crease of the inlet which insists that Noah's dove plucked its olive branch from a local tree after the deluge and commemorates the event on its town seal. The Gothic church of San Martín is a sea-view fortress to a mighty God, noted for a fine sculpted portal and rose window. A medieval bridge merits a look, and so does the shady Plaza Mayor. Next to the 14th-century church, Santa María de Noya, the cemetery is filled with ancient headstones, carved with Celtic and pagan symbols mingling with the more familiar Christian signs. Many relate to the trades of the buried, but more than a few still baffle scholars.

It's tempting to stay on the winding road that keeps revealing coastal surprises, but a classic journey's end is just 36km inland on the C-543. **SANTIAGO DE COMPOSTELA**, the fabled cult destination for 11 centuries of European pilgrims who 'took the cockleshell', still overwhelms even seasoned travellers.

SANTIAGO DE COMPOSTELA, pop: 93,695 Tourist Office: Rua de Vilar, 43. The tradition is to eat a scallop on arrival and to tuck the shell into your hatband to mark your pilgrimage. When a journey to holy medieval Rome became hazardous due to religious civil war, and the Crusades made Jerusalem a no-go area, the 'tomb of St James' drew thongs of the faithful, by sea and overland. Every road leads to the great cathedral, but the best approach is face on, from the Plaza del Obradoiro. The building lives up to all its promises and outdazzles the sundry imitations in tribute built all along the Way. An extraordinary Baroque façade keeps the inner Romanesque entrance a beautiful secret until you pass beneath it, marvelling at the 12th-century carving of Maestro Mateo. Enthralling as the cathedral is, there are other attractions which are lesser lights here only because of the sheer preponderance of beauty: The Collegiate Church of Santa María del Sar which has looked on the brink of collapse since the 12th century, Palacio de Gelmírez, Colegio Mayor Fonseca and Palacio Ranxoy stand out, but there are dozens more which anywhere else would be landmarks. In the Santo Domingo convent, a remarkable stairway plaits together three separate unsupported stone spirals.

After centuries of rain, all the old granite monuments have a patina which adds to the slightly mystic atmosphere about the place, and green plants sprout from the oddest spots. Yet the university keeps this town lively, not overly reverent, and cheap meals can be found. The very pricey state **parador**, the **Hostal de los Reyes Católicos** (Plaza de España; 58 22 00) is worth a visit out of historic interest. Fernando and Isabel commanded a hostelry worthy of Santiago and this was the result. Kitted out for comfort in 1954, it didn't lose its 16th-century spirit. **Suso** (Rua del Villar, 65; 58 66 11) is reasonable, central and quite pretty. *Hospedajes* cater to the less well heeled. Basic lodging at the **Villa de Cruces** (Patio de Madres, 16) costs just 400 pesetas per person. Good cooking can be found around the University plaza for about the same rates, but a truly memorable meal can be savoured at **Vilas** (Rosalia de Castro, 88; 59 10 00; closed Sun, mid-May to mid-Oct) or **Anexo Vilas** (Avda de Villa-garcía, 21; 59 83 87) run by the same family of Gallego cooks. The annex is closed Mondays. If you visit on 25 July, St James will be celebrated with a rain of fireworks and skyrockets that matches the best displays any-where.

Picos de Europa

2 days / 225km / from Ribadesella

When sailing gold-laden galleons back to La Coruña from the New World, home-bound sailors would spot these peaks and know that Europe was close at hand. Though not especially high (2,400m), the Picos are rugged enough for alpin-ists to seek out, yet provide plea-sant walks easy enough for a child to stalk the wildlife in the meadows and woods. The scenery is savage: dark gorges, great clefts where water surges, snow never melting off the highest jagged summits.

Still, small villages have scratched a living in their shadow for centuries. A blue ewes' milk cheese — *cabrales* — is traditional, and sunny protected slopes can produce walnuts and cherries. Some mining continues in the area, which is divided into two regions: a National Park to the west and a hunting reserve. Jeeps are for rent in many of the villages bordering the park, but even a rented Panda, not too loaded, can handle all but the roughest tracks. Plan to do some hiking, for a sense of personal discovery, and come prepared for a sudden shower — clouds blow in swiftly from the Atlantic seaboard. Walking boots are recommended, for it's easy to slip in the loose shale.

RIBADESELLA, on the estuary, is a town and port-cum-resort. It is the finishing point for an international kayak race each August on the first Saturday when the population and excitement quintuple. A special train runs along the river course to cheer on the paddlers. If crowds and hysterical celebration are not your scene, be elsewhere on that date. Nearby, the Tito Bustillo Cave, unlike the famous Altamira Cave, is still open to anyone who turns up. Estimated to date from 20,000BC, the chambers lie at the end of stalactite galleries and feature red and ochre animal shapes, some up to 2m long, painted within an engraved line on a smooth 'ceiling'. Horses, stags and does are the main subjects. Guided tours cost 125 pesetas for ¾ hour, during the season from 1 April–30 September. Hours 10–1; 3.30–6.30. Closed Mondays.

From here, head inland towards Arrionadas on the N-634, then bear left for **CANGAS DE ONIS**, just beyond the Romanesque hump-backed bridge over the Sella River. In effect, Cangas was Christian Spain's first capital when the 8th-century Asturian kings set up court here after their triumph over the Moors at nearby Covadonga. A Celtic dolmen with one unusual engraved stone marks a tomb beside the Santa Cruz church where the royals worshipped. With all the mountain scenery beckoning, it's wise to stop for detailed maps at the tourist office: Emilio Lara, 2.

The C-637 road out of Cangas follows the river course and divides at its junction with the Ponga. Bear right at the sign for the gorges (*garganta*), strewn with huge boulders that nearly block the way. Getting back to the main road, continue south through the Los Beyos Defile, a narrow slash through sheer limestone cliffs which the Sella River carves for 10km. Below that, there's a left turn to a lookout point, at Oseja de Sajambre, which provides a stunning overview of the defile and the basin with the Niaja rock spike rising from its midst like an enormous sundial. Going back to the C-637, ascend to the corniche road with its spectacular views, then wind between the elms as you climb towards the massive western mountain range. Pontón Pass, at 1,280m looks over the Sajambre valley at a higher angle. Branch off to the left here and drive towards the Panderruedas Pass, where woods give way to bare limestone outcrops that surround high pastures. A foot trail climbs up to a

Soto de Valdeón, Picos de Europa

95

lookout point at Piedrafitas, where a viewing table maps out the panorama, including the Cerredo — (2,648m) the highest peak in the range. Between this pass and the Puerto de Pandetrave to the east lies the beautiful Valdeón Valley. A track leads up to Posada de Valdeón, the largest of this enclave of farming villages with their characteristic *hórreos*, raised stone granaries that defeat the moisture.

Perhaps the prettiest hamlet of all is **SOTO DE VALDEÓN**, a short walk from the road, crossing a little bridge over the Franana Creek. It boasts two small chapels which are blessed by the soaring spires of the peaks. The stone walls of the houses are thick against the cold, and wooden balconies which catch the late afternoon sun display local wood-carvers' skill. Some houses do let out rooms for the night, or you can go over to **POSADA DE VALDEÓN**, slightly bigger, and bed down at the 2-star **Hostal Abascal** (no phone) or one of the fondas. A mile's hike from Posada takes you up to **Mirador El Tombo**, which is marked with a statue of the chamois goat. From here is one of the best vistas in all the Picos, face on. The Valdeón valley is serene and a good base for serious hiking. The remote village of **CAIN** to the north is the usual starting point for the hike to **Cares Gorge**, a good 25km with sheer drops but safe trails cut into the mountainsides.

Travellers who prefer car-touring can backtrack to the C-637 and continue to Riaño where the road bears left along the Yuso River, over which harsh southern mountainfaces glower down. At Portilla de la Reina, turn off for a lookout point at the Pandetrave Pass, which takes in all three of the Picos' distinct massifs. Returning to the main road, follow on through the delicate colours of the Yuso Gorge, which is guarded by the village of **LLÁNAVES DE LA REINA**. From there, drive through the harsh scenery past the San Glorio Pass, when lonely mountain pastures will open up. Near **BORES**, switchbacks descend to a poplar-planted valley and then on to the bustle of **POTES**, where cheques can be cashed, maps bought, hunting and fishing permits obtained, jeeps hired, and meals eaten in traditional restaurants. From the bridge, look back for a view of the city's wooden houses and squared-off Infantado Tower, reflected in the Deva. A narrow 3km road goes up to the Romanesque Monastery of Santo Toribio de Liébana, where a large splinter of the True Cross is on loving display.

Outside Potes, there are stables at **TURIENO** which can arrange tours on horseback and also rent mounts by the half-day. The road branches off and skirts the Deva River along meadows and woods through the village of Espinama and on to **FUENTE DÉ**. Here a Parador overlooks the crests and the wild rocky source of the river. **Parador Río Deva** (73 00 01) also has a dining room serving mountain specialities. In season, try the game dishes. Nearby, a cable car dangles high over a sheer cliff (250 pesetas round trip). Watch wild chamois, ibex and eagles during the dizzying ride to the Mirador. A refuge at **ALIVA**, 4km ahead, has a simple restaurant and cosy rooms. (Open 15 June–30 Sept, no reservations taken.) On the path from the lookout, erosion on the limestone has sculpted long plinth-like forms and abrupt sinkholes.

The road north leads through tiny **LA HERMIDA**, in the midst of a shadowy ravine that snakes up the basin some 20km, absolutely devoid of plantlife. **PANES**, the park's east entrance, has a couple of passable restaurants and a reasonable hotel, **Hostal Covadonga** (Pío Virgilio Luares; 41 41 62). The tourist office on Mayor is quite helpful with area maps.

From Panes, the road traces the mossy course of the Cares River up to **ARENAS DE CABRALES**, production centre for the strong local blue ewes' cheese (Blue Whew). A number of the stone granaries are festooned with corn cobs. Turn left here and drive to **PONCEBOS**, through a cleft near the small reservoir. You can park here and walk to the remote villages of **BULNES** (with a refuge) or **CAMARMEÑA**, both with vistas of the fanged peak, **Naranjo de Bulnes**, which taunts climbers to tackle it. If it's early, more ambitious hikers might cross the gorge to **CAIN**.

On the way from Cabrales to **LAS ESTAZADAS**, there is a fine view of the rock wall that seals the Casano Valley. Continue on this C-312 road and take the third turning on the left, marked for **COVADONGA**. Be aware that afternoon mists are frequent and try for a morning drive.

The Basilica here displays a statue of Pelayo, the Visigothic Spaniard who began the Reconquest when he defeated the Moors at Covadonga and began to avenge the fall of Toledo in the 8th century. In the Cueva Santa, the patron of Asturias — Virgen Santina — guards over the tombs of the Asturian kings Pelayo and Alfonso. Gifts of veneration to her, on display in the Treasury (entry fee 30 pesetas), include a crown studded with over 1,000 diamonds. A steep road continues past the town, up to the Queen's Lookout (*Mirador de Reina*) with views back to the basilica and out over the jagged mountainscape of the Sierra de Covalierda. Two lakes, near pastureland used by herds of shy Asturian horses, are within reach. Retrace the road back to our starting point at **CANGAS DE ONÍS**. From here, it's a quick ride to the Cantabrian coast or south into León.

Sierra de Ancares

1 day/165km/from Lugo
The country is wild, the tales wilder; pack a big meal and a sense of adventure. This route may seem to traverse meadows carpeted in wildflowers but legends claim that werewolves prowl by night and spirits are about. Lizards are said to hold trapped souls. Certainly there is every reason for there to be ghosts in these high passes: hundreds of Sir John Moore's troops perished in the blizzards up in the pass by O Cebreiro in 1809. In their rush to reach the coast in La Coruña, thousands of pounds worth of heavy gold payment and horses were dumped over the cliff while the camp followers were left to starve. Centuries before that episode and long after, pilgrims on the Way would dread this as the last big hurdle before the descent to Santiago. They have left their mark on these isolated villages, as have the shepherds, who still shelter in the Celtic-style

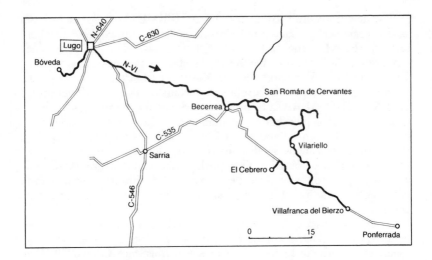

pallazos. These round stone huts are topped with pointed thatched roofs with profiles rather like local Tertulla cheeses.

LUGO pop: 73,986 Tourist Office: Plaza de la Soledad, 15. The ancient centre of Celtic Galicia, Lugo's modern name isn't far removed from the original, *Lug*, after the sun god. The slate walls which gird the city, nearly 2½km around have four ancient gates and nearly 50 towers still intact and rank as Spain's most important Roman military architecture, dating

A pallazo — a shepherd's straw-roofed stone hut

back to the 3rd century. Here and there, Roman inscriptions can still be read. A ring road circles them, allowing a fine view, and there is also a sentry path along the ramparts, reached by stairways beside the gates. The Cathedral is grand yet peculiar, an 1177 copy of Santiago wrapped in a Baroque cocoon. The three great towers define Lugo's skyline. Take time to visit the Provincial Museum, in a cloister of San Francisco Church. Displays include Celtic and Roman finds, coins, ceramics, sundials and even the kitchen of a country cottage.

Once outside the imposing walls, follow roadsigns towards Orense. After 4km, turn right towards Friol but bear left again after 2km. Continue 7km and turn right to **BÓVEDA**. A visit to **Santa Eulalia de Bóveda**, a palaeo-Christian church, reaffirms just how long worshippers have been in the area. Excavated next to the parish church in 1924, Santa Eulalia is built on top of a Roman Nymphaeum, with traces of a Celtic temple beneath that. The vestibule is open to the sky while archaeologists still ponder over the shards. Motifs of dancers, birds and leaves adorn the walls. Supposedly the tomb of St. Prisciliano, Galicia's first Christian martyr (beheaded for heresy by fellow Christians rather than Romans) is here, in keeping with his blend of Celtic rites with the orthodox Christianity. Yet a number of scholars assume that it is his headless body which is lying in the crypt at Santiago, a colossal case of mistaken identity. To visit, call first at the house across the way for the key.

Retrace the route back through Lugo and pick up the N-VI southeast to **BECERREA**. Just north of town are the edges of the rugged **Sierra Ancares**, now a national reserve. Turn left and take the winding secondary road through the wild country, threading its way through tiny shepherds' hamlets and hillsides thick with blooms in the spring. Look out for capercaillie (comical fat grouse with ruddy Groucho Marx eyebrows), ibex, chamois and roebuck. Hunters will be stalking. Salmon and trout crowd the streams. Some remote villages are little more than a huddle of *pallazos*, thatched huts for herdsmen and their small flocks built along Celtic lines.

VILARIELLO is easily reached, but others take courage; brave rutted tracks or walk north to **DONIS**, **CERVANTES**, **PIORNEDO**, **SUARBOL** or **BALOUTA**. When the flowers fade, the mountains are bleak. Stone summits peak and crest like a petrified sea. The climate is harsh, too: count on rain in summer and snow in winter, though there's a slight chance of being surprised. When the road descends to intersect again with the N-VI highway, turn right. After about ten minutes bear left at **PIEDRAFITA**. Traditional *pallazos* are much used at **EL CEBRERO (O CEBREIRO)**, and four have been done up as a Folk Museum (*Museo de Artes y Costumbres Populares*) which closes in the afternoons. Spinning wool is one of the traditional crafts here. And if you get a chance, buy some of the fresh cheese, peaked like the huts, on sale in the village. The French influence is evident in the blend of flavours. The old stone chapel, Santa María del Cebreiro, dates from about the 9th century and was the scene for the Miracle of St. Grial, in the 14th century, when the village was on the French Road to Santiago. An ill-tempered priest, giving communion for a lone pilgrim, muttered that it was a long way to come just for a bit of bread and wine. Before his eyes, the host and holy wine were transformed to flesh and blood. It can be seen today, preserved in a crystal chalice and a silver plate supplied by Queen Isabel in 1486. Both Catholic Monarchs passed through this windswept place and commanded that lodging for the passing pilgrims be erected. Today's travellers can stay at **San Giraldo de Aurilac** (Piedrafita, no phone).

Return to the highway and turn right, backtracking a bit, and continue to **VILLAFRANCA DEL BIERZO.** The valley town seems so civilised after the rough country, with churches and palaces that

Galician bullock cart

complement the castle and the handsome Romanesque Church of Santiago, recently restored. This was once a sort of consolation prize for pilgrims too ill or weak to handle the last rough section of the Way, and they could receive indulgences here. Shops now sell mostly local bread and wine plus home-grown pimentos in jars and bottled cherries alongside the turnip greens. The state **parador** here (Avda Calvo Sotelo; 54 01 75) is not a noble historic building, but it is snug and has all modern conveniences. It seems a real refuge after a visit to the harsh Sierra de Ancares.

Peddler's Trek

3–4 days/395km/from Ribadeo

From the harbour and recreation centre of Ribadeo, journey into the interior along the route of peddlers who still traipse between the rural villages with tools and haberdashery heaped on their shoulders. They are welcomed for their gossip as much as for their goods. Incomparably bucolic, with old men scything green grass and heaping it into bullock carts, the countryside is rife with grazing cows. Herds of wild horses run in the hills as well. Allow time to navigate rather ill-kept roads that will make travelling a true challenge.

RIBADEO, on a northerly *ría* of the same name, seems to tame the Eo River, with its fighting salmon and trout, into a docile inlet between flat

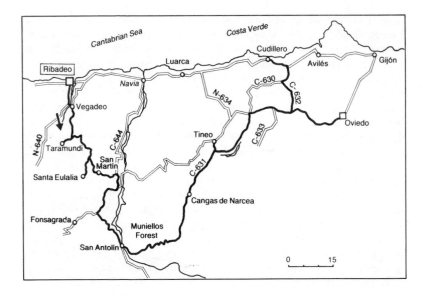

green banks. From the Santa Cruz Church, a high vista looks over low slate-roofed houses onto the inlet, which is the frontier between Galicia and Asturias. The fishermen's quarter in town is a lively place, not inundated with tourists, and has a few inexpensive bars that serve good *empanadas*, savoury individual fish pies.

Leave the harbour town by following the roadsigns toward **VEGADEO**. The road seems to teeter on a startling corniche with views across the inlet and the Asturian valleys, and **CASTROPOL** juts out on its rock spur across the *ría*. From Vegadeo, take the small road towards Bres and then bear right. **TARAMUNDI**, a small village known for its 24 artisans who fashion traditional iron jackknives, now is the centre of a project to promote travel in the rustic interior. Good area maps and information about fishing and farmhouses which will put up visitors can be obtained in the **Hotel La Rectoral** (63 40 60). The small hamlets of **AGUILLON**, just outside Taramundi, and **TEIJOIS**, up a dirt road in the nearest mountains, both preserve old hydraulic complexes for traditional metal refining. Much like Wales in the lay of the land, Asturias is also a mining region.

From here return to the main road and ascend the **La Garganta** pass. You are apt to see nomadic shepherds herding their flocks along the ancient *Trashumancia*, a route which covers open pastures the length of Spain. You may also spy frisky wild horses with unkempt manes covering their eyes. An old refuge marks the pass and looks foreboding as the fog swirls around it. If fine weather prevails, look for the narrow forest road up to the Bobia summit. A panorama extends from the Cantabrian Sea to the peaks of the Ancares. In the dark woods on the eastern slopes, the **Selva de Murias**, wild boar and wolves take refuge and provide a focus for shadowy tales. A little farther on, a track runs up to the deserted mine of **Excomulgada**, a detour which only the most adventurous drivers should attempt. This continues past **La Arrunada**, a country house which offers hospitality to travellers, and the parish church of San Pedro de Ahio. From there, a steep swoop and corkscrew turns bottom out at the Soutelo River, where an old watermill still churns away. It is a secret spot for a picnic.

Keeping to surfaced roads may be more your style. From La Garganta, bear left to **VILLANUEVA DE OSCOS**, where the mossy pile of an ancient monastery is open. If you're hungry, take the left fork into **SANTA EULALIA DE OSCOS**, and drive to **Méson La Cerca** (no phone). Besides the hearty *fabada*, a bean stew with morsels of pork, sausage and black pudding, washed down with the local hard cider, specialities include meat cooked over an oakwood fire, *chostes* and *botiellos*. After a suitable feast, retrace the route past Villanueva and on to **SAN MARTÍN DE OSCOS**, which hosts a rip-roaring local livestock fair on the last Sunday of each month. Across from the local convent, the town's sole café sells rum tortillas. Strong moonshine liquor (*aguardiente de alambique*) is also available. On the outskirts of the village, a number of paths and tracks lead off to grand homesteads on the old watercourses. **La Coba**, tucked beside a wild canyon, is nearly as impressive as **Mon**. Here, they claim that the 18th-century palace is enchanted. Built by a local after a stint as governor of Florida, back when it was still a Spanish colony, the palace's hermitage is perched over an abyss where the Ahio River surges forth.

The road improves on the way to **GRANDAS**. When the Navia River nearby was dammed in the 1970s, many of the villages were cut off and then abandoned. Not so **VILLARPEDRE**, which commutes by boat to the main municipality in **GRANDAS**. Hire one of the boatman's two boats for the most pleasant way to explore the green Navia valley, with old mansions isolated along the shore. A few artists' communes have cropped up in some of the more remote ones. **FOXO** is within reach by boat. **RIODEPORCOS**, with its suspension bridge, makes a lovely stop. Sample fresh baked bread and rough *tinto* wine in the little cantina.

If you can arrange to have your car driven to meet you at Boadil bridge, you may save some time; but in the long run, it's probably faster to do a circuit back to the embarking point and pick up the car. Get on the C-630 south from Grandas and take the first left to reach the bridge at **SAN ANTOLÍN DE IBIAS**. Climb the switchback road to the Connio Pass, and look down on the eastern side to a rare sight in Europe: a completely virgin valley. Ahead is the **Muniellos** forest, an ecological reserve. From an old mansion at **MOAL**, drive right up to the park's entrance at **TABLIZAS**. There is a small lodge on the outskirts where you can eat and spend the night. Access to the Muniellos forest is by foot only.

Enormous thousand-year-old oaks, the last relics of the woods which once covered the Iberian peninsula, shade the paths in the Muniellos. Butterflies of a hundred hues flit between wild blossoms, and the profound silence is broken by otters in the streams. Deer, wild boar, wolves and even rare Iberian bears share the protected forest. It is also a refuge for the red-browed capercaillie, a rare grouse. It takes between 5 and 6 hours to hike through the reserve. Afterwards, follow the road along the streambed 17km up to **CANGAS DE NARCEA**, a nondescript modern town which can claim a proper inn: **Conde Pinolo** (Uria, 21; 81 02 50). From this largest town in the district it is an easy drive north to **TINEO**. Several medieval churches survive from the time that the road to Santiago veered off through here, and the parish church dates from the 13th century. The trout fishing in the streams here is supposed to be exceptional. Bear right where the road forks and head east on the N-634, past *hórreos* (granaries on stone stilts) and pasturelands to Oviedo, the Asturian capital.

OVIEDO pop: 190,123 Tourist Office: Pl. de la Catedral, 6. The ancient quarter in the midst of this industrial centre is near the large San Francisco park and pleasant to visit. The cathedral tower, the city's main landmark, helps guide you through the narrow streets to the asymmetrical Gothic temple. Next to it is the Cámara Santa, built in the 9th century to hold relics spirited away from Toledo when the Visigoth kingdom fell. Asturias was very much the refuge of defeated Christians in the 9th century. Daily tours of the Cámara Santa cost 50 pesetas, but shut down between 1 and 4 for siesta. Much was devastated by battles in 1934 and again in 1936, though many original artworks, especially gold and silverwork, are displayed in the rebuilt chapel. The older Asturian churches are the real draw, however. While post-Visigothic, they nevertheless pre-date the French Romanesque influence that was to overwhelm architects. Santullano, just outside town, is the finest example. See also the Palace of Santa María del Naranco and San Miguel de Lillo, its church, which both overlook the city. They have almost Byzantine influences in their designs of pale golden stone adorned with delicate tracery. Oviedo's modern prosperity comes from mining iron and coal; Romans stripped the gold from the nearby valley. An important University of Mining Engineering adds verve to the new town, plus plenty of inexpensive student restaurants and *tapas* bars. There is a wide range of hotels. **Hotel de la Reconquista** (Gil de Jaz, 16; 24 11 00) is a converted 17th-century palace and utterly sumptuous.

For a daytrip in marked contrast to the city, head past the mining country northwest on the N-634 towards Cornellana and turn right. Before reaching the regional airport beyond Soto de Barco, bear left and then **CUDILLERO** is at the next right turn. Here, clinging to a steep promontory, the red tiled fishing village is clustered around its single real street, which runs down to the pier and around its only plaza. Some claim that Viking fishermen sheltering from a storm founded the village and were so delighted by it that they never left. It is true that even today the villagers have some distinct ethnographical differences from their neighbours along the coast and that custom prevented the *pixueto* fishermen from marrying outside Cudillero for centuries. They retain their own dialect of *Bable*, plus the custom of the *pregón*, a kind of ironic rhyming riddle. La Amuravela on 29 June is the big fiesta, honouring St Peter, the fisherman, when the folklore and dances can reach a frenzy. Simple fish restaurants line the pier, where great nets are hung to dry. The country house, La Quinta El Pito, merits a visit.

7 THE LEVANT

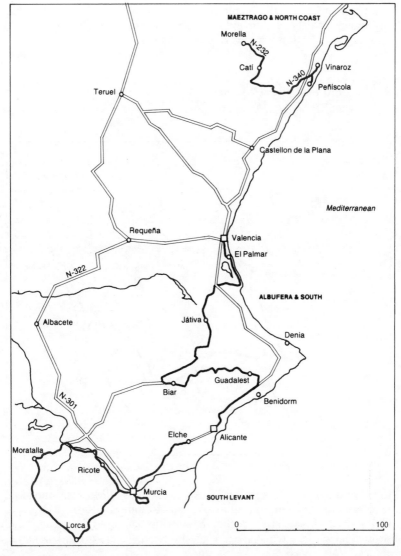

Valencia and its environs on Spain's east coast haven't yet been thoroughly tapped by the tourists, regardless of how many charter flights arrive. With most visitors prone on the beach, the green interior and the mountains still maintain their own brand of regional Spanishness. Fountains and cool, narrow streets take the edge off the heat and give an inkling of the fierce past when warriors were the principal visitors. The Middle Ages are not long gone in some of the mountain villages behind the orange groves, and even on the coast, many farmers go their own sedate pace, oblivious of the disco delights. The Moors, first to irrigate the land here, had nearly the impact that they did in Andalucía, though they were driven out of this terrain long before they left Granada. Aside from the placenames and the architecture, from fortresses to thermal baths, one legacy is the honey-almond sweetmeat, *turrón*. Typically Spanish, this Christmas confection is a ringer for Arab *halva*.

Maeztrago and North Coast
2 days/120km/from Morella

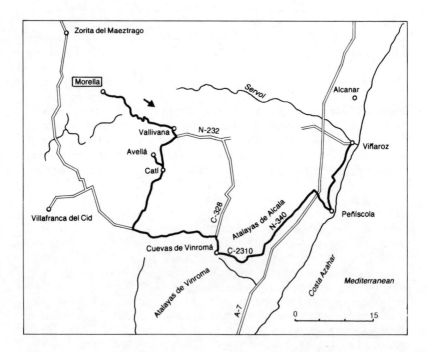

In the arid uplands, villages fortified by the Knights of Montesa (the local successors to the Templars) still look ready to stand up to the Moors. El Cid stalked these parts, as did the Carlists centuries later, and the stronghold villages remain in archaic isolation. Nearing the coast, the climate and the landscape soften. Mild winters and hot, windy summers account for the lush garden crops. The Mediterranean Sea swirls benignly beneath the dramatic castle at Peñíscola.

MORELLA, on the N-232 from Zaragoza, is a daunting village, surrounded by 2km of stout Gothic walls with 14 towers and overseen by a fortress-castle atop a brutal rock. It's no surprise that the place has seen its share of fighting: the Moors resisted El Cid twice here before falling. The Carlists battled with a vengeance: General Cabrera earned his nickname 'Tiger of the Maeztrago' in these rugged hills. Napoleonic troops occupied this strategic point, and Civil War battles ensued years later.

Six massive gates lead through the walls, but the grandest is San Mateo. By far the most impressive church is the pure Gothic basilica Santa María la Mayor, with its great blue tiled dome. The two monumental portals — the Apostles and the Virgins — are said to have been carved by father and son, who finished the job simultaneously without having looked at one another. A marble stairway within spirals up to the choir and the stained glass windows are particularly fine. Completed in 1330, the church is held to be the finest Gothic work in the entire region. San Francisco convent, founded even earlier, in 1272, today stands in ruins. After use as a prison last century, it was abandoned completely. Most of Morella's houses are unpretentious whitewashed affairs, usually three storeys high, with wooden balconies. Looking down from the decrepit castle high above the basilica gives a sentry's view of the village. Streets run in semi-circles, cutting terraces in the steep hillside until interrupted by a rough bullring. Beyond the walls, grey scrubland looks as if it might still hide a stray guerrilla or two, though they'd be apt to freeze in the harsh winter. A Gothic aqueduct is visible to the northeast. **Cardenal Ram** (Cuesta Suner, 1; 16 00 92), a converted palace, is the best hotel; **Méson del Pastor** (Cuesta Jovani, 5; 16 02 49; closed Wed) serves pleasant mountain cooking, with an emphasis on young lamb and pork.

Continue east along the N-232, but take the first turning right, on a local rutted road just past Vallivana. This begins along a dry river course, past a little hermitage to Santa Ana, and on to **CATÍ**. This tucked-away village, founded by Moors, became Morella's rival in the cloth trade and hawked its fine wools and silks as far away as Genoa, Florence and Venice. The legacy of such prosperous trade lingers in the architecture, especially the town hall's *Lonja* (exchange), though textile wealth is centuries gone now and sheepfarmers live in the mansions enscribed with proud family crests. Some of the most impressive medieval palaces lining the main street are now cafés or civil servants' offices. The elegant parish church, La Asunción de la Virgen, dates from 1350 and has two Romanesque portals — one with a double arch. Its choir developed a following and toured cathedrals and the wedding circuit throughout the Valencian provinces until the end of the 18th century. Most of the village ramparts remain, though the San Vicente gateway has been transformed into a public fountain. Just before the entrance to Catí, a narrow track turns off into the hills. Follow this, through a 300m tunnel, and 4km ahead is the **AVELLÁ** sanctuary, a small 19th-century spa known for bicarbonated mineral waters that soothe skin problems.

Continuing south past Catí, the road passes distant rows of olives, almonds and grapevines. Bear left towards **ALBOCÁCER**, a Templar village which is topped with a ruined castle. Eastwards, the road snakes through the **Barranca de Valltorta**, a narrow canyon with stark striations in the rock, and proceeds to **CUEVAS DE VINROMÁ**. Franco had plans to turn this place into a sort of Falangist Lourdes through a propaganda stunt involving false visions of pro-Ribera virgins. The *Calvario* (an outdoor stations of the cross) is a labyrinth of low white walls rising to a hill with a sculpted crucifix, but the sightings of virgins spouting political profundities ceased in the mid-1940s. Palaeolithic ochre drawings are visible in the caves nearby.

From here, go north along the fast N-340 rather than the motorway and avoid both trucks and tollbooths. The right turn into **PEÑÍSCOLA** is well marked. Perched on its rocky promontory with the Mediterranean whisking around it and boxy white houses clustering beneath the powerful castle, the town is truly special. Cars cannot negotiate the tortuous streets within the old walls, and a stroll will go past widows who have set up their rush chairs right in the street to catch the best of the afternoon sun and the latest gossip.

While the town can trace roots back to the Iberians, its strategic placement made it a commercial port for the Phoenicians (who named it after Tyre) and later the Greeks, ousted by the Romans, who considered Peñíscola a frontier between themselves and the Carthaginians. Hannibal had an early taste of Roman empiricism here, which evidently fired him up to chase them off his turf. Papa Luna, the last of the Avignon Anti-Popes, retired to this fortress and stubbornly held his claim to be Benedict XIII. Among other acts, he was responsible for confirming the 1411 founding of St Andrew's University in Scotland. His final refuge was the great Templar Castle (open 10–1.30, 4.30–8 in summer, 10–1, 4.15–6 in winter. Entry 100 pesetas). It was modified by Luna, and his crescent moon coat of arms marks the southeast gate through the town ramparts. Quite near the castle, the 18th-century church Virgen de la Ermitana has military motifs. The parish church, on the far side of the highest gate, Portal Fosc, holds some of the anti-pope's finery. His cross of rock crystal mounted with sapphires and delicate enamelwork is very flashy, almost a jewelled version of the bright *azulejo* tiles which are Valencia's trademark. In high summer, the narrow streets can teem with visitors, and arriving in early evening can allow for a bit more breathing space. Besides, after a Mediterranean sunset the spotlights turn the old stones to gold. To stay right on the promontory, choose **Hostal del Duc** (Fuladosa, 10; 48 07 68; Apr–Sept), in an old mansion near the centre. Dozens of beach-side rooms, with a view back to the castle, are offered all year round.

North of town, the road skirts along vast sand beaches, plugged by the tourist board as the 'Orange Blossom Coast' (*Costa del Azahar*) and still short of the overblown development that blights those to the south.

BENICARLÓ, at the end of the beach, has an 18th-century parish church in the typical Valencian Baroque style, blue tiles gleaming on the dome and a tower surveying it all. A fishing port and a modern lighthouse are the only other real diversions beyond the beach, unless your visit is on 24 August, when the patron San Bartolome Apostol is saluted with bull calves charging through the streets and getting their debut in the ring. An unapologetically modern parador (**Parador Costa del Azahar**, Avda Papa Luna, 2; 47 01 00) serves up the regional specialities of paella and seafood *par excellence*. You might be tempted to try the local sturgeon, fresh from Viñaroz, the next big port up the coast.

Albufera and South

2 days/260km/from Valencia
Short drives uncover abrupt changes on this route. An industrial town hiding a gaudy tiled centre gives way to a wide lagoon, where frogs and eels dodge the flat-bottomed boats making slow progress across the sunset. The bright green of the rice fields darkens as stumpy citrus groves and fruit orchards proliferate on the irrigated plain. Further inland, the mountains rise up and castles still offer protection from bogus Moors when the villagers re-enact the Reconquest in a setting which has changed remarkably little over the centuries.

VALENCIA pop: 751,734 Tourist Offices: Paz, 46 or Plaza del País Valenciano, 1. Valencia, Spain's third biggest city, is an initial disappointment. The mosaics and orange blossoms shown on postcards are mostly hidden by industrial plants, factories and shipyards. Yet burrowing deep into the old centre will uncover an interesting Cathedral, commercial silk exchange (*Lonja*), a couple of palaces and churches. Most architecture is flamboyant Gothic. The National Ceramics Museum, in a fine 18th-century building, is both amusing and instructive. While Valencia has produced artists of note, their distinctive styles can be found displayed in less built-up parts of the province. Unless it is the season for *Fallas*, when, after a week of flower processions and giddy celebrations, huge papiermâché caricature floats are torched on 19 March beneath a sky full of mega-decibel fireworks, don't linger long.

Follow the signs to La Albufera, leading off from the Gran Vía Marqués del Turia. Just south of the city, the source of all that paella rice is evident in the paddies. Closer to the coast, wind-stunted pines root down the sand dunes to keep them from blowing into the rice plantations. Adobe shacks with pointed thatched roofs, *barracas*, still can be found along the shore, though development is on the books. The freshwater lagoon, **La Albufera**, was named 'small sea' by the Moors, despite the Mediterranean being kept at bay by a large sandbar. It is only a tenth the size it once was owing to intense cultivation. Since the Middle Ages, rice growers have worked the flat shallows; it is an evocative place, the water and sky

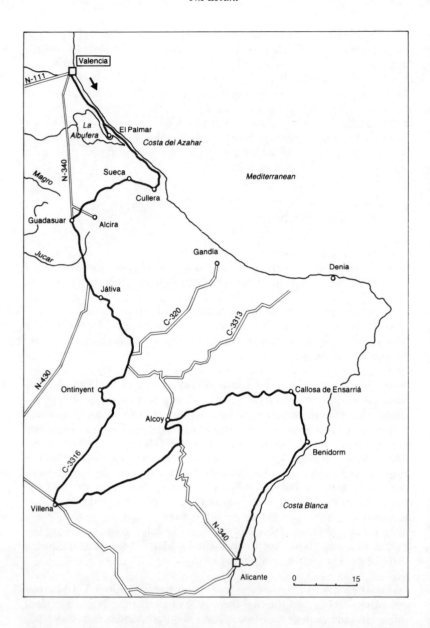

changing colours by the hour, the rice shoots green or golden depending on the season. The calm is broken only in autumn when coots and wild ducks dodge shotgun blasts.

Continue south along the coast road and turn right, following the road 3km up to the shores of La Albufera at **EL PALMAR**. The road was only built in the 1930s, and the traditional rhythms persist as stubby boats traverse the lagoon and eel catchers inspect their contraptions. It's worth-

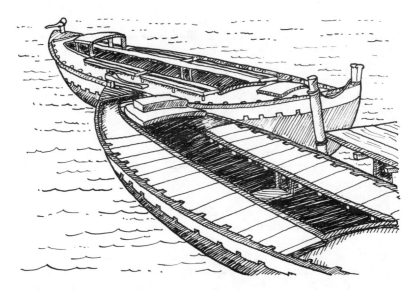

Boats in La Albufera, Valencia

while to bargain down at the little dock for an afternoon boat trip to capture the feel of this place. For flavour, go into any of the informal bars and order up a plate of *all i pebre*: fresh eels fried in garlic and served with green pepper sauce. Quite a few *barracas*, thatched with rushes or rice straw and whitewashed a searing white next to the soft greens of the district, stand in the geometric streets, though few are the main residence of fishermen as in days past. **EL PERELLÓ**, farther along, is a main fishing port along one of the natural channels where the freshwater hits the Med. **LAS PALMERAS**, with its wide beach, is beginning to cater to tourists, and even the harbour town **CULLERA** is putting up highrises out towards the lighthouse. Near the ruins of a castle, the hermitage of Nuestra Señora del Castillo has a panorama over the rice fields, the green *huerta* with its glossy-leaved citrus trees, the new resort and the old town. Follow the signs towards **SUECA**, driving past endless rice plantations, and at Sueca bear left along the Júcar River toward **ALBALAT DE LA RIBERA**. The road threads through two irrigation canals beside orange groves. In November they are heavy with fruit, and in April the sweet blossoms nearly blot out the tang of the sea air. However, orange trees can bloom and bear fruit at the same time, which is why brides often carry a few blossoms in their bouquets. Symbolically this promises fertility without losing beauty. Cross the Magro River and at Guadasuar, head for L'Alcudia. Peach and apricot orchards begin to appear between the citrus groves. At the N-430, bear left and head south on this main road for 26km, bearing left for Játiva.

JÁTIVA (XÁTIVA) pop: 23,755 Tourist Office: José Espejo, 30. From a distance, Játiva rings the two tallest hills with ramparts and spreads out comfortably in between. Dry countryside is coaxed into growing rows of gnarled vines with tall cypresses as windbreaks or exclamation points. Dry riverbeds, which can flashflood in the sudden downpours come spring or autumn, are softened by pink oleanders. At last count there were over 500 fountains in the town, and their waterplay combats the moderate traffic noise in the new quarter. In the Plaza del Cid, a polygonal stone fountain has splashed without interruption since the 15th century. Birthplace of two Borgia popes — the notorious Alexander VI and Calixtus III — as well as the painter José de Ribera, this is no ordinary small town. Philip V, incensed by its opposition during the War of the Spanish Succession, burned much of it and renamed it San Felipe, to remind the citizens just who was in charge. The traditional name didn't come back onto the maps until 1822.

The main Plaza del Seo leads onto the monumental Collegiate Church, bigger even than Valencia's cathedral, which houses Renaissance marbles from the Borgias. Facing it is the Municipal Hospital, with a wonderful Plateresque façade that shows an orchestra of angels tuning up above the door. From the Plaza, both a walking and a driving tour are signposted and a new tourist office on the Plaza provides explanatory pamphlets. The museum in the old granary building on Carrer de la Corretgeria displays archaeological finds alongside several paintings by native son José de Ribera. It also has a surprising effigy of Philip V hanging upside down, in belated retribution for his heavy-handedness (open 10–2 weekdays; closed Sun and Mon). San Felix, a Visigothic chapel on the hillside, contains some beautiful Valencia Primitive paintings (open 10–1, 4–8; closed holiday afternoons). To get there, take a steep path marked 'Castillo' from the Plaza del Espanoleto. This continues up to the ruins of the two castles, linked by a double wall, which stand on the town's original site. Dismantled by Philip V, they have been partially restored, with damage from Bourbon troops and an earthquake in the 18th century recently repaired. The view is extraordinary from this height: it overlooks the tile roofs of the town, split by the Alameda de Jaime I into old and new sections, and extends past the green *huerta* to the rice fields. On clear days, Valencia and the Mediterranean hover on the far horizon. **Vernisa** (Academico Maravall, 1; 227 10 11) is a pleasant place to stay, and **La Abuela** (Reina, 17; 227 05 25. closed Sun) serves good regional dishes with some original flair.

Go south to Albaida on the N-340 and turn right on the C-320 towards Ontinyent. Bear south again, picking up the C-3316 which twists through the green slopes past hidden hermitages. The road straightens out on the plain, passing a couple of zinc mines. Just after Cañada, the road leads to the striking castle at **VILLENA**, where most of the houses are contemporary with this 15th-century squared-off fortress overlooking the plain. Santiago, the Gothic church, has unusual fluted columns and motifs. Visit the town hall for the Archaeology Museum's display of a treasure unearthed in 1963. Solid gold coronets, bracelets, rings and bowls give credence to all the stories of treasure beneath any lump in the ground anywhere in Spain. These are dated from mid-Bronze Age, approximately 1000BC, fashioned by predecessors of the Iberians. Outside town, bear left on a local road to **BIAR**.

Long an agricultural village, Biar is also noted for its pottery, particularly crockery and jugs. Two old fountains, which irrigated the adjoining *huerta* in the 18th century, still operate. The parish church, Virgen de la Asunción, has a graceful Renaissance doorway. With a reputation for honey and toy dolls, Biar has eclipsed its warrior past, but the old houses still huddle at the foot of the hill, shielded behind an austere castle of bleached mustard-coloured stone. The castle stares back to the neighbouring one almost 7km away at Villena, with the valley between them looking ready for a company of knights to set out with flags unfurled. A double wall with crenellated lookouts built into the angles encircles the castle and its homage tower. The Moors held out here for 5 months, the last obstacle to the reconquest of Valencia by James I. Long narrow streets, elegant pointed arches, coats of arms displayed on old ochre mansions all bring these struggles to mind, especially the remains of the Moorish walls around the San Roque neighbourhood.

To commemorate the days when all this terrain was a continual battlefield each village has its own festival of Moors and Christians. The citizens divide up into elaborate fancy dress squads, complete with blackface, scimitars and turbans, or chain mail and helmets, then proceed to wage fierce mock battles, with an invariable Christian triumph. Biar's celebration varies whimsically, but in **IBI**, just down the road, the fights always break out at the end of August. With an even larger manufacture of toys than Biar, Ibi claims that one local factory has the world record for producing dolls' eyes. Leaving the village, your own eyes will boggle with the views around the hairpin turns going up from the plain to Carrasqueta Pass, over 1,000m up, on the approach to Alcoy along the N-340.

ALCOY pop: 66,100 Tourist Office: Avda Puente San Jorge, 1. The grandest Moors vs. Christians fest is here each 23 April, when to thank St George for his personal intevention, which assured final victory in 1276, everyone battles on for three days in epic style, interspersing fireworks and parades. If you miss the event, costumes and records relating to it are on display in the Casal de Sant Jordi. The Baroque Santa María church and the Archaeological Museum, with Iberian relics from nearby Puig and Serreta on exhibit, are both worth seeing. From the Cristina Bridge, a dizzying view down the road to Callosa emphasises the mountain fortress setting of this now-industrial town. The water power from the confluence of three rivers accounts for the development. Try a can of anchovy-stuffed olives, one of the area's specialities. Just north of town, **Venta Pilar** (Ctra Valencia, km 2300; 59 23 25; closed Sun and all Aug) is an 18th-century inn, which serves good regional food along with some international dishes, though it's a little disconcerting to be offered spring rolls in this setting. **Reconquista** (Puente San Jorge, 1; 33 09 00) or **San Jorge** (San Juan de Ribera, 11) are both comfortable overnight stops.

Take the C-3313 east from town, 36 winding kilometres along the Sierra, with the extensive views tempting your eyes at every bend. **CASTELL DE GUADALEST**, carved out of rock over the jade-coloured reservoir, stands on a pinnacle with terraces of olives and almonds putting a geometry on the valleys beneath the new town. Little is left of the castle: what a 1644 earthquake left standing was finished off during the War of the Spanish Succession when the buildings were blown up. The houses are humble, clinging to the limestone ridges, and narrow streets tunnel gingerly through the rocks. The church, Asunción de la Virgen, incorporates twisted rock in its simple design. High on a crest, the bell tower sits in its own whitewashed cubicle, linked to the plain white chapel by a great wall of rugged stone. James I wrote that his soldiers needed wings attached to their armour in order to take the castle. While the tunnel makes the climb possible for visitors, it is still not a place for those with vertigo.

On the descent towards the coast, the land becomes greener and less rocky. **CALLOSA DE ENSARRIÁ**, the capital of this fertile region of fruit trees and cultivated valleys, sits at a crossroads where links to any of the small villages nearby can be followed at random. **POLOP**, on a plump hill ringed by crests, is especially pretty and offers a couple of lodging places. It is a pleasant pause before descending 15km down the road to the dread Benidorm, or preferably Alicante, the regional capital 57km farther on.

South Levant
3 days/360km/from Elche

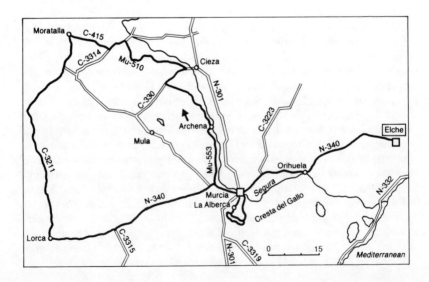

One of the first and last strongholds of the Moors, who irrigated the parched land here and also nurtured a couple of esteemed mystics, Murcia (Levant's most southerly province) has lately gained an undeserved bumpkin image amongst all the Spanish provinces. While not considered a full-fledged member of the Valencia Comunitat, it gets lumped together with it due to common geography. This route goes from the date groves of Elche, in Alicante province, and climbs up to the coastal mountains, where old Moorish outposts, ruined castles and monasteries are too out-of-the-way for most tourists to visit. Despite the intense heat and torrid wind, Murcia does more than compete with neighbouring Almería as good background footage for spaghetti Westerns. Excellent early produce is coaxed from the land through irrigation and is now exported throughout the European Economic Community as well as in Spain. On the coast, shrimp farming is a booming business.

ELCHE pop: 126,873 Tourist Office: Parque Municipal (45 27 47). Few European cities have the exotic look of Elche, fringed by a vast grove of date palms. Now numbering over 200,000 trees, the palms were first planted by Phoenicians and are the only ones in Europe to produce a reliable crop. The palm fronds are used as well, cut and sunbleached, then transported around the country for use on Palm Sunday. The forlorn branches you spy tied on balconies are not necessarily leftovers from this festival: they traditionally are used as low-tech lightning rods. Visit Huerto del Cura, gardens where bright flowers are planted in patterns beneath the city's oldest palms, for the ultimate view of these trees, including the seven-branched Imperial Palm believed to be 150 years old. (Open 8 am–9 pm. Entry 75 pesetas.) The city's best hotel overlooks the palms and is associated with the state paradors: **Huerto del Cura** (Federico García Sanchiz, 14; 45 80 40). Its restaurant, **Els Capellans**, serves a poolside buffet of good seafood and rice dishes. The blue-domed Basilica of Santa María, a Baroque hulk from the 17th century, was designed specifically as a setting for the Elche Mystery, a medieval tale of the Virgin always performed on 14–15 August. See also the Arab minaret, La Calahorra, plus the Altamira Palace and the Museum of Contemporary Art.

Directly south of town, just 2km away, is **La Alcudia**, a rich archaeological source where nine successive civilisations have been uncovered. Relics are exhibited in a small museum on-site (10–2; closed Mon). The real prize, unearthed in 1897, is the Iberian polychrome stone bust, *La Dama de Elche*. But wearing her exquisite headdress and an impenetrable gaze, this mysterious lady is on permanent show at the National Archaeological Museum in Madrid. Double back on the N-340 and head south to Orihuela, skirting the Segura River and extensive groves of lemons and oranges and another big stand of date palms.

ORIHUELA pop: 49,851 Tourist Office: Plaza Condesa Villamanuel, 1. Under the Visigoths and the Arabs, this city was the seat of power in

Murcia, though it became linked to the Kingdom of Valencia in 1304. Visit El Salvador Cathedral, with unusual spiralling vaults, which is mostly Gothic, but graced with a delicate Renaissance style north doorway. Velazquez' *Temptation of St Thomas Aquinas* hangs near Ribera's *Mary Magdalene* in the adjoining museum (10.30 am–1 pm). Santo Domingo College, for two centuries a university but now a Diocesan school, has a rather sober façade but the coloured frescoes in the chapel are lovely. Santiago Chuch, with a legacy from the Knights of St James, is also noteworthy. On Thursday of Easter Week singers perform the traditional *Canto de Pasiones*, religious melodies which share some of the intensity of flamenco *cante hondo*. On the Saturday of Semana Santa, the devil himself rides amongst the holy images from the churches. One float, *La Diablesa*, represents Satan with the nude bust of a woman. July sees a vigorous mock battle between Moors and Christians. **Casa Corro** (Palmeral de San Anton; 30 29 63) specialises in local rice dishes and also rents out rooms.

Continue south on the N-340, just 9km past Murcia, to **ALCANTARILLA**. (Weave through Murcia, following the signs to Plaza de Gonzalez Conde in order to find the marked exit.) On the outskirts of the village is a Huerta Museum, surrounded by orange trees and vegetable gardens, alongside old-fashioned peasant *barracas* thatched with straw (the English word barracks conceivably could be traced back to these ancient shacks, in use before the Crusades). An enormous Arab waterwheel, a *noria* used in the early irrigation schemes here, is also displayed.

Follow the country road MU-534 alongside the banks of the Segura, towards Las Torres de Cotillas. Continue up towards **ARCHENA**, on the MU-553. The Romans first exploited thermal springs here, followed by the Arabs, and this spa village is an outgrowth of their settlement. Near the baths an ancient stone slab lauds their curative waters and quite a few Roman utensils have been dug up in the area. Traces of the original Roman vaulting remain, but the *balneario*'s atmosphere comes mainly from bright Moorish mosaics and stucco tracery around the graceful horseshoe arches: all remodelled in 1898. The technical equipment was updated in 1980 and 1982. Swimming outdoors in the warm green mineral waters is positively sybaritic. It's not difficult to picture saddlesore knights recovering from a Moor-bashing battle with a long soak. These very baths were owned by the Knights of Santiago during the Middle Ages, and were later handed to the Order of St John of Jerusalem. Four hotels linked with the spa provide rooms. The best is **Hotel Termas** (67 01 00). Nearby, concert halls, a video game parlour, a cinema and even a casino bring you back to the 20th century with a thud.

Farther up the riverbanks, the rutted roads lead on to **RICOTE**, an isolated village where the Moriscos held out against expulsion orders until 1618 and were the very last to abandon the former realm of Granada. From a distance, the hills rise up around an expanse of tiled roofs, with lemon groves crowding the village walls. Under the Moors, Ricote had great importance and was named the 'Mount of Moors' in 1228 by emir Ibn Hud, who united all Muslim Spain. Ibn Sabin al Ricote, a local mystic, was the most brilliant of his court's wise men. Although the Knights of Santiago appeared on the scene in 1285, they were so overwhelmed by sheer numbers that they took over three centuries to carry out the banishment. Many of the most historic buildings were damaged by time and neglect, but some of the doorways at least remain. The local seat of the Inquisition, on the Calle Santiago, is now indistinguishable from the other severe houses along the street, but the *Casa Grande*, headquarters of the commandante of Santiago, is still impressive despite its dilapidated state. Built in 1702 in florid Baroque style, its elaborate iron grilles are protected by the cross of Calatrava wrought in the iron. Another is carved in the stone lintel above the doorway. In the centre of the village, the old palace of the military order has been converted into a Dominican convent and College while the slender tower of the 18th-century church, San Sebastian, could pass from a distance as a mosque. Follow a forest trail up to the nearest peak to look back over the village and try to fathom the strong hold this land had on the Moors. The Sierra de Oro, the Golden Range, rises in the north. Head for it over the C-330, towards the wide Segura River, and turn left at La Torre. Where the road splits, bear left by the still blue lake formed by the Alfonso XIII dam.

Continue through this wild backcountry, hawks soaring on the updrafts between the crags, the mountains dark with trees. Turn right on the MU-510 and drive past San Miguel crest. The road clings to the ridge, and overlooks the Benamor River valley beneath. At Las Murtas, turn left and cut over to **MORATALLA** on the C-415. A medieval fortress castle dwarfs the two-and three-storey stucco houses which look heaped around it. The narrowest streets are only wide enough to let a couple of donkeys pass each other, so park at the church plaza and then proceed on foot. Many of the climbs are steep enough that iron handrails are necessary even for the iron-legged residents. Many of the houses bear family crests above their doors and date from about the time of the impressive homage tower on the church. Most of the village activity centres here, card games in the shade most of the year and sombre penitents on the march through the web of streets during Holy Week.

CARAVACA DE LA CRUZ pop: 20,231 Tourist information in Museums. Just 14km south of Moratalla, this town shows the former power of the region through its proliferation of Baroque churches and mansions. An imposing pink Baroque Sanctuary, *Real Alcázar–Santuario de la Vera Cruz*, commands the highest hill outside town. According to legend, a Moorish chieftain ordered an imprisoned priest to say Mass just to satisfy his curiosity about the rites. As the liturgy began, two angels flapped through the window, toting a cross to replace one that was missing from the altar. The Moor became an instant convert. The Sanctuary was erected in the 17th century to commemorate this miracle, but the cross disappeared during the Civil War. (The Vatican has since replaced it with a replica, which supposedly contains a splinter from the cross at

Calvary.) Both the Jesuits and the Carmelites have convents in town. The castle, dating from the 12th century, was dedicated to the Knights Templar, who figure in the town's festivities during May. The miracle of the cross is celebrated, and fancy-dress Moors have another go at the Christians, but to no avail. Two good restaurants merit a visit in Caravaca: **Caballos del Vino** (Carretera de Murcia; 70 20 19) serves succulent roast lamb, washed down with local wine from Jumilla, and lets out rooms for the night. **El Canota** (Gran Vía, 41; 70 03 34; closed Thurs and Sun nights) dishes up fine regional stews and soups.

Descending the C-3211 for 60km through the wooded hills brings you to Lorca, on the main highway.

LORCA pop: 60,627 Tourist Office: Casa de los Guevera, Lopez Gisbert. Long an outpost against the Moors of Granada, this town became an artistic centre for sculptors, embroiderers and tilemakers before it took the lead as the main marketplace in this dry corner of Murcia province. Its squared-off castle and many of its Baroque palaces have been tastefully restored. The main square, Plaza España, shows off to fine advantage the town hall, the law court and the Collegiate Church of San Patricio, all Baroque façades. Almost an institution is **Candido** (Santo Domingo, 13; 46 69 07; closed summer Sun), going strong on its home-style cooking for 50 years. Lorca is noted for devout celebrations of Easter Holy Week, with Roman and Biblical characters joining the processions with the more standard hooded penitents. A rivalry between two major brotherhoods lightens the mood just enough.

The main highway N-340 goes north 65km to the regional capital at a good pace, except that heavily laden lorries can sometimes slow things down.

MURCIA pop: 288,631 Tourist Offices: Tomás Mestre (city) or Alejandro Seiquer, 3 (province). Straddling the Segura River, Murcia's modern appearance belies its age. Founded in 831 by the Arabs, it was captured by the Catholics in 1266, not long after the death of Murcia's Ibn Al-Arabi, a sort of Muslim St. Augustine still highly revered in the Arab world. Murcia soon took over from vulnerable Cartagena as the seat of the bishopric. The cathedral sports a bell tower that was designed by committee: four different architects put their mark on it over 270 years. You can ask the keeper to unlock the door and climb to the top for a good view over the river and its farmland, encircled by grey mountains. Once past the Baroque exterior it is mainly Gothic, and the Vélez chapel has beautiful star vaulting. Just off to the left gallery is a skeleton. The Francisco Salzillo Museum (9.30–1, 4–7; closed Sun) exhibits the *pasos* — polychrome wood carvings carried in the Easter Week processions — at which this Murcian sculptor excelled. Just as interesting are his small terra cotta figurines which show the daily rounds of 18th century peasantry, active in creating the wealth from farming and silkweaving. More idealised Bible characters are mainly working models for the great wooden carvings. More worldly is the men-only casino on Calle de la Trapería, apparently worth a look for its 19th-century sumptuousness, if your gender is correct.

Hotel Conde de Floridablanca (Corbalan, 7; 21 46 24) is a palace in the town centre which has been pleasingly converted into an air-conditioned hotel. **Rincon de Pepe**, more modern and very comfortable, also has the best dining room in town (Apostoles, 34; 21 22 39; restaurant closed Sun pm). Fresh salmon with lemon leaves is typical of their inventive approach to traditional cuisine. For afters, *fresas al vinagre de Jerez*, wild strawberries in sherry vinegar, are recommended.

Head out of town on the N-301 and, after crossing the railway tracks, bear left towards La Alberca, then left again at the canal. Look for signs pointing to Fuensanta, and turn right before Algezares. The **sanctuary of La Fuensanta** (the sacred fountain) is the scene of a big pilgrimage during the first two weeks of each September. The Baroque chapel, dedicated to La Virgen de la Fuensanta, the patron of Murcia, was built by a rich, repentant actress in the 17th century. The church terrace overlooks Murcia's rich farmlands. From here, follow the signs to the **Cresta del Gallo**, a jagged red ridge which does look like the comb of a Titanic fighting cock. A lookout point at the base of the peak has a panorama over Murcia, bisected by the Segura River, plus the orchards and fields fanning out all around it. Follow the unpaved road another 5km for a lovely view of the *huerta* from a different angle. Farther along, the Sierra de Columbares comes into sight, its naked crags cratered and casting weird shadows. Descend for about 5km until you encounter a paved road, leading through **EL VALLE** and **LA ALBERCA**, dusty farmtowns, back to the city of Murcia.

8 NEW CASTILE, LA MANCHA AND MADRID PROVINCE

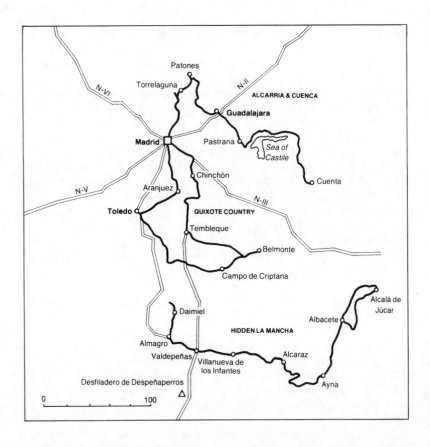

Solid, interior Spain none the less shimmers with the shade of Don Quixote and his windmill jousting. La Mancha's flat fields of grain or vines seem to stretch on forever except in the spring, when bright wildflowers lend a touch of anarchy between the rows. Purple crocus are cultivated for the saffron harvest every autumn. And the *noria* water-wheel, hitched to a blinkered *burro* that plods round and round to draw cupfuls of well water which wet the irrigation channels, still measures out the tedium of farming the arid southern meseta, tipped slightly east. Man-made lakes to the north and the swamps in the south provide some relief and, like all of Spain, there are mountains — these mostly eroded and bare — within reach. Settlements are far apart, but the roads are generally level and quick. The bustling national capital, known for its art museums and its non-stop nightlife, is anything but rural with at least 3½ million inhabitants, yet within Madrid's *comunidad* are some rustic villages which haven't been overrun by city folk looking for weekend retreats. One is so isolated that it was its own minuscule kingdom for centuries after Spain was united.

Quixote Country

3 days/410km/from Madrid

This is classic La Mancha, arid and so monotonous that the daily grind — using windmills — becomes exalted. The beautiful Bourbon gardens at Aranjuez seem like a true oasis in this bleak setting. Toledo retains an overriding glory gleaned from history and legend that almost radiates from the still-beautiful buildings left by three communities — Arabs, Jews and Christians. Castles seem to marshal rows of olives and vines that stretch to distant flat-topped mountains and bright glazed pottery glints from roadside stands. Meeting the garrulous Manchegans presents no problem, and each stop finds a new character ready to talk on any subject.

From Madrid, set out on the N-IV motorway south and keep your foot down on the accelerator for 47km. The Plaza de la Libertad in **ARANJUEZ** is unavoidable: the lanes of the busy artery to the south go right under the arches.

ARANJUEZ pop: 35,936 Tourist Office: Plaza de Santiago Rusinol. This town is almost unbearably hot in summer, despite the English elms, the gardens and the slow-flowing Tagus River (Río Tajo). In spring, it lives up to the romance promised by Joaquin Rodrigo's famous *Concierto de Aranjuez*. Once the palace gardens are in bloom and the rest of the town is fragrant with strawberries and abristle with asparagus, it comes into its own. Since it passed into royal hands from the Knights of Santiago, Aranjuez has been the spring hunting grounds of the Royal Family, and the Bourbon Palace standing there now is an outgrowth of this interest. Philip II had the first purpose-built royal residence, and subsequent fires led to much restoration and new building. The buildings have intricate collections of treasures and fripperies, with the guide droning on enthusiastically about each piece of furniture. For many, the gardens are the main attraction: the Prince's Garden once included a model farm, stables for exotic animals and glasshouses for even more exotic plants. Within it now are the Labourer's Cottage — a real misnomer for a neo-Classic trianon which would be at home in Versailles — and the Sailor's House, a riverside museum of the royal pleasurecraft, both worthwhile (100 pesetas to visit by car). Parterre, the formal palace gardens designed by Boutelouin in 1746, and the Island Garden, a less rigid one that Philip II enjoyed on a fake isle in the river, are closer to the main palace. The surrounding town is in a strict grid plan and a little run-down. In season, try the fresh strawberries and cream from any of the little stands, or from one of the riverside restaurants. Partridge or pheasant in season is the speciality at **Casa Pablo** (Almibar, 20; 891 14 51), along with Pablo's stellar winelist.

South of town, veer left onto the N-400, clearly marked for Toledo.

TOLEDO pop: 57,769 Tourist Office: Puerta de Bisagra. Holy Toledo: this town was paramount for centuries in the fortunes of Spanish Moors, Jews and Christians and, with its towers and spires reaching up from a granite perch above the Tagus River, it looks every inch a shrine. Though not a large place, the streets wind and seem to tangle, making the geography seem nearly as complicated as the history. Most buildings are monuments of some kind, so that the tacky tourist shops with armour, swords and nifty Rambo-style jungle knives come almost as comic relief. Few Roman traces have survived, other than the circus now devoted to manufacturing arms, and the Visigoths were not noted builders.

An exhaustive checklist of sites would require a book in itself. Highlights include: the Cathedral (13th–18th century; extraordinary stained glass, carved walnut choirstalls depicting the conquest of Granada, Mudéjar plasterwork, and much more); the Alcázar, still pockmarked by bullets from the Republican seige during the Civil War, though damage by shelling has been repaired so that the palace-fortress looks as it did when Charles V made it an imperial residence. Church of Santo Tomé, with Mudéjar tower and El Greco's masterpiece, *The Burial of Count Orgaz*; El Greco House and Museum; El Tránsito Synagogue; Santa María la Blanca Synagogue; San Juan de los Reyes Monastery; Hospital de Tavera with its stunning collection of canvases by El Greco and Titian, Ribera and Tintoretto; San Roman Church, a Mudéjar church revamped into a Visigothic Museum; Plaza del Zocodover, the heart of the town; Puerta del Sol; Cristo de la Luz — multi-layered worship takes place in a Mudéjar church on top of a mosque erected three centuries earlier over a Visigothic temple. El Cid's charger supposedly dropped to its knees in front of this mosque during the regal pomp of Alfonso VI's entry to Toledo. Let there be no thought that the horse couldn't keep up with its master's changing loyalties. An ancient Visigoth lantern was found walled inside, illuminating a crucifix. El Cid and steed were vindicated. Every corner in town seems to have its own dubious legend. Daytrippers swarm the streets, and mediocre restaurants jack up prices accordingly. For cheap fare, **El Nido** (Barrio Rey) stands out. **Hostal del Cardenal** (Paseo de Recaredo, 24; 22 08 62) is for self-indulgence. Roast suckling pig or lamb, stuffed partridge, and Manchegan specialities are served with style in an 18th-century palace near the old walls. For dessert, try the marzipan at least once. The **Carlos V** (Escalerilla de la Magdalena, 3; 22 21 00) is a comfortable and central hotel with good views from most rooms. Outside town, the **Parador Nacional Conde de Orgaz** (Paseo de los Cigarrales; 22 18 50) has stage-set views of the town but is less convenient for sight-seeing and usually packed with tourists.

Leave on the C-400 southeast to **MORA DE TOLEDO**, which has a utilitarian castle just outside the village on the C-402 road. This narrow little keep commands a view over most of La Mancha, and olive trees seem to march on parade in all directions. To climb up to the castle, allow about ten minutes. Go back to the C-400 and drive on to **CONSUEGRA**. An undistinguished town spreads out beneath a ridge with the ruins of a 14th-century castle beside a line of windmills. They are genuine, though the sails are rigid after a recent remake, all the better to pose against. In October, the town comes to life with a Saffron Harvest, when the purple crocuses that carpet the surrounding fields are pain-stakingly pulled apart. Harvest competitions, bullfights, folksong and dance contests in traditional dress, a disco, plus a tawdry funfair beneath crocus flowers in fairy-lights, mark the occasion.

Keep heading east, through Madridejos. Before Alcázar de San Juan, get on the N-420 to by-pass the centre and arrive in **CAMPO DE CRIPTANA** with another skyline of windmills, three with the old machinery intact. Most of the religious monuments, which harkened back to the Knights of St John of Jerusalem and the Order of Santiago, were destroyed in the Civil War battles.

Just past town, head left up the local road to **EL TOBOSO**, which Cervantes mentioned by name as the home of Don Quixote's sweet Dulcinea. The town is prettified to welcome visitors on literary itineraries and the streets are swept daily. Dulcinea's house has been refurbished and transformed into a humble museum of the errant knight's exploits, and the earnest efforts seem a bit bogus. Iglesia Santiago is a surprisingly mas-sive late Gothic church in such a small town's plaza. Follow the local road on to **VENTA DE DON QUIJOTE** on the N-301. Picture-tiles on a line-up of rough buildings depict the imaginary scene when Quixote was knighted by an innkeeper when he mistook the tavern for a castle, not quite claim-ing that it all happened here. Toast Cervantes with a glass of Manchegan wine and go east to Mota del Cuervo, the junction with the N-420. Bear left and follow the road 16km to **BELMONTE**.

On a small rise, above orderly rows of grapevines and wide grain fields that ripple under the gusty winds, poses Belmonte's 15th-century castle.

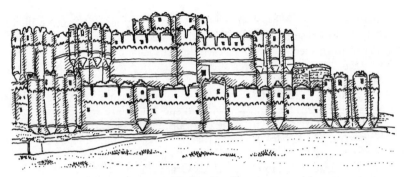

Medieval castle

With its hexagon shape and triangular patios, it rivals Coca castle for geometric fantasy and the drawbridge and dungeon help you imagine medieval life inside, under the whims of the Marquis of Villena, court favourite of Henry IV. Pale pine Mudéjar ceilings and Gothic tracery stand out and the Marquis' bedroom chamber is most curious. A carved walnut ceiling, complete with a handle to crank it round and tiny bells attached to mask the creaking of the contraption, must have relieved bedroom boredom. In the corner, a stairway spirals down to an emergency escape from the basement. The castle ramparts link up with most of the old town wall, which retain three of the original five gates. The slope between the castle and the town is quite steep and planted with umbrella pines. Within the town, lime and whitewash cover much of the old stone and the hidalgos' homes are distinguished by tall windows protected by sturdy iron grilles, *rejas*. Most impressive of all the buildings in town is the Collegiate Church, dating from the 14th century and embellished by the Marquis. The Santiago scallop shell atop the Calatrava cross recurs throughout the church, and with high positions in both of these military orders the ruling families maintained their might. Fray Luis de León, the revered theologian from Salamanca, is the most famous native son, and his family chapel is set off by a remarkably carved Renaissance retable of the Virgin.

From here, double back on the N-420, turning right at the local road towards Monreal del Llano. Veer left at Los Hinojosos and head for Quintanar de la Orden. This is all flatland, fit for little else besides knights' battles and for fast driving, so continue on to **TEMBLEQUE**, 42km farther along the C-402. It seems like another faceless Manchegan town until you reach the centre, an extraordinary Plaza Mayor. The smooth stone supports of the double arcade all around the dusty square are graceful, and the delicate triple wooden galleries which bridge over the road have a vaguely Oriental feel to them, almost as if they were pinched from Christian Istanbul. The peaked tiled roof displays the Maltese Cross, reflecting that the town was mostly under the sway of the military knights of Saint John of Jerusalem. The Baroque palace of Fernandez Alejo as well as a fine Renaissance parish church both deserve a look.

Leave on the north road, following signs to **OCAÑA**, a sober town which witnessed the Spanish Army knuckling under to Joseph Bonaparte in 1809. Once past the *alfiz* framing the town's 15th-century entrance, leave the main road for the N-400 as far as Noblejas, then head north through Colmenar de Oreja up to **CHINCHÓN**.

The sound of clinking glasses and the toast 'Chin chin' is very frequent in Chinchón. The town's biggest industry is making the potent anise fire-water, *aguardiente*, which is practically synonymous with the name Chinchón, and is distilled near the old castle above town. In botany handbooks, *Chinchona* identifies the quinine plant, brought from Peru to Europe by a local countess in the 17th century. During her stint as vicereine of Peru, she was cured of jungle fever by its application. Thus, gin and tonic drinkers can trace the quinine bite of tonic back here. Much drinking and celebration goes on in the Plaza Mayor when it is cordoned off for the summer bullfights. The whitewashed buildings are highlighted by painted wooden galleries which command the most prized views of the *corrida*, and the hulking parish church of La Asunción, conserving its precious Goya painting behind thick stone walls, faces right on the plaza. The **Meson de la Virreina** (894 00 15), also on the main square, serves plain Castilian grilled and roast meats along with salads and fresh bread. Pitchers of local wine complete the meal, and a shot or two of the Chinchón liqueur after coffee is practically obligatory. The **National Parador** (Avda de Generalisimo, 1; 894 02 06) is installed in a 17th-century Augustine convent, and has managed to soften the ascetic lines with terraced gardens and a swimming pool rimmed with shade trees, yet hasn't sacrificed ambience to comfort. Madrid is only 45km from Chinchón, and supplies quite a few of its week-end revellers.

MADRID pop: 3,188,297 and growing! Tourist Offices: Maria de Molina, 50; Plaza Mayor, 3; Torre de Madrid, Plaza España; Princesa, 1; Barajas Airport and Chamartín railway station. Madrid is a come-lately by the ancient standards of most Spanish cities, and the capital seems to be making up for lost time. While it can be claimed that the place has been inhabited since palaeolithic days, it was little more than a village until Charles V and his son Philip II discovered that the dry heat eased their gout. Philip II stopped the peripatetic royal roaming, which had traditionally avoided rows between proud cities vying for patronage, and declared Madrid capital in 1561. The citizens have long been nicknamed *gatos* (cats) by other Spaniards because they prowl around so late at night, and Madrid does offer entertainment round the clock. In the go-ahead 1980s, even the siesta can be avoided in some establishments here.

The fountains are an elegant city feature, and are even indexed in the official street atlas. One of the best, at the downtown Plaza Colón, is unabashedly modern. Here Christopher Columbus surveys the horizon from a tall pedestal, and beneath him a flat expanse of water roars over an edge like the far reaches of the sea would have in a world that was not round. In the scorching heat, the fountain provides shade and spray, with a marble-cooled passage underneath it. Columbus' routes of discovery are mapped out on the wall and the power of a falling wall of water drowns out the formidable traffic. Big pink Cyclopean blocks, carved with some of the most evocative passages from Spanish poets and philosophers, mark the other edge of the plaza, and a ship-shaped terrace bar, complete with rigging, is a trendy place to station yourself. Not far away is the Cibeles Fountain, a graceful 18th-century creation in which the Greek Goddess of Fertility rides her chariot through spurting water jets in one of the capital's busiest intersections.

No one should miss the Prado Museum, with its inspiring art collection, and though the displays are often woefully lit, the paintings command attention. At least 24 other museums are open to the public, and the Centre Reina Sofía, recently opened, is a showplace for more contemporary art. The Real Academia de Bellas Artes de San Fernando is a treasure house of Goyas and Riberas, if you can manage to be there the sole morning or afternoon it opens its doors each week. To complicate matters, opening day rotates sporadically. Madrid's Old Town, around the Plaza Mayor, has a down-at-heel charm and also impressive buildings near the Plaza de la Villa. The national parliament, in the 19th-century Palacio de la Cortés, is surprisingly modest. Now that scaffolding is coming down after a blitz of restoration, the area's churches are visible again. The 17th-century San Isidro Cathedral is joined by San Miguel Basilica and San Francisco El Grande as the city's most distinguished churches, though the capital is filled with them, having headed Catholic Spain for four centuries. One in the new part of town resembles a Mexican sombrero! Down by the Manzanares River behind the railway tracks is San Antonio de la Florida, rarely visited by tourists. This little chapel is decorated with wonderfully spirited Goya frescoes, and the artist is buried here, though his skull has been misplaced. The Royal Palace is open to the public, for the King normally prefers his Zarzuela Residence just outside the city, and is a study in Bourbon excess: 2,800 rooms. The displays of carriages and royal armour have a certain appeal, and the gardens have a lovely outlook to the mountains.

Madrid's big parks, the Retiro, Casa de Campo and Parque de Oeste, are used mostly for strolls in early evening and present a truly Spanish scene. When exploring Madrid, and there is much much more to uncover, don't overlook the new city, with modern architecture that is sometimes off-beat, sometimes just off, but frequently exhilarating. Salvador Dalí, egotistical surrealist and Marques de Pubol, was commissioned by the King to create a monument to himself in his own square. His arch-rival Picasso is honoured with a square as well, with a building fronted by a Joan Miró mural tauntingly nearby. Restaurants abound, from the humblest stand, to hundreds of pavement terraces, to the outrageously expensive **Zalacaín**, begrudgingly ranked 3 stars by the French snobs of Michelin in early 1987. Hotels come in all price brackets. **Gran Hotel Victoria** (Plaza del Angel, 7 near Plaza Santa Ana; 231 45 00) is where many of the old bullfighters stayed and is close to the old part of town, in a lively plaza close to the theatre and filled with inexpensive restaurants. **Hotel Sanvy** (Goya, 3; 276 08 00) is more upmarket, right on the Plaza Colón, but with friendly management that avoids the expense account atmosphere which riddles many of Madrid's 4- and 5-star hotels.

Hidden La Mancha

4 days/480km/from Daimiel

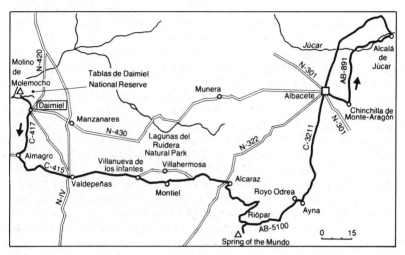

This view of La Mancha happily sees the region breaking most of the norms that castigate it as a dry and flat impediment between Madrid and anywhere worth going. Great marshes which draw migrating birds, hidden springs that bubble forth in mountain caves and other rivers that dive underground for their own diversion, narrow canyons, steep villages with Renaissance pretensions, even Spain's oldest stage overlooked by Flemish windows: these are some of the unexpected treats of Hidden La Mancha.

DAIMIEL, on the fast N-420 south across some of the most parched plains of La Mancha, is the gateway to a national park for waterfowl. **Las Tablas de Daimiel**, known as a hunter's paradise since the Knights of Calatrava controlled it, has King Alfonso XII's royal hunting lodge stranded in the midst of a marsh on the *Isla de los Asnos* (Asses' Island). Surprisingly enough, this is the traditional name and not a recent sardonic comment from ecologists once the bird sanctuary was finally declared a national park in 1962. Part is still set aside for hunters. Information centres are in Daimiel town, which is also known for its pottery with distinctive green glazes. From the entrance just past the old windmill 11km west, at **Molino de Molemocho**, hikers can follow an itinerary that includes camouflaged observation posts for watching the wild ducks, geese and terns who stopover here. In the northern part of the park, **Ojos de Guadiana** marks the place that the Guadiana River sinks out of sight only to reappear a few kilometres west. **Las Brujas** (N-420 highway, 85 22 11) offers reasonable food and a few rooms if you want to stay and explore the Gothic church, Santa María, or the Carmelite convent. Unless your visit is at the end of August or in May, when the images of the Virgin are paraded through the town with fervour, it's best to head south on the C-417, past the castle at **Bolaños de Calatrava** to **ALMAGRO**.

A traditional lacemaking town, where the women still sit at their old-fashioned bobbins, Almagro bears the influence of the rich Flemish bankers who came just as the warrior-monk Calatrava founders submitted to the Crown. The main square, especially, with its double glass galleries set

Ceramic pottery, La Mancha

with green-painted panes, has the Fugger family's touch of Flanders. But what really stands out is the *Corral de comedias*, on the south portico. Refurbished in the 1950s after a century of neglect, this Golden Age theatre was the stage for Spanish drama in the 16th century and is the sole surviving example of early theatre in the entire nation. Classic works are still performed here during San Bartolomé (24–28 August) plus the final two weeks in September (open 9–2, 4–9).

Great mansions with elaborately carved heraldic crests line the narrow streets, while palaces merit a little plaza of their own. The university is impressive, and reminders of the Calatrava knights are on almost every corner. The old Calatrava convent, now a Dominican college, is worth a visit for its Plateresque stairway alone. The former prison is now the tourist office (José Antonio, 11) and a magnificent 16th-century Franciscan convent has been converted to a state parador. **Parador Nacional de Almagro** (Ronda de San Francisco; 86 01 00) has patios and galleries that lighten the sober religious architecture, and the dining room serves rustic regional specialities such as *ajo de patatas con conejo* (garlic potatoes with rabbit).

From here, go east on the C-415 across the former domain of the Calatrava knights, passing straight through **VALDEPEÑAS** with its wineries and noise, the road lined with huge terra cotta wine vats now that more prosaic concrete ones are being used in the processing. After a total of 70km, arrive in **VILLANUEVA DE LOS INFANTES**. This graceful Golden Age town was once Montiel country, where the military Knights of Santiago ruled. Independence was won through the efforts of four princes (*infantes*) of Aragón, sons of Ferdinand. The main plaza has a neo-classic harmony of arched supports, pillars and grand balconies of worked wood, all overlooking the 16th-century church of San Andrés. Quevedo, the poet and satirist, is buried here. The Casa de Arco has a beautiful entrance and patio, and the 16th-century Convent of the Dominicans, whose Santo Tomás was born here, merits a visit as well. Branch off to the right outside town and head for the fortress village of **MONTIEL**. Continue on until you rejoin the main road and follow it to **ALCARAZ**, where the mountains begin to rear up again.

Alone on a clay mound, Alcaraz looks over the fields at its feet which may have inspired the carpetweavers who first brought the city fame. A few arches with crumbling stairs are reminders that the city was once walled off and patrolled by local knights who refused to submit 'even to the king himself' in a dispute over dubious inheritance taxes and calmly locked the royal messenger out. King Juan II admired such spirited independence and declared Alcaraz a full-fledged city, craftily gaining their support by his action. The fine Renaissance architecture comes as a surprise in this isolated shepherd's town, until the discovery that Andalucía's most active Renaissance architect was a native son: Andres de Vandelvira, born in 1509. The main street has a genteel air, with two-storey mansions graced by wrought iron balconies and elaborate entrances. On the Customs-house (*aduana*), Plateresque decoration distinguishes the doorway. The main square, a refuge with a small garden, has a glorious Gothic church, Trinidad, whose tower twins with the Tardon, a more slender one on the adjacent 16th-century prison (originally a Dominican convent). A modern clock keeps the time now and the bells only ring out when a citizen is imprisoned or set free. The town hall and the old exchange, both from the 16th century, complete the Plaza Mayor, which annually rings out with the full pageantry of a bullfight.

Just beyond the town are the remains of an aqueduct which brought water to the Romans and later the Moors. The Reconquest here took over 3 centuries until Alfonso VIII, with the Archbishop of Toledo at his side, marched in with a cross and a sword held high. All mosques, save one, were wiped out and a church, now disappeared, was set up inside its grandeur. September brings the celebration and pilgrimage up to the hillside sanctuary of the Virgen de Cortés, where Aragón forged links with Castile to continue the Reconquest. From here, the view of the town's dark roofs and towers in exhilarating. Rooms with private baths are available at a simple hunters' inn, **Hostal El Cazador** (no phone), out on the main highway.

Go south on the C-415 towards the Alcaraz mountains, whose lower flanks are covered in olive groves. The road dips down through a wooded valley and goes through **RIÓPAR**, known for its bronze foundry where some enormous sculpture is cast. About 5km past this village, turn right for Siles. Follow along for 6km more and take the turn-off to the **Cueva de los Chorros**. Here, inside the grotto behind a curtain of leaves, the Río Mundo comes bubbling up as a small spring, or *nacimiento*. The road traces the young river down the steep course back on the C-415, which you follow east past Fuente Higuera and then turn left on the narrow AB-5100. This winds its way through mountain crags and ravines, to snake its way down from the stunning pass at **Royo Odrea** to a lookout over the canyon.

Continue the descent into **AYNA**. This little pueblo comes like an apparition around a bend in the road, teetering on the steep side of the Mundo Ravine. A few remains on the highest outcrop verify that La Yedra castle witnessed battles against the Moors in the early 15th century, and a document in the town hall signed by King Philip II in 1565 founds the little municipality. The lower part of the village is the most traditional, and many of the homes here are simple constructions of adobe, wood and plaster, with an occasional rock thrown in. **Cueva del Niño** just outside the village contains ochre paintings dating back 20,000 years and the hermitage of Nuestra Señora de los Remedios, not far away, has Mudéjar styling.

Some 59km onwards, along the fast C-3211 which cuts across a flat plain planted with rows of feathery artichoke thistles, sprawls Albacete.

ALBACETE pop: 117,126 Tourist Office: Avda España, 3. This dreary city heads the regional government and even claims a state parador, but the only worthwhile activity is a look at the Provincial Archaeological Museum in the city park. The most engrossing exhibit is the collection of tiny ivory and amber dolls taken from a Roman necropolis (10–2; 5–7; closed Mon and Sun pm. Entry 150 pesetas). A good place to eat is **Nuestro Bar** (Alcalde Conengia, 102; 22 72 15) where the quick service matches the imaginative local food. *Queso frito* (fried cheese) is done with just the right touch and the home-made sausage is scrumptious. You can even trust the waiter's recommendations.

Set off from Albacete following the signs towards Alicante for a quick detour over the **CHINCHILLA DE MONTE-ARAGÓN**, 14km away. The only sizeable hill in the region is crowned by a castle, and this town, the former provincial capital, huddles beneath it. Wander through the labyrinth of narrow streets and be surprised by the elegant Gothic and Renaissance mansions which hint at the town's prosperity under the sway of the Marquess of Villenaon. The flamboyant 18th-century town hall, with a bust of Charles III glaring down, dominates the main square. The plaza shades itself with an arcade on wooden pillars and the old exchange (*Lonja*) echoes them in a gallery. the Gothic church of Santa María del Salvador is also worth a look. Today, potters still peddle the traditional ceramics which made a name for the town throughout the province.

Retracing your route back towards Albacete, the **Parador Nacional de la Mancha** (Highway N-301, km 260; 22 94 50), built in an old country house, is a pleasant stop for rather pricey regional food such as *monje de* *tomate*, and the swimming pool and tennis courts make an overnight stop worthwhile. There are plenty of more luxurious hotels back in the regional capital proper.

If the area's flatness threatens to destroy your soul, an afternoon excursion to the uplands will remedy the problem. Go northeast on the AB-891, but veer left towards the canal, following signs to Tinajeros and Valdeganga. The road suddenly becomes wicked and spectacular along the River Júcar, the same one that sculpts the landscape near Cuenca to the north. Turn right to reach **ALCALÁ DEL JÚCAR**, just as scenic but on a much more intimate scale. The village is squeezed between a castle tower and the church, cut right into the cliff. Below, the river rings around the cliff like a natural moat. Open to the public, the Masago gives a good idea of the weird cliff-dwellings hollowed out of the rock. Long passages lead to balconies which gaze out at the other side of the cliff. (Visits Sun and holidays, 9–2, 4–10; closed winter afternoons. Entry 50 pesetas.) Even by night the village is impressive, and afterwards, head north on the AB-863, which will intersect the N-322 back down to the hotel in Albacete (52km) or north to the Valencian wine town of **REQUENA**, equidistant through the mountain passes.

Alcarría and Cuenca

2 days/255km/from Madrid

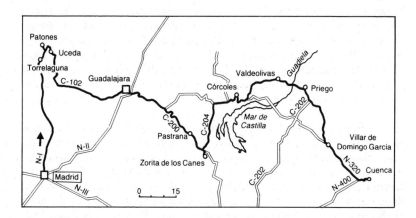

North and then east from the capital, this route goes past stumpy mountains and by dammed rivers which now help sweeten the harsh face Castile and La Mancha presented to its knights, errant or not. The Alcarría especially is carved by rivers and gives a foretaste of the sinkholes and canyons that penetrate the limestone range near Cuenca. This lively city is a literal cliff-hanger and it avoids a time-warp mentality with its *avant garde* museum, creating futuristic controversy now for over 20 years.

Taking leave of the art museums and nightclubs of Madrid, make your way from the ring road M-30 and onto the N-I motorway to Burgos. Delicate manoeuvres these, and an enormous motorway sculpture — a Calderesque black stabile bird — sees you off on your flight from the city. The mountains will be ahead of you, urging (if not blocked out by a petrol tanker). The exit from the N-I is easy to miss, so look out for kilometre mark 45.5, marked **LA CABRERA**, and exit to the right. (All destinations are measured from an official central compass point in the midst of Madrid's Puerto de Sol.) You will already have passed El Molar, and driving past Cabanillas means you've missed the turn and will have to double back. The first main settlement will be **TORRELAGUNA**, birthplace of Cardinal Cisneros, not far from the Jarama River. This was one of the post-Reconquest repopulation projects of the ambitious archbishops of Toledo, though there is evidence that prehistoric hunters and Iberian tribes passed this way before it was a Roman agricultural community. The 15th-century church of la Magdalena is certainly grand for the present size of the town, and the supports for the arcades in the main square are worth a look. A Franciscan convent founded by Cisneros also fronts on the plaza. And the grand 16th-century town hall also bears his blessing, carved on a stone plaque. The beginning of September sees 'giants' and 'fatheads' adding to the patron's fiesta, which also features bullfighters and bulls in the streets.

Follow the local road off to the right towards **PATONES**, and don't be dismayed on arrival at a dismal modern village with breeze-block construction. **PATONES DE ARRIBA** is marked with a sort of minibillboard on the left, and a rough road corkscrews up for 2km. Slate-spiked hills rise up on each side and the village houses are built of dark stone that blends into this fold above the river. It was here, well away from the battles between the Moors and Christians which swept over the valley, that a tiny group of shepherds lived on the fringes under their own 'Rey de Patones', a privilege which they kept until Carlos III consolidated his own kingdom. Streets are incredibly steep and lead up eventually to high pastures for goats and sheep. The wildflower honey sold here is special, and it is also a surprise to find a restaurant with dinner-jacketed waiters just up the road from where the village women peddle their eggs. **El Rey de Patones** (843 04 49) serves huge portions of meat cooked on the wood-fired oven, as well as home-made pastries for afters. Service is attentive, though slow, and the Bar La Cabaña right next door grills up *pinchitos*, meat kebabs, and *tapas* with more speed if less style. The road is fairly recent, and the tower village didn't come about until the hungers of the Civil War drove some of the villagers to a more accessible site.

Go past **PATONES DE ABAJO**, taking a look at the turn-of-the-century dam on the heights above the left side of the road. Go over the bridge to **UCEDA**, a town as rich with religious architecture as Torrelaguna. La Varga church, with a Romanesque appearance, is outshone by the parish church built in 1553 by Siliceo, archbishop of Toledo. The Plaza Mayor is brightened by some carefully tended gardens beneath the crested mansions. Continue on, bearing right through Valdepiélagos and then left at the intersection with the C-102, which heads to Guadalajara.

GUADALAJARA pop: 56,922 Tourist Office: Travesia de Beladiez, 1. Much of Guadalajara's past was blasted away during the Civil War, leaving a modern industrial outpost for Madrid. The Mendoza family, who based their fief here in the 14th century, constructed the most impressive palace, right at the north edge of town. The Duke of Infantado's Palace had a glorious double-storey patio which still needs damage rectified, although the distinguished diamond-patterned façade is now complete. Don't bother with the hotels and restaurants here, but move on, bearing right at Alhóndiga onto the C-200 which leads to the former ducal ville of Pastrana, 47km southeast.

Grouped on a mound in the midst of a low plain, the brown tiled roofs of **PASTRANA** form a geometric patchwork and resemble a huge tortoise, basking in the sun. Patches all around the village are intensively cultivated and on the surrounding hills grow lavender, rosemary, marjoram and thyme which flavour an aromatic wild honey known throughout Spain. While the village is extremely old, with Iberian origins, it became known as a stronghold of the Calatrava Order and also as a sanctuary for Moriscos from Granada, who took refuge from expulsion orders in the 16th century and worked miracles on silk tapestries. Many of these are on exhibit in the remarkable Collegiate Church, including eight of the Flemish style which were commissioned locally by the Dukes of Pastrana. Velazquez' famous painting, *Las Hilanderas* (the spinners), may well represent a tapestry workshop in this village. The four tapestries woven in Brussels between 1471 and 1476, recounting the North African exploits of Portugal's Alfonso V, who challenged Isabella's right to rule, are the pride of the church. A wooden crucifix from the 13th century is also outstanding.

The main plaza is curious, with one side completely open and dropping away to the River Arias below. It's called La Plaza de la Hora, because of the one-eyed Princess of Eboli, who was permitted only one hour's daily glimpse of the place during her banishment to the Palacio de los Duques de Pastrana, which overlooks the square. As a young widow she had a notorious liaison with the king's secretary which besmirched her reputation so much that Santa Teresa's nuns fled town to seek holier surroundings. A large Franciscan monastery stayed on. Los Cuatro Canos, an ancient stone fountain with four faces spurting out the precious water, lends its name to a small plaza near the shopping district. Citizens would reach up with a hollow bamboo cane to guide the water jet to their pails, not splashing away a drop. The **Hostal de Santa Teresa** on the main square provides simple lodging and meals. At weekends, try out the **Figón Princesa de Eboli**, run by the Concepcionista nuns in their own convent. On the last day of April, there is a midnight concert in the Collegiate Church when the youngsters 'sing in' the month of May. On 19 January, the scene is a bit more carefree with dancing and singing accompanied with instruments such as bottles and brass mortars in front of the town

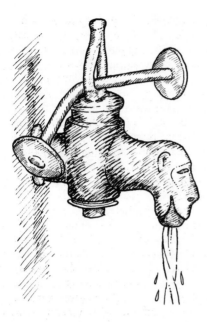

Zorita: public tap (detail)

hall, followed by street serenades well into the night.

Just 9km down the road, bearing right past the power station, **ZORITA DE LOS CANES** has shrunk to only 94 inhabitants after a glorious past, having been the regional centre for the military brotherhood of Calatrava in the 13th century. The castle which remains on a strategic rise over the green Tajo (Tagus) River was probably fortified using stones filched from the Visigothic ruins of Recropolis on nearby Oliva Hill. Long before Alfonso VIII grabbed the castle from the Castro family and handed it over to the Calatrava, it was the scene of battles during a distant civil war which split the Caliphate of Córdoba. Moorish and Jewish neighbourhoods used to thrive here during the prosperous Middle Ages. The view from the ruins is extensive and startlingly modern, with Spain's first nuclear energy plant nearby. The village still boasts several noble mansions and a village church just inside the old gate. Handwoven willow baskets are hawked in the village centre.

Get back on the C-200 and return to the fork, then loop up to **SAYATÓN**, first travelling close to the river before tunnelling right through the rocky strip which separates the Buendia and Entrepeñas reservoirs. Together these manmade lakes are grandly dubbed the *Mar de Castilla* or Sea of Castile. The road climbs up past the humdrum village of **SACEDÓN**. Ahead, **CÓRCOLES** is easily missed, for the earth-coloured tiles and houses blend in with the countryside. Turn left just past **ALCOCER** on a local road. After about 10km, turn right again at the junction and go on to **VALDEOLIVAS**. The olive groves close by, from which the village takes its name, break out of the usual regimented rows, and stunted trees seem to swarm over to the flat-topped ridges. Rusty-coloured fields are broken up by streams lush with beeches and poplars along their banks. A Romanesque church with a pointed barrel-vault graces the village and is set off against a backdrop of the wide water and table-top mountains. Don't miss the pair of windmills on the way out, for they haven't been done up for the tourists like the ones closer to the Toledo daytrippers. Continue straight on the local road until it intersects the C-202. Turn left for **PRIEGO**.

Now a timber town, Priego is impressive beneath its great escarpment and stands guard over the entrance to the Escabas Ravine which winds north. A trout stream waters the flat canyon floor, which is cultivated,

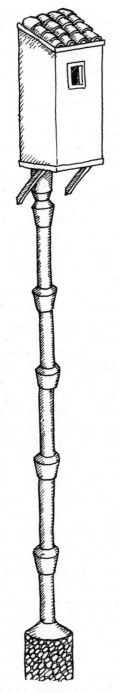

A cliffside toilet from Cuenca

and vertical cliffs look up on either side. A Renaissance town hall doesn't outdo several of its contemporaries, mostly large mansions, though the 16th-century church is masked by a Classical revamp. Turn left south of the village at **VILLACONEJOS** (translation: Rabbitville!) and follow the streams and market gardens along the pleasant road to Albalate and Villar de Domingo García. Here the route links up with the N-320, heading for Cuenca.

CUENCA pop: 41,791 Tourist Office: Fermín Caballero, corner of García Izcara. Skip the modern section and head across the Huecar River for the old quarter, standing on a cliff top with precipices on three sides. With such an impregnable position, Cuenca was spared many of the invasions which complicated life in the rest of New Castile. Note that there isn't a castle. Park in the main square, after driving through the arch in the 18th-century town hall, and explore the steep narrow streets on foot. The Cathedral fronts on the Plaza Mayor de Pio XII and, with unweathered rebuilding after a partial collapse in 1902, looks distinctly odd. Inside, the 16th-century altarpieces and the wrought iron screens stand out, along with a 16th-century Knights' chapel. The treasury holds two El Greco paintings. *Casas Colgadas*, or hanging houses, are Cuenca's real trademark and these 14th-century structures clamber down the cliff-sides defying gravity with as many as a dozen storeys. Three houses have been knocked together to form the Museum of Abstract Act, which presents New Wave Spanish artists in a medieval setting (Closed Mon and Sun afternoons, otherwise 11–2, 4–6 (till 10 on Sat); 100 pesetas entry).

For the best view of the houses, follow a path down to Puente San Pedro, an iron footbridge with a non-slip walkway of wooden slats which is suspended 40m above the Huecar, definitely not recommended for vertigo-sufferers. The path descends right into the gorge of the Huecar with small strips of gardens and pine woods far below those dangling houses. The Torre de Mangana, which has been transformed from a minaret to a clocktower, and the Archaeological Museum are both worth seeking out. Only one lodging place is in the old quarter proper: **Posada de San José** (Julian Romero, 4; 21 13 00). Just a couple of streets north of the cathedral, some of its rooms have gorgeous views. **Torremangana** (San Ignacio de Loyola, 9; 22 33 51) in the new section is very comfortable. **El Figón de Pedro** (Cervantes, 15; 22 68 21) is far and away the best restaurant and its linked hotel is undergoing improvements. The same owner is taking over the operation of **Mesón Casas Colgadas** (Canonigos; 21 18 22) which up till now has had mediocre food which was a poor second to the view. Just once, taste the local brew called *Resoli*. This is a potent potion of corn-brandy, coffee, cinnamon, orange rind and sugar.

9 OLD CASTILE AND LEÓN

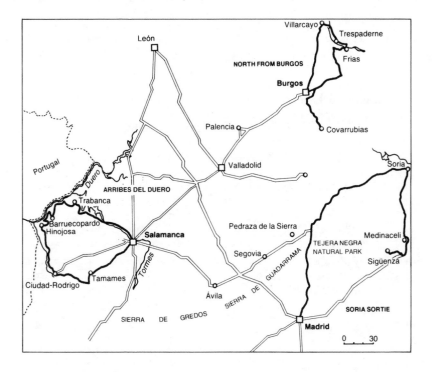

This is the heart of Spain, where ancient alliances were forged and castles were erected on strategic hills to ensure that small gains were not lost. These strongholds were braced against the Moors but also wary of each other. So many maps here seem to start from a central point and go outwards, conquering. Boundaries were political and mental rather than physical geography alone. Aside from a few ranges in the south and León's share of the Picos, most of Castile is a high *mesa*, littered with great rocks. Curious stone bulls or boars (*verracos*) mark the extent of an early Celtic tribe, with one quartet of the beasts eternally grazing at Guisando, a field south of Ávila. The weather can be fierce: bitter winters and baking summers, belied by a shield of blue sky which practically dares the towers of churches, castles and universities to try and pierce it.

Stone bulls, Guisando

Arribes Del Duero
2 days/325km/from Salamanca

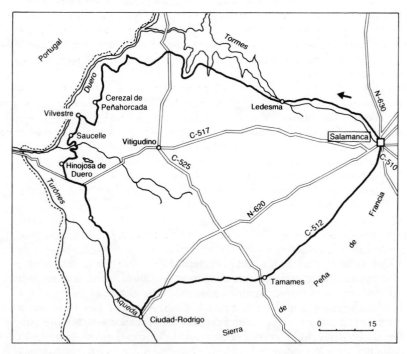

West of the proud university city of Salamanca, where contemporary pro-
fessors of international law challenged authority and branded the Spanish
conquest of the New World as blatantly illegal, Castile touches Portugal.
In this little-traversed corner of Spain, carp and eels ply the wide Duero

River that dramatises the frontier with a steep-sided limestone canyon. Looking at the wild stone escarpments in this region, the philosopher Unamuno declared, 'Lord, it is the most beautiful, most savage, and most impressive landscape of Spain in its entirety!'

SALAMANCA pop: 153,981 Tourist Offices: Gran Vía 41 or Plaza Mayor. A monumental university city in golden-hued stone, Salamanca is a hymn to the Churriguera architecture and its beautiful Plateresque buildings nearly overwhelm the earlier history here. Hannibal took the city from the Iberians in 217BC, and it later fell to successive waves of Romans, Vandals, Visigoths, then Arabs, until its Reconquest by Alphonso VI. The Roman bridge, arching 25 times over the River Tormes, leads the way into *La Vía Plata* (the silver way). The grandiose Plaza Mayor is one of the most harmonious in all Spain, and still acts as a focal point for student life with its bars and cafés tucked into shady arcades. The *tuna*, student minstrels in Renaissance garb, often stroll here. Founded in 1215, the University reflects the renown of its scholars and the patronage of the Kings of Castile with its exquisite architecture and sculpture. Maybe the elaborate ceilings overhead helped inspire the highbrows: in the *escuelas menores* (preparatory schools), part of the 15th-century library ceiling is preserved, and shows Fernando Gallego's four winds, constellations and zodiacal signs in intricate detail. All the main buildings are daubed with ochre graffiti: traditionally, scholars on passing their doctorate, would come exultant from a bullfight and make their mark in bulls' blood mixed with olive oil. This has since evolved into a craft with dye and stencils and is used for commercial signs as well.

Though the university continues today, it no longer ranks in the world's top five as it did under Unamuno's rectorship. But in its long heyday it brought Salamanca considerable influence and power, evident in its two cathedrals, set side by side. The older and smaller one, dating from the 13th century, is famed for its *Torre del Gallo*, a scaled tower with odd Byzantine turrets, topped by a weather cock. The new cathedral, from the 16th–18th century, is elegant and eclectic. The carving is capricious, with monkeys, birds, beasts and unholy faces peering out. Inside, among other treasures, is El Cid's lucky talisman, a simple Romanesque cross which he carried into each battle against the Moors. Walking through the narrow streets of spires and domes and open plazas, there are palaces, convents, monasteries and churches galore. *La casa de las conchas* (House of Shells), covered with 400 carved cockleshells in tribute to Santiago, is one of the loveliest mansions. With so many students in the city, inexpensive meals are easy to find, especially around the Plaza Mayor. For a little more outlay, traditional Castilian roasts can be had at the pricier establishments. **El Mesón** (Poeta Iglesias, 10; 21 72 22; closed Nov) specialises in regional fare. Down the road **Gran Hotel** (Plaza del Poeta Iglesias, 3–5; 21 35 00) has luxurious rooms overlooking a garden.

Northwest of the city, along the River Tormes, wide beaches on the banks contrast with the fields beyond, where black fighting bulls fatten underneath holm oaks. On the approach to **LEDESMA**, at the edge of a vast reservoir, the landscape becomes increasingly wooded and non-Castilian. Cross a mainly Roman bridge — the French blew up the central arch — to enter this stonewalled town, with its San Nicolás gate still intact. Iglesia de Santa María, dating from the 12th century, merits a visit and two medieval palaces are also worth a look-in. Roman baths 7km away have evolved into the spa of Ledesma and provide the only full-fledged lodging around.

Continue west through Trabanca to Villarino de los Aires, very close to Portugal. It is here that the upper reaches of the Duero branch off, mighty from the start. The name alone is evocative of Spanish history. This ancient boundary, which set apart the heathen frontier 'Beyond the Duero' (extreme dura), comes to life as a forceful green river, cutting through great limestone cliffs like the sword of El Cid. Viewing it from ancient Catholic hermitages, such as nearby Fayo, seems historically right. Ask anyone in the tiny village of **PEREÑA** to point out the Zahorra road which leads up to the **Ermita del Castillo**, scene for a local pilgrimage and jamboree every 14 May. After 2km on this narrow and rugged track, arrive at a small sanctuary in a meadow bordered by an ash grove. On a granite outcropping stands an old Celt–Iberian structure, and vultures circle alarmingly low, making you fear some loathsome sacrifice until you realise that they ride the canyon air currents, waiting to see what floats past on the Duero 500m beneath.

Back on the local road, avoid **ALDEADÁVILA DE LA RIBERA**, which is the site of a nuclear waste dump for the entire Common Market and has become the economic centre for this isolated rural district. By contrast, **CEREZAL DE PEÑAHORCADA** seems untouched by the 20th century and there, as in neighbouring **MIEZA**, delicious *repelaos*, a concoction of cheese with almonds and pine nuts, can be bought at the local pastry shop, not signposted but located through the smell of fresh baking. From here, go on to **VILVESTRE**. A carved stone pillar welcomes you to a tidy village of cobblestones and traditional houses but doesn't prepare you for the cemetery, where high above the village, a well preserved neolithic tool site stands near the neighbourhood tombs. Close by, look for a country house called Masueco, where a little road leads off to the Humos del Uces. Follow this to arrive at 'the vapours', a cascade 50m high where the tributary Uces falls to the Duero low in the canyon. Petroglyphs are inscribed on the walls of a cave which views the falls.

BARRUECOPARDO is a tranquil willow-weaving village similar to **SAUCELLE** — which has an inn for the weary. They are especially lovely in late January when the pale almond blossoms soften the landscape. Either would be a good stop before tackling the winding pass of Molinera, a road devoid of straight lines, zig-zagging down to the valley of the Huebra River. Aside from the sound of water falling and wild boar snuffling through the brush, be alert for apparitions, ghost riders and robbers, which local legends warn against. More likely encounters will be with keen botanists, who seek out rare wild plants which grow only here owing to the micro-climates that change with the lie of the land. Above

700m, oak and yellow broom flourish and the air is nippy in the winter. But less than a kilometre away is the lowest point of the canyon where frost never reaches and prickly pears, olives, pomegranates, oranges and almonds thrive. It's a weird plunge into a Mediterranean climate in the midst of harsh Castile.

HINOJOSA, the closest village, produces a fine ewes' cheese, and nothing washes it down better than the local light claret-type wine. Try ordering a round at the little bar in **LA FREGENEDA**, facing the town hall. From here, drive on the C-517 to Lumbrales, turning off to the right at the sign for Ciudad-Rodrigo, 50km farther on. The road, though narrow, is fast and castle ruins on a parched plain reaffirm that this is Castile. **SAN FELICES DE LOS GALLEGOS**, defended by a 15th-century fortress, also boasts a couple of fine old churches and very few visitors.

CIUDAD RODRIGO pop: 15,766 Tourist Office: Arco de Amayuelas. On approach, Ciudad Rodrigo looks every bit a frontier stronghold with a warrior past. A Roman bridge crosses the Agueda River and leads up to the hilltop town, encircled by magnificent walls, built on Roman foundations in 1190 and now forming an unusual starburst pattern. Walking atop these medieval walls like a sentry on his 2.4km round is one of the highlights of a visit here. They were refortified with modern gun positions in the 18th century. Reconquered from the Moors by Count Rodrigo Gonzales back in the 12th century, Ciudad Rodrigo continued to be an important fortress post. After driving the French troops from it in the 1812 War of Independence, Wellington became a Duke of Ciudad Rodrigo and Grandee of Spain.

Cannonball pits are still visible on the cathedral tower, though most of the damage has been repaired. Built mostly of grey stone during the 12th century and again in the 14th, the Cathedral is rather dim inside. The choir stalls are special, with carved armrests represented by the arched backs of a dozen different beasts all stroked to smoothness over the centuries. But walking through the narrow streets is the real delight, with carved stone escutcheons decorating the odd corner and pleasant plazas opening up beneath the trees. Since the 11th century, the town has been noted for its carnivals which herald the first bullfight of the season, with young bulls charging through the alleyways beforehand. The town hall in the main square has a Latin American feel to it, and not unsurprisingly; Francisco Montejo, the conquistador of Yucatán and Cozumel in Mexico, hailed from here. A state **parador** has been fashioned from the castle of Enrique II (Plaza del Castillo, 1; 46 01 50), which has beautiful views over the walls out to the river and the fields beyond. **Conde Rodrigo** (Plaza San Salvador, 7; 46 14 08) is less expensive and friendlier, and is none the less a palace. Eat at **Mayton** (La Colada, 9; 46 07 20 closed all Oct), which roasts suckling pig, the regional speciality, to crackling perfection if you want to venture outside the parador's pricey restaurant. **El Rodeo** (Gigantes, 6; 46 00 07; Closed Thurs eve) is the place for *tapas* and conversation.

Rather than return directly to Salamanca on the N-620, turn off at Valdecarpinteros and take the local road to Tamames, riding along beneath the ridges of the Peña de Francia mountains. At Vecinos, the road becomes the C-512 and completes the circuit back to the University city, Salamanca.

North from Burgos

2 days/250km/from Burgos

Castles guard each strategic outcropping against the next invader bound to come charging over the battle plains between them. Almost nine centuries after his death, El Cid still is indomitable in this part of Castile, and his name and image recur along this route. Burgos gives his bones the place of honour in its beautiful cathedral, and one settlement of direct descendants basks completely in his glory. Farther north, the Ebro River and mountains rear up, signalling the nearness of the other provinces, and providing a cool diversion from the stifling summer heat of the Meseta.

BURGOS pop: 156,449 Tourist Office: Plaza Alanso Martines, 7. On first impression, this industrial city is appallingly ugly, but it has compensations: the Paseo de Espolón, where everyone strolls in late afternoon, with its fantastic topiary trees is one. Another is the round central Plaza José Antonio, with its shady portico. The huge Gothic Cathedral, the third largest in all Spain, is one reason to linger briefly in the city. The sculpted detail on the grey stone exterior demands careful examination, and the interior, which spans three centuries of building, is harmonious. Outstanding features are the Golden Stair, and the *coro*, almost a church unto itself, with a magnificent lantern hanging above the simple marble slab that marks the final resting place of the warrior El Cid and his wife, Jimena. Their remains were entombed here with royal pomp in 1921, after suffering the indignity of French troops plundering through the original 700-year-old vaults in San Pedro de Cardeña and then being shuffled about by civil servants or monks for 112 years. The side chapels are as full of sculpture and painting as the main cathedral.

The Mudéjar church of San Martín, and the Gothic churches of Santa Águeda, San Nicolás, San Esteban and San Gil, will interest students of comparative architecture, but don't measure up to the Cathedral. The Santa María arch, a 14th-century city gateway done up to honour Carlos I two centuries later, is quite impressive. At the top of the high street, Calle Santander, stands the Casa del Cordón, named for the stone carving over the door that mimics the thick cord binding a Franciscan cassock. This restored 15th-century palace was the scene of Columbus' reception by the monarchs after his second voyage when he brought back considerable gold booty, and where Ponce de León was saluted by Ferdinand before setting out after the Fountain of Youth. Philip I died here suddenly after a game of *pelota*, which may have helped send his queen

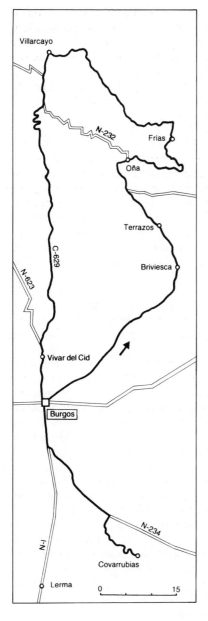

Juana La Loca into despair. Puente San Pablo, a bridge over the frog-filled river, is a litany to El Cid, with 8 chunky modern statues commemorating important people in his life. A statue of the old mercenary himself, sword drawn and astride a bronze steed, stands on the north side of the river.

Just 1½km west from the city centre, the Real Monasterio de las Huelgas is a pleasure palace converted to a Cistercian convent in 1180 by Alfonso VIII and his English wife, Eleanor, Henry II's daughter. Great powers were given to the abbess here, who extended her influence over more than 50 towns and had the ear of all the royals who used the convent as a retreat. As a convent for queens and princesses, las Huelgas became a pantheon for their tombs, and the royal families of 12th- and 13th-century Castile and León-Asturias were buried here. The 16th-century revolving iron pulpit in the church gives a hint of the machinations needed to operate in a place where religion was so politically potent. Another mechanical wonder is a wooden statue of Santiago rigged so that the sword arm can extend. This would be employed so that monarchs, untouchable by mortal hand, might be knighted by the saint himself. Don't miss the Museum of Rich Fabrics, taken from the one tomb that the French troops spared from desecration in 1809. The 13th-century court regalia on display shows a strong Eastern influence. There is also a surprising English Gothic church and the chapterhouse where Franco assembled his first government. (Visiting hours for all 11–2, 4–6; closed all day Mon and Sun pm. 100 pesetas entry.)

As a provincial capital, Burgos offers plenty of accommodation. South of town, on the highway to Madrid, the **Landa Palace** (N-I, km 236; 20

63 43) offers every modern comfort in a faultless Gothic setting. Even the indoor swimming pool has medieval vaulting supporting the ceiling. The restaurant **Hostal Landa** is considered the region's best, and the Castilian roast lamb and suckling pig is wonderful, though innovations such as grated asparagus and salmon also work well. In town, the **Hostal Mesón del Cid** (Plaza Santa María, 8; 20 59 71; closed Feb), just across from the cathedral, has a fine restaurant in a multi-level medieval building and rents out rooms as well.

Head north on the N-I towards **BRIVIESCA**, the centre of cereal growing in the province, unremarkable except for its octagonal church of Santa Clara. Fork left on the local road to **TERRAZOS**, where the parish church stands on a grassy knoll like a statue on a plinth and the spire soars above the grain fields. At Cornudilla, turn onto the N-232 and follow it north to **ONA**. Built in a cleft carved by the River Oca, this old village has a curious main square on three different levels. The parish church remains from the monastery founded in 1011 by Count Sancho and contains the family tombs of the early Castilian kings. The fortified walls were erected by Abbot Sancho after the place was sacked in 1367, and three towers still stand.

Turn off towards Barcina de los Montes for the scenic village of **FRÍAS**, with a crumbling castle — one of the first in Castile — that thrusts its sole remaining tower skywards. It's nicknamed *La Muela*, the molar. The view from up here is splendid: the Ebro, dammed by the Sobron *embalse*, fans out into a long lake squeezed between limestone cliffs. Market gardens make green patches down to the near bank of the Ebro, where a Gothic bridge with a fortified gatehouse spans across. The oldest quarter, first founded in the 8th century, is near the castle, and has tall half-timbered houses clinging to the cliffsides, some with rounded roof tiles. A few private houses rent out rooms for the night, but more reliable lodging can be found up the road in **MEDINA DE POMAR**.

Go to the farther side of the Ebro, one of the earlier boundaries of Christendom, and turn left at the crossroads towards Trespaderne. The road runs beside the railway and a distant castle marks the village of **MEDINA DE POMAR**, which still has the rubble of early fortified ramparts. Walk up to the castle — the streets are too narrow for easy driving — and a sturdy shell with a great double keep hints at the former power of this corner of Castile. Nearby, the Convent of Santa Clara has lovely star-vaulting inside its early Gothic church as well as the 16th-century Velasco tomb of the fourth Constable of Castile. **Hotel Las Merindades** (Somovilla; 11 08 22) boasts the best village restaurant and has comfortable rooms upstairs in the atmospheric old building.

Pass through **VILLARCAYO**, a trout-fishing centre 8km on, which sits on a plain encircled by hills. From here, take the N-232 south as far as **VALDENOCEDA**, with its square-cornered fortress and a parish church with a Romanesque tower. Here, bear right on the C-629 and gear down for a steep climb up the Mazorra Pass. Glancing back from the top of the pass, the Ebro River winds west beneath tabby-striped mountains.

Straight ahead, a dour moor stretches for 30km. Worn stone pylons show the way in case of heavy snows, and there are mountain ranges either side of the road — the jagged Picos de Europa crowd the horizon to the far right while the Demanda mountain range, closer on the left, casts shadows. At **PEÑAHORADA** the road escapes from the moor through a narrow hollow, and links up with the N-623. Turn off when the old castle at **SOTOPALACIOS** appears, and continue along the rough road a bit farther to **VIVAR DEL CID**, where about three dozen lowrise houses cluster around a statue of Rodrigo Diaz de Vivar, the notorious El Cid. This is his ancestral land, extending to the mill but not the old castle, built long after his demise. Everyone in the village claims some family link to the hero, and the venerable coat of arms looks a bit preposterous on some of the smallest squared-off houses.

From here, skirt along the eastern side of Burgos, following the signs to **Miraflores**. The road runs beside the Alarzon River, through the wooded Paseo de la Quinta for 3km, and arrives at this Carthusian monastery built on the grounds of an ancient royal hunting lodge. Only the church is open to the public (open 10–3, 4–6, except Sun; Sun 11.15–12.30, 1–3, 4–6); the 15th-century monastery still in use. The master sculptor Gil de Siloe carved the remarkable alaster tombs for Queen Isabel's parents, Juan II and Isabel of Portugal — the only pair missing from the Toledo cathedral's royal chapel. A less elaborate tomb for the Infante Don Alfonso, whose early death opened up the monarchy for his sister, shows the sculptor's playful touch in mischievous angels romping in the grapevines and a host of birds and beasts at his feet. Much of the florid Gothic retable, the Life of Christ, is his work and is just as exceptional, gilded with New world gold from Columbus' second voyage.

Leave the monastery, forking left through Cardenajimeno, and drive on 6km to **SAN PEDRO DE CARDENA**, the abbey where the family of El Cid waited out his banishment and where his widow, Jimena, carted back his body from Valencia. Now a Trappist monastery, the church retains one Romanesque tower which the Cid would recognise, though it was all restored in 1950, as well as part of the cloister which pre-dates him. Though the elaborate original tombs of El Cid and Jimena now are empty, a stone marks where his warhorse Babieca lies buried in the forecourt. The man has become almost eclipsed by his legend since he died in 1099; but the Vatican did manage to reject Philip II's pressure to canonise this warrior who would burn mosques or churches with the same zeal.

Head back towards Burgos, but follow the roadsigns to go south on the N-I motorway, avoiding congestion in the centre. Branch left at Saracín, onto the N-234, then right again at Cuevas de San Clemente. The local road arrives at **COVARRUBIAS**, probably the prettiest town in the region. Twin hills, called Las Mamblas, hunch over the bright red tiled rooftops of the medieval city with its solid stone towers. The Collegiate Church of San Cosme and San Damian, built atop Visigoth and Mozarab foundations, dates from 1474. It does its double namesakes proud with the treasures inside: the triptych Adoration of the Magi and a 17th-century organ which still is in working order. The town hall, formerly the palace of Fernán González, is quite impressive. Even more so is the riverside tower of Doña Urraca, named for the spirited daughter Fernán González allegedly locked away inside. A broad base narrows slightly so that it forms a truncated stone pyramid, one of the grandest examples of non-religious Mozarabic architecture left in Spain. It connects through a tunnel to the house where Doña Sancha, sister of King Alfonso VII, lived. Like many of the mansions lining the cobblestoned street, it is elegant and carries a noble family shield. The humbler ones, with wooden supports and balconies bursting with bright blooms against the whitewashed façades, capture much of the character of this old Castilian stronghold. **Arlanza** (Doña Urraca, 11; 40 30 25; closed Nov–Feb), in a mansion on the principal arcaded street, is an associate parador. The restaurant is decent, but **El Galin** (40 30 15) on the plaza is better and cheaper. Roast lamb is the speciality.

Soria Sortie

3 days/440km/from Madrid
Rumpled brown hills and castles crumbling on the horizon, flat fields of sunbleached grain, and lonely pinewoods: Soria's beauty is desolate. This route goes northeast from the national capital to discover villages which had might in the Middle Ages and now are suffused with a dusty melancholy.

Head north from **MADRID** on the N-I motorway, the Burgos Road, and turn right at km 104, through the town of **CEREZO**. On the far side of the railway tracks is **RIAZA**, a town which now makes its living from cattle and mining, but has all the echoes of bygone Castilian power politics and religion. The round Plaza Mayor of this hill town is surprisingly grand, lined with 18th-century mansions which have wooden galleries and weird zinc gargoyles on the rain gutters plus ornate wrought iron grilles over the windows. Most of the heavy oak beams were logged in the extensive forest which darkens the range just south of the river. The town hall, with its metal campanile above an elaborate stone-carved municipal shield, is distinguished. The Parish church, Nuestra Señora del Manto, was originally Gothic, with later Renaissance touches from the 18th century, and was a proud possession of the Segovia bishops for three centuries. **La Trucha** (Avda Dr. Tapia; 55 00 61) not far from the town centre, is a pleasant inn, complete with garden and pool. No less than three eating places, all specialising in roast lamb, line the Plaza Mayor. The village acts as a gateway to excursions into the mountains, which are serviced by ski-lifts in the winter. The second Sunday of September sees in the annual village festivities, with bulls running through the streets and much rowdy celebration.

A worthwhile detour up to the hermitage of **Hontanares** is reached by heading north on the N-110, and turning right just before the third kilometre-mark. The road to the hermitage is posted, and goes for 2km up

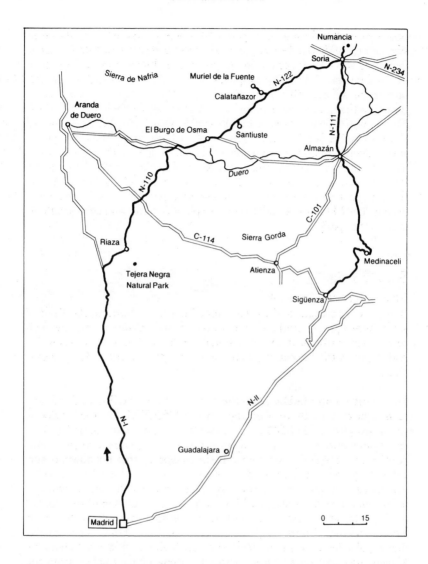

the Merino hill. A vast meadow (over 50 hectares) with picnic tables, fountains, grills and facilities awaits the throngs who come up on the pilgrimage and jamboree each May and September, though it is available all year round. The 16th-century hermitage, with the worship-worn virgin guarded inside, is striking but doesn't rival the view from the *mirador* at Peñallanas, which looks out over the mountain peaks.

Back down on the main road, continue north through the pass. The tall Baroque tower that looms up ahead through the trees belongs to the cathedral of **EL BURGO DE OSMA**. Just 2km beyond **OSMA**, with its Roman ruins, this monumental city has porticoed streets and elegant Baroque buildings, along with traces of its original ramparts. From its

major role in Castile, peaking in
the 1700s, it has retreated into a
calm village, proud of its architectural heritage, but getting on
with more agrarian life as market
gardens and fields approach its
glories. San Agustín Hospital on the
Plaza Mayor is harmoniously pro-
portioned, and the University of
Santa Catalina merits a look simply
for its patio. But the real jewel is
the Cathedral with its 13th-century
façade (9–1, 4–7, 100 pesetas
entry). San Pedro de Osma, whose
exquisite 13th-century tomb is
within, vowed to rebuild the original Romanesque cathedral which
the Moors had defiled. The realis-
ation of this magnificent temple
over the centuries reflects Burgo de
Osma's increasing power. A white
marble pulpit inside is particularly
impressive, and an extraordinary
11th-century crucifix, with the
figure covered in buffalo hide, fea-

*Pedraza, just off the N-1 motorway,
typifies medieval villages in Castile*

tures prominently among the treasures. The illuminated manuscripts,
especially the rare *Beatus Apocalypse* from 1065 and a 12th-century century signs of the Zodiac, are worth seeking out. Should all the heavenly
imagery work up an unearthly appetite, go to **Virrey Palafox** (Uni-
versidad, 7; 34 02 22) where the house speciality is pork in all possible
guises. Unique is the *cerdali*, a cross between pork and wild boar,
marinated and served with mild mushrooms. Mountain trout in season is
a delicious alternative. The management runs a simple but clean hostal as
well, or there are a couple of 2-star hostals on the same street.

Continue east on the N-122, and bear right for a detour over to **SAN-
TIUSTE**, one of a score of villages which came under the jurisdiction of
El Burgo de Osma. It is distinguished by a carved column of sabina wood
topped with a figure, arms outstretched, which declares the village's liberty far and wide; one of the few remaining examples of early wooden
sculpture.

Farther along the N-122, the turning to **CALATAÑAZOR** goes past
the Romanesque hermitage of **Soledad**, which is next to the ruins of another
— San Juan Bautista — overgrown by trees. Just 2km past this, a
stranded archaic village still venerates the spot where the fierce Moorish
warrior, Almanzor, fell in battle with a mortal wound. From Calatañazor's
appearance, not much has happened since. The houses are odd mixtures
of adobe, stone and wooden struts, propped up on great wooden supports
which teeter over the cobblestone streets. Primitive conical chimneys

make an odd skyline, and the surrounding walls are crumbling. The grassy main square near the foot of the castle is so irregular that it is almost unrecognisable, save for the fountain nearby, the ancient elms and a lichen-covered stone cross. The parish church, Santa María del Castillo, is a Gothic building on Romanesque foundations, but has an odd Celtic motif on the moulding and a pre-Romanesque stone panel which still baffles archaeologists. The church, proud of its sculpture, is open for inspection in August; otherwise, ask for the judge (*juez*) or the mayor (*alcalde*), either of whom will be pleased to unlock it for you. **Venta Nueva** (N-122, km 181), out on the main road, is reliable and provids fair meals.

The best view of the village is looking back from the road which proceeds to **MURIEL DE LA FUENTE**. The Padilla Castle juts out on its stone crag on the far right, while the yellow earth is cut away in terraces like an old step-pyramid below the remnants of Calatañazor's walls. Ahead, the plain gives way to a greener valley. Instead of touring Muriel de la Fuente, which offers little aside from a monumental pillar sculpted from sabina wood, turn off on the rough road marked *piscifactoria* (fish farm) and continue to the refuge. Park here and hike along the stream bed, braving it as the plants close in, until a narrow canyon with steep walls leads to the spring, *La Fuentona*. A deep clearwater swimming hole, circled by pines and cliffs, is usually deserted except for hawks coasting on the updrifts.

However reluctantly, retrace the way back to Calatañazor and over the pass on N-122 to Soria.

SORIA pop: 32,039 Tourist Office: Plaza Ramón y Cajal. The burnt sienna tinge of the province's furrowed hills changes on the approach to this city, which seems almost unduly grand in comparison to the underpopulated villages surrounding it. Here, two bare grey hills frank the Duero River, which has poplars lining its banks, and Soria's early medieval monuments seem unperturbed by the dreary modern blocks which blight the outskirts. A holy site since remote antiquity, the town's origins are obscure, though it is known that late-Palaeolithic shepherds roamed the near pastures. Nomadic flocks remained big business in Soria, which lodged the senior branch of the *Mesta*, a powerful sheep-owners' lobby in the 13th–15th centuries when flocks had the right-of-way through cultivated lands the length of Spain. Even today, the migrant long-distance drives persist in the *Trashumancia*. Wealthy sheep-owners settled in impressive mansions along three principal streets: Aduana Vieja, Calle Caballeros, and Calle Real. An opulent Palace of the Counts of Gómara, with a thrusting 16th-century tower and a two-storey patio, far outdoes them all. But architecture fans are drawn to the fine Romanesque churches, with Morisco touches, which include Virgen del Espino, San Juan de Rabanera and Santo Domingo, with its single portal carved in incredible detail. The Cathedral of San Pedro, though mainly gothic, also has three Romanesque galleries in its graceful cloister. Over on the far side of the river is the monastery San Juan de Duero, founded by the Hospitallers of St John of Jerusalem (open Tues–Sat, 10–2, 4–7). Abandoned in a field, the remains of the 13th-century cloister huddle together, a linked series of pointed arches. The neighbouring church is in better repair, and its museum displays some fine Roman mosaics as well as an exhibit of cut stones.

Many of the artifacts reveal the large Jewish culture which flourished in Soria back before the kingdoms of Castile, Navarre and Aragón united, and a go-between was paramount. Farther along the bank is the path up to a Templar monastery over the shrine of San Saturio, the hermit patron of Soria. On the other hill is a ruined castle, circled by a park dedicated to poet Antonio Machado, who penned evocative lyrics to the city grown old by the green Duero. A long bridge crosses the river just below. You might attempt a visit to the museum by the post office, but as I write it has been closed for over 2 years for remodelling. It houses most of the finds from the Celt–Iberian tribe at Numancia. While a state parador (**Parador Antonio Machado**, Sainz de Vicuña; 21 34 45) has a glorious view from the castle's hill, it is quite overpriced for the region. Better value can be had in town, at **Mesón Leonor** (Paseo de Mirón; 22 02 50) or several other 3-star inns. Restaurants in all ranges offer good roast lamb, and **Maroto** (Paseo del Espolón, 20; 22 40 86) tops the lot in imagination, with offerings such as wild mushroom soup with truffles.

NUMANCIA, a 7km drive northeast up the N-111, is a sombre destination. Broken columns litter a bleak field and harsh winds blow off

the hills. Vestiges of a 6.4km wall and the remnants of a Roman grid of streets barely hint at what Spanish schoolchildren learn was the ultimate gesture of defiance. Here, the Iberian Arevaco tribe struggled 19 years against Roman legions who would come storming across the Meseta. They actually routed the Romans on five separate occasions, but in 133BC were held under siege for eight gruelling months and defeat was imminent, despite desperate measures. Rather than submit to the outsiders, they set their dwellings on fire and nearly every man, woman and child perished. The conqueror Scipio retained 50 survivors for his Triumph, sold the remaining few as slaves and razed the city. A few underground chambers are all that could remain of the Iberian city.

Roman arches, most impressive in Segovia's famed aqueduct, recur throughout Castile

(Open 10–2, 4–7, Tues–Sat only.) The details which would flesh out the story are back in the provincial museum at Soria, still being sorted out for display.

Double back through Soria and rejoin the N-111 south to **ALMAZÁN**. San Miguel, a 12th-century church with a dome that recalls the interlocking arches over the mihrab in Córdoba's mosque, is the pride of this ancient fortress village. Farther south, **MEDINACELI** announces itself with a triple triumphal Roman arch which can be seen from the road. The inscription, dating back to the 2nd or 3rd century, is so worn that it is unreadable; other records confirm that the arch lauds the consul Marco Marcelo. The fortified town retains more a medieval look than a Roman one and has long vistas across the Meseta and to the marshes southwards. Northeast, on the N-11, an easy drive goes through the brick-red Jalon Gorges for an exhilarating morning excursion. Medinaceli's proud past, caught between the struggles of Castile and Aragón, is reflected in noble mansions with ornamental wrought iron grilles on windows and balconies. The Alhóndiga, the old grain store in the Plaza Mayor which is now the tourist office, is the prettiest of the undistinguished buildings there. On dark November nights, a strange rite combines two ancient obsessions: the bull and the fire. Bonfires are set alight in the main plaza and a bull, protected from the flames, is led through ritual movements with sputtering torches. The village goes into paroxysms of celebration and youths dare one another to best the bull, though he is not harmed. On the edge of the village, the great Moorish fortress has been taken over as the Christian cemetery.

A bizarre graveyard for elephants only is the focus for a sidetrip, 10km east just past the village of **AMBRONA**. Traditionally known by farmers as 'Hill of Bones', this mound has been excavated and now is a shack with the grand name of *Museo Paleontologo*. What is sheltered are the remains of mammoths, lying here some 300,000 years, so ignore the fanciful folk-tales of Hannibal's rogue runaways. Experts doubt that this was a secret spot where the pachyderms came to die. Most theorise that hunters drove them to a watering hole and slaughtered them while they had no room to charge. Should there be no sign of the guard in his hut, check back in Ambrona.

From here, head southeast on the local road to **SIGÜENZA**, over in New Castile. The castle and the cathedral towers dominate the skyline, and the town descends from the fortified castle in grassy tiers. It took a real beating during the Civil War, and the old towers are still pockmarked by bullet holes. The 12th-century cathedral, with its French air, shows off over three centuries of religious architecture which flowered under the bishops pf Sigüenza. The cathedral's showpiece is the tomb of Martín Vazquez de Arce, a young page who died battling Moors in Granada. His alabaster image, head propped on his elbow and dreaming over a book, is known as *El doncel de Sigüenza* and is one of the best loved carvings of medieval Spain, though the artist is anonymous. Extraordinary Mudéjar filigree work is also noteworthy, as are the rose windows. Across the plaza from the cathedral is a museum which displays religious treasures in proper style and also includes paintings by El Grec and Zurbarán.

Other monuments worth a visit are the churches of San Vicente and Santiago, the plaza de la Carcel, the Arco de San Juan, the Casa de Doncel and the Renaissance town hall. The castle, revamped as a parador after serving Visigoths, Arabs and finally the Bishops of Sigüenza, commands a strategic overview of the town. It has been completely rebuilt and retains much of its atmosphere, without appearing squeaky-clean. **Parador Nacional Castillo de Sigüenza** (Los Martires; 39 01 00) is the leading hotel and its dining room offers delicious quail and partridge. Better value food can be had along Calvo Sotelo, especially at **El Motor** (Calvo Sotelo, 12; 39 03 43) which does so well, it can afford to shut down June, November, and every Monday.

10 RIOJA/NAVARRA

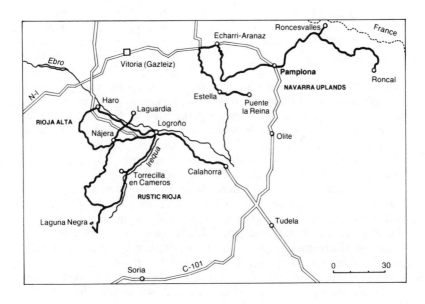

Unlike Rioja, which is known for wine and pilgrim waystations, Navarra doesn't fit into any easy categories. While the Basques would claim it as part of Euskadi owing to the Basque minority which traditionally live in the North, the conservative majority will not have it. More even than Catalonia, Navarra has turned towards France in the past, though Ferdinand I, the first king of the Spains — Navarra, Castile, León and Galicia — hailed from this region. Even the landscape refuses to conform to typical geography. Abrupt contrasts between forested sierra and mountain pastures, dry prairie with clay-based soil and tiny stonewalled smallholdings of maize, turn the region into a jumbled jigsaw with pieces taken from the entire country. The fiesta at Pamplona draws most of the tourists here, but only for the one week. Others drift up on genteel tours of the vineyards, an important industry in both provinces which has put neighbouring Rioja on the map especially for its rich, oaky tasting red wines.

Rioja Alta

2 days/180km/from Laguardia

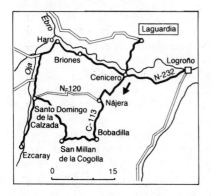

From the 'Rioja Balcony', coming into the province, the Ebro Valley along the riverbanks appears tawny and not particularly fertile. **LAGUARDIA**, with its square towers thrusting up against fat clouds and hectares of vineyards stretching beneath, could be posing for a wine label. The medieval fortifications and gateways are in good repair and ancient stone houses line the streets with their wrought iron balconies facing one another. Most of the village is caught up in winemaking, and in autumn, during the harvest, the narrow streets reek of grape marc. Once inside the massive Late Gothic doorway of the parish church, Santa María de los Reyes, look for the remarkable polychrome statues. St John the Baptist is the patron here, so the Summer Solstice, his saint's day, is seen in with much celebration. The fiesta drink is a wine punch, *zurracapote*, local wine stirred with lemon, sugar and cinnamon.

Head southeast, across the Ebro River and the daunting motorway, going through Huercanos to **NÁJERA**, the historic capital of Rioja. Pines and poplars fringe the approach and the town's old quarter lies between the Najerilla River and sandstone hills. Rows of crystal galleries shine along the riverbank. As the court of the kings of Navarra in the early Middle Ages, the town gained stature and the Road to Santiago was diverted through here. A bridge and inn were built for wayfaring pilgrims, along with the 11th-century basilica of Santa María la Real. Rebuilt in the 15th century, it is massive, with a lovely Renaissance cloister, and houses the curious royal tomb of Blanca, wife of Sancho III. In the hills is a wealth of archaeological finds, Roman funerary stelae and ceramic shards. The hermitage, Los Arcos, on the slopes above town was built mainly of Roman finds.

Directly south through the Sierra de la Demanda on the C-113, turn right at Bobadilla and follow the country road until it arrives at **SAN MILLAN DE LA COGOLLA**. It is a gateway to two old and isolated monasteries in the hills above. **Suso**, higher on the hill, dates from the 10th century and is an early Mozarabic construction with intricate arcades and horseshoe arches. **Yuso**, a Benedictine abbey down the hill, is later. The 11th-century buildings were revamped in the 16th. A delicately carved ivory chest, dating from the abbey's foundation, is the prize exhibit.

From here, a network of minor roads leads north, to Villar de Torre, then cuts over to the main highway N-120. **SANTO DOMINGO DE LA CALZADA** lies just to the left. This dusty town was once a main stop along

the trek to Compostela, and the 13th-century cathedral and stone archways sheltering the main street hint at the former splendour. Barnyard
sounds emit from one shrine inside the Gothic temple, and it seems odd
that a holy hen roost is tolerated here. It all stems from one of the
miracles of the Way: a hapless German pilgrim, after spurning the
advances of a housemaid at the inn, was accused of thievery and hanged
when she planted false evidence in his bags. Passing by the town on their
return from Compostela, his bereaved parents saw that he was still alive
on the gallows. Overjoyed, they rushed to share the news of the miracle
with the judge who had condemned him. The judge, about to tuck into
roast fowl, dismissed them as holy fools, reckoning that their son was no
more alive than the birds on his plate. At this, his supper sprouted
feathers and flew away. Ever since, a hen and a rooster have been kept
inside the cathedral to commemorate the event, and passing pilgrims
would pluck a lucky feather for their caps. Each 12 May, the chickens are
replaced and the old pair stewed.

Hardly more conventional is the sepulchre of the town's namesake,
with the blessed scythe he used to fell forests along the Road to
Compostela, just beside him. The very founder of the Dominican Order
set up a hospital here for ailing pilgrims too feeble for the journey, now
transformed into the **Parador Nacional** (Plaza del Santo, 3; 34 03 00).
Less pricey is **Santa Teresita** (General Mola, 2; 34 07 00).

Follow the road along the River Oja to **EZCARAY**, near the pine-
covered Mount San Lorenzo. There are few villages less like a ski resort
than this. Pink sandstone mansions bearing coats of arms stand next to
the humbler houses of woolspinners and weavers. The tiled roofs of all the
buildings, even the handsome 16th-century parish church, are weighted
down with stones against the strong mountain winds. While this church,
Santa María La Mayor, has a slight fortress feel to it, the Baroque hermitage of La Virgen de Allende up in the woods is unabashedly militaristic.
Inside are five paintings of the archangel St Michael, kitted out in an
18th-century officer's uniform and firing a harquebus. Pistol-packing
angels seem quite apt for this area: the woods are rife with quail and
partridge, with plenty of hunters in pursuit.

HARO, reached by backtracking along the Río Oja until the confluence with the Ebro River (just follow the road straight up!) is at the very
heart of the wine region. Surprisingly enough, it has kept much of its elegance, with streets of grand 16th-century houses lining the old quarter.
The town hall and the church of Santo Tomás are distinguished, as are
the Basilica de la Vega and the palacio de los Condes de Haro, now
known as the Casa de Cultura.

If you plan to tour the vineyards in town or beyond, it's a good idea
not to start off with an empty stomach. **La Kika** (Santo Tomás, 9; 31 14
47) serves hearty lunches. Just down the street, **Beethoven** (Santo
Tomás, 3; 31 11 81) works wonders with *setas*, local wild mushrooms, and
other traditional dishes. You may drop in unannounced at Bodegas
Bilbainas (closed for siesta), though other wine cellars in town prefer
advance arrangements. It is a pleasure to explore the cavernous store-

rooms with countless bottles and huge casks. After the autumn harvest everything hums with the expectation of an untried vintage in the making. During Haro's patron festival each 29 June, a solemn mass on a rocky hillside, *Peña de Bilibio*, suddenly erupts into a wine battle. Villagers, clothed traditionally all in white, squirt, spray and throw red wine at one another for a couple of hours. The usual weapon is the goat-skin *bota* bag, but once a helicopter was hired to douse those below. It's normal to go through some 50,000 litres of wine in this Bacchanalian rite which dates back to medieval times when Haro won a territorial dispute with neighbouring Miranda del Ebro over the rights to the local peak. Stop at **BRIONES** for a look at the slender Baroque tower reflected in the Ebro River, then get back on the N-232 east. **CENICERO** and **FUENMAYOR** both have important bodegas and are worth a tasting stop. End up in the provincial capital, Logroño.

LOGROÑO pop: 110,890 Tourist Office: Miguel Villanueva, 10 (25 54 97). This commercial centre is somewhat lacking in charm, full of tanker trucks and diesel fumes. Cathedral aficionados, though, can examine the one here for influences of the Pilgrimage Trail. It is a conglomeration of Baroque and Rococo styles tacked onto the original 15th-century building. Two other churches, San Bartolomé and Santa María de Palacio, deserve a look. Besides the winemakers and merchants (documents refer to Rioja wine as early as 1102), the city is known for textile manufacturing plus exquisite coffee caramels. **Gran Hotel** (General Vara del Rey, 5; 25 21 00) has retro charm and a nice garden. But reward yourself by dining out in an 18th-century palace: **La Merced** (Marqués de San Nicolás, 109; 22 11 66; closed Sun). It has an astounding wine list, and the cook is innovative with the season's best. **El Cachetero** (Laurel, 3; 22 84 63) serves good pork chops or stuffed pimentos. Closed Wednesday nights and Sundays, and usually crowded.

Rustic Rioja

2 days/260km/from Logroño
South of the more bustling wine country, Rioja's rough highlands are rarely visited by outsiders, though hidden troutstreams and even a Black Lagoon attract Spaniards from the simmering *Meseta* in summer. Sierra villages are peaceful, though excitement mounts during a fiesta when young boys don bright golden skirts and dance precariously over the cobblestones on stilts. Meadows with extensive orchards become a sea of blossoms come spring.

Leaving Logroño on the N-232, continue on the N-120 and fork left onto the C-113. First stop is **BAÑOS DE RÍO TOBIA**, where the salami-style local sausages are the perfect pairing for a bottle of full-bodied Rioja wine. Drive on until the turn-off marked **ANGUIANO**, which is along the banks

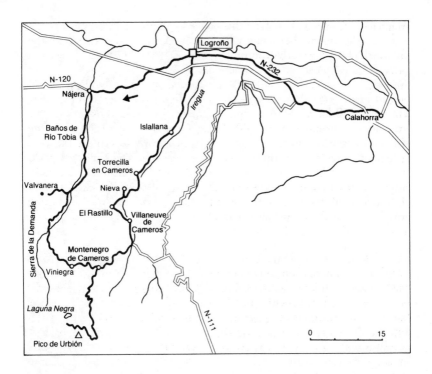

of the swift Najerilla River. It is here each 21–22 July that the weird *Danza de los Zancos* takes place, drawing a big crowd to see daring dances on wooden stilts. Until September, the stone streets are as calm as the still crags high above them. Then the fiesta of Gracias, a sort of harvest thanksgiving, brings out the clatter of stilts once again. Balance and rhythm are utmost in this ancient ritual.

Continue on, turning right for the **Valvanera** monastery, dedicated to the patron virgin of Rioja. All year round the Benedictine monks operate the *hospedería*, or wayfarers' inn, and visitors may tour the old buildings and sample the monks' home-made liqueur.

Back on the 113, keep going past the twisting streams until **VENTA DE GOYO**, where the Urbión and Neila Rivers join up. Bear left here at the signs to **VINIEGRA DE ABAJO** and **VINIEGRA DE ARRIBA**, villages well placed for hikes up into the Sierra Demanda. Quail and partridge are plentiful up here, and frequently there are signs of wild boar and deer. **MONTENEGRO DE CAMEROS**, which leads out of the Demanda, is the departure point for further excursions into Soria province. Go farther south up a wickedly curving road to the summit of the 2280m Pico de Urbión or turn right on a signposted forest road 8km through the pines to the Black Lagoon, **Laguna Negra de Urbión**. Here, two slender waterfalls pour over a curved cliff into a deep glacial lake. The dark rocks on the bottom seem to suck up the light rather than reflect it. The water is clear and very, very cold, celebrated in the poetry of

Machado. In high summer, this remote place can be amazingly crowded, but an early morning often evades most of the other visitors.

Just east of Montenegro de Cameros, **VILLOSLADA**, a small ski-station during the winter, becomes a centre for hunters and fishermen in the spring and autumn. The buttes and woods around here can ring with gunshot, so bright clothing for hikers who want to avoid becoming targets is well advised. Turn left onto the N-111 and stop at **VIL-LANUEVE DE CAMEROS**, a small mountain hamlet where the half-timbered houses are roofed with round tiles. Bear left again at the next turning, signposted **ORTIGOSA**. This is a potholers' paradise with several still partially explored caverns nearby. La Paz, a well-known grotto, is worth a look. The road loops back through **EL RASTILLO**, a lakeside boating area, and on to the N-111. The river here runs along the bottom of a deep ravine, slicing through

Trout fishing in the river

yellowish and grey banded rock. Just past **NIEVA**, with the remains of its old fortress, a left turn leads to the largest village in these parts, **TORRE-CILLA EN CAMEROS**. The ancient quarter in the town centre is well preserved and San Martín, the old parish church, deserves a visit. The road out descends through the high valley, following the course of the Iregua River which jumps with trout and splashes between reddish boulders. After the two tunnels, the valley begins to widen and becomes a bit leafier. Near **ISLALLANA**, the landscape changes suddenly and two immense windsculpted rocks rear up like ruins of an ancient temple. As the road levels out, the landscape becomes much tamer, with fruit orchards stretching ahead for kilometres. Rather than return to Logroño, turn right on the N-232 and proceed to **CALAHORRA**.

With only some of its Roman ramparts still standing, Calahorra doesn't look nearly its age: as an Iberian–Celtic alliance, it held out against Pompey's legions and only fell to African forces in 71BC when a long siege killed all defenders, by sword or starvation. Its main attraction now is a Gothic cathedral beside the Ebro River. The churches of San Andrés and Santiago are not as impressive, though the Carmelite convent has a magnificent carving of Christ. August is the time for repeated bullfights and bulls running through the streets, should you be too late or too retiring to tangle with the mob at Pamplona. **Chef Nino** (Basconia, 1; 13 20 29; closed Thurs) specialises in fish dinners, though good regional dishes are also offered. The **Parador Nacional Marco Fabio Quintiliano** (Era Alta; 13 03 58) lacks the history or majesty of many of the chain, but is comfortable and has a good dining room.

Navarra Uplands
2 days/255km/from Roncal

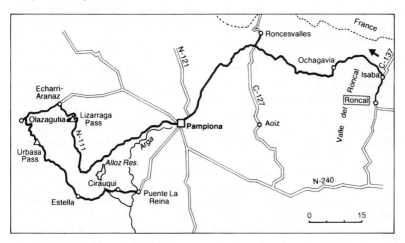

These high pastures with bright rivers, grazing cows and Basque milk-maids may have been enough to attract medieval rogue pilgrims to these parts even without the lure of travel-weary worshippers toting valuables. This trip contrasts the sheer natural beauty of the uplands where epic battles were fought with the wealth of art inspired by the Road to Santiago and the early monarchs of Navarra. One annual pilgrimage, to the streets and bullring of Pamplona, is still going strong, though the revelry frequently verges on international excess.

RONCAL, a bucolic valley town, is known for mild cheeses and for qua-lity timber logged from the dense pinewoods on the slopes above the Esca River. While 20th-century convenience and efficiency have made inroads into business practices here, the villagers still harken back to older times by donning traditional Basque dress on the slightest excuse. One curious fiesta is the annual Tribute of the Three Cows, when the French Basques from Bearne, across the border, present a trio of bovine beasts as settle-ment for an obscure feud. Just north, along the C-137, **ISABA** is a pretty village and a fine base for forays into the Pyrenees. A heavily fortified

16th-century church guards the misty village, and contrasts with the newest hotel, **Isaba** (89 30 30). More modest is **La Lola** (Mendigatxa, 17), a restaurant which also lets rooms.

Turn right and take the Lazar Pass through the mountains for 24 twisting kilometres until you reach **OCHAGAVIA**, in the Salazar Valley. Crooked narrow streets run between shingled houses the same way the trout streams cut through the pines above. Stone crosses mark the Pilgrim's Trail. Santa María de Muskilda, the 12th-century church, still stands, spared from the fires of French troops in the War of Independence. The hermitage of La Virgen de las Nieves, nearly as old, is reached by an idyllic hike through the Irati beech forest. Though very green, the land can support only potato growing and sheep grazing so most of the village youth are forced to commute to distant manufacturing jobs. In September, everyone turns out for the village fiesta, when the celebrated local dance troupe goes through its paces. Eight men in conical caps are led through the streets by a harlequin, performing some of the region's ancient war dances. Records of witch trials back in 1539 note the dances and jubilation in the streets of Ochagavia. There are several small lodges providing rooms in the village.

Head through **ESCAROZ** and then right, again through the mountain passes, with clusters of small houses with bold family crests dotted alongside the roads. The most legendary village of them all if ahead, after a right turn on the C-127. **RONCESVALLES** — the Valley of Thorns — where Charlemagne's rearguard was massacred by Basques, was immortalised in the French epic, *Chanson de Roland*. The fittest pilgrims would reach Compostela from here in 20 days walk; many others were laid to rest in the 7th-century ossuary here beneath the Church of Santi Spiritus. An Augustine monastery, zinc roofs blue under the overgrown vines, was long an important pilgrims' hostelry and funeral chapel. More interesting is the Collegiate Church founded in the 12th century by Sancho the Strong, whose tomb lies in the chapterhouse alongside his queen's. The treasury displays a huge emerald, which tumbled from the sultan's turban when Sancho defeated him at Navas de Tolosa in 1212. **La Posada** (76 02 25), next to the Collegiate Church, retains the feeling of a wayfarers' stop along the Road, though the beds are more comfortable; the restaurant is in the same inn which served the pilgrims in the Middle Ages. Yes, the oil in the deep fryers has been changed in the meantime.

PAMPLONA pop: 183,126 Tourist Office: Duque de Ahumada, 3. Navarra's best-known town, courtesy of Papa Hemingway, is Pamplona, 37km southeast along a quick road. The Pyrenees taper off completely here and Pamplona lies on a flat plain. The name reputedly honours Pompey, whose sons founded the city. Much of the city history is recounted eloquently at the Navarre Museum, in a 16th-century hospital building, where the collection of Roman mosaics and artifacts outdazzles the paintings. Outside the giddy days of San Fermín (6–17 July), when locals and foreigners run in the streets before the bulls and dance all night afterwards, it's a pretty quiet place with only a big private university sparking the scene. Gob-stopping coffee caramels are the town's most noted product. The old quarter — Navarrería — encircles a Gothic cathedral where the alabaster tomb of Charles III and his queen is kept. A Diocesan Museum adjoins the cathedral and has a wide range of religious artifacts, highlighted by polychrome Madonnas from all over the province. Unicorns cavort in an early chase scene on the reader's rostrum, perhaps a precursor to the abandon of *los Sanfermines*. Don't count on running in the fiesta if you are a female; the police are liable to yank you out of the way 'for your own protection'. Though there are a couple of prestige hotels in Pamplona, **Hostal Europa** (Espoz y Mina, 11; 22 18 00) is comfortable and conveniently near the Plaza Castillo with its arcades of old plane trees and elegant Cafe Iruna. If you attempt to join the mob in July, book well in advance and be prepared to pay exorbitant rates or else to sleep rough.

Leave Pamplona on the N-240 which skirts along the River Arga by the Taconera Gardens in the northwest corner of town. Turn left just after the bridge, and go on to Echauri. Soon after, the road climbs through the beeches up to a pass 840m up and a lookout point back over the Arga valley. Keep straight on now, past the tip of the Alloz reservoir until the N-111, where you bear right. **Iranzu Monastery** is signposted from here, a detour of 3km. The old buildings have stood at the end of a stark canyon since the end of the 12th century, and now are used as a college. Unusual along the Santiago Road, the Cistercian style is a bridge between Romanesque and Gothic and is stout and graceful at the same time. Triptych windows are a special feature.

Returning to the N-111, head for the Lizarraga Pass. The broad vista comes suddenly after emerging from the tunnel, and seems like a pause on a green roller coaster before the road dips down through pastures and woods. Carry on to Echarri-Aranaz, bear left on the N-240 as far as Olazagutia, then turn left again, towards Estella. Get into gear for a steep climb through a landscape strewn with huge boulders and huddled trees before it gives way to a broad and leafy dale. On the other side of the **Urbasa Pass** — 920m high — limestone cliffs loom up and then seem to swallow the road, as it wriggles through a set of gorges carved by the Urenderra River. Where this tributary joins up with the Ega River an extraordinary medieval town rises up on both banks.

ESTELLA La Bella, passing pilgrims called it, and even today it is clear why. Many of the fine stone churches and brick mansions have been well kept since the 12th century when the Navarran kings lived here. It later became a centre for Carlist sympathisers in the 19th century. Distinct neighbourhoods have kept their character over the years: a quarter for Jews sheltering from persecution and ultimate expulsion flourished before Navarra's alliance with Ferdinand; another for Franks, freemen who'd come south to seek fortune; and a third for the local Navarrans. Plaza de San Martín, once the hub of the Franks' parish, is overlooked by the Palace of the Kings of Navarre, perhaps the oldest civil structure still standing in Spain. The legendary Roland battles the giant Ferragut on a supporting capital, one of the first depictions of the hero. Opposite, on a rock spur which lost its guardian castle in the 16th century, stands the grand church of San Pedro de la Rua, with its oddly Moorish doorway. Inside, a relic of St Andrew has had pride of place since 1270, but the cloister, partially damaged when the castle was blown up 400 years ago, is much more impressive with its exquisite carving. The church of San Miguel Arcangel, over on the far bank where the locals quartered, is a haphazard mix of styles but the delicacy of the reliefs carved on the lower walls redeems it completely.

The Puente Azucarero (sugar merchants' bridge) across the river leads on to the main monuments. The Royal Palace now houses a collection of paintings by Maeztu, with erratic opening hours, and Santo Sepulcro Church has been converted to a Road to Santiago Museum, with an even less reliable schedule. In July, a festival for medieval music suits the venue perfectly. What a contrast to the rowdy celebrations the next month when, as part of the town's patron day jamboree, a yearling cow with padded horns is set loose in the streets. Whether the padding is to protect the ancient monuments or the women who are permitted to run in this *encierro*, unlike most, is not quite clear. Eating out at **La Tatana** (Garcia el Restaurador, 3; 55 38 70) offers a choice of traditional Navarran fare or a touch of the *nueva cocina*. While a few fondas are available in town, **Irachi** (Stra Logrono, km 43; 55 11 50), just south of Estella, is comfortable.

Join the N-111 east to travel over the actual Pilgrim Road, now transformed into a wide dual carriageway. Stop in **CIRAUQUI**, with narrow streets so steep that they are broken up with stone steps. It's a jumble of whitewashed houses. Most have wrought iron balconies and heavily sculpted cornices to balance out the ornate family coats of arms. At the very top of the village stands the parish church of San Ramón, with an elaborate but deteriorated entrance which recalls Estella's San Pedro de la Rua.

Continue on the N-111 to **PUENTE LA REINA**, where an 11th-century bridge spans the Arga River. It was here that the two main Pilgrim trails over the Pyrenees came together and it was a natural stopping place for gathering strength, swapping stories and praying for perseverance. The village is incredibly well preserved and is a patchwork of stone, brick and adobe among the ancient monuments. The Church of the Crucifix, founded by the Templar Knights, is actually outside the fortified walls and towers, though the porch connects directly with the odd pilgrims' hospice. It is noted for its unusual second nave and for the old gift a 14th-century passer-by left: a wooden crucifix with Christ nailed to a Y-shaped tree, said to have come from Germany. The narrow main street, lined by elegant crested houses with carved eaves, passes by the Santiago Church before crossing the bridge. Most of the carvings on the portal are very worn by the touch of so many believers. At the north entrance of town a bronze pilgrim statue greets the influx of modern travellers, many of whom still come for religious *romerías* to the carved virgins in the churches and hermitages around Puente La Reina. The Day of the Apostle (25 July) initiates a week of processions, folkdances, morning bullruns, *pelota* games and a general spree that attracts people from all over the district to join in. Most are farmers, and in their oxcarts rattling along the cobbles to the sound of ancient church chimes, it seems as if time never touched Puente La Reina. To enhance this sense of being a time-traveller, stay in *Mesón El Peregrino* (Ctra Pamplona–Logroño, km 23; 34 00 75), which is old enough to have lodged pilgrims on the march. Its modern swimming pool comes as an anachronistic delight.

BIBLIOGRAPHY

There is a bewildering number of books on Spain. Any aspect of this vivid country seems to be dissected in detail by foreigners: architecture, Reconquest, Inquisition, victory and defeat in innumerable battles, chivalry, the pageantry of bullfighting, Surrealism, the whys and wherefores of the Civil War, the transformation from dictatorship to democracy. Some of the best and most romantic travel books of the last century were set south of the Pyrenees, which was too savage to be included on the typical 'Grand Tours' of the day. Quite a few modern classics have been inspired in the Iberian peninsula as well. I've listed a selection below, but suggest first a glance at literature of the country itself. Even in translation, these works can set the edge for a personal discovery of Spain.

Spanish Literature
Anon (tr. Hamilton & Perry), *Poems of the Cid* (Penguin)
Cervantes, Miguel de, *Don Quixote* (numerous editions)
Garcia Lorca, Federico, *Three Tragedies* and *Five Plays* (Penguin)
Jiménez, Juan Ramón, *Platero y Yo*
Machado, Antonio, *Castilian Camp* (Aquila)
Ortega Y Gassett: *Collected Essays*
Perez Galdoz, Benito, *Jacinta and Fortunata*

Literature and Travels
Borrow, G., *The Bible in Spain* (1842, often reprinted)
Brenan, Gerald, *South from Granada* (Cambridge University Press)
Ford, R., *Gatherings from Spain* (1846; reprint Everyman, 1970)
Greene, Graham, *Monsignor Quixote* (Penguin)
Hemingway, Ernest, *Death in the Afternoon* (Jonathan Cape)
—— *The Sun Also Rises* (Jonathan Cape)
Irving, Washington, *Tales of the Alhambra* (numerous editions)
—— *The Conquest of Granada* (Darf)
Lee, Laurie, *As I Walked Out One Midsummer's Morning* (Penguin)
—— *A Rose for Winter* (Penguin)
Michener, James, *Iberia* (Fawcett): long-winded but fascinating detail
Pritchett, V.S., *The Spanish Temper* (Chatto)
Starkie, Walter, *Spanish Raggle Taggle*
—— *The Road to Santiago*

History

Brenan, Gerald, *Spanish Labyrinth* (Cambridge, 1943)

Elliot, H.H., *Imperial Spain 1468–1716* (Pelican, 1983)

Gates, David, *The Spanish Ulcer: A History of the Peninsular War* (Allen and Unwin, 1986)

Gibson, Ian, *The Assassination of Federico Garcia Lorca* (Penguin, 1984)

Heningsen, Gustav, *The Witches' Advocate: Basque Witchcraft and the Spanish Inquisition 1609–1614* (University of Nevada Press, 1986)

Hooper, John, *The Spaniards* (Viking)

Laxalt, Robert, *In a Hundred Graves: A Basque Portrait* (University of Nevada Press)

Mitchell, David, *The Spanish Civil War* (Granda, 1982)

Page, Julia (ed.), *Intelligence Officer in the Peninsula; Letters and Diaries of Major the Hon. Edward Charles Cocks* (Spellmont)

Thomas, Hugh, *The Spanish Civil War* (Penguin, 1977)

Art, Architecture and Photography

Bronstein, Leo, *El Greco* (Abrams)

Brown, J. & Elliott, J.H., *A Palace for a King* (Yale University Press)

Canton, Sanchez, *The Prado* (Thames & Hudson)

Descharnes, R., *The World of Salvador Dali* (Macmillan)

Gudiol, J., *The Arts of Spain* (Thames & Hudson)

Harvey, J.H., *The Cathedrals of Spain* (Batsford)

Leymarie, J., *Pablo Picasso* (Macmillan)

Muller, J.E., *Velasquez* (Thames & Hudson)

Palol, P. de & Hirmer, M., *Early Medieval Art in Spain*

Pohren, D.E., *The Art of Flamenco* (Musical News Services)

Smolan, Rick *et al.*, *One Day in the Life of Spain* (Collins): new coffee table book with 100 photographers' shots of a 24-hour period in 1987

Thomas, Hugh, *Goya: The Third of May, 1808*

Language

Ellis, D.L. & Ellis, R. *Just Enough Spanish/Traveller's Spanish* (Passport Books/Pan Books): an essential phrasebook for getting by in Spanish

Truscott, Sandra & Escribano, José, G., *Just Listen 'n Learn Spanish* and *Just Listen 'n Learn Spanish PLUS/Breakthrough* and *Breakthrough Further Spanish* (Passport Books/Pan Books): complete cassette and coursebook programs for learning Spanish

Other Guidebooks

Michelin Green Guide to Spain and *Michelin Red Guide to Spain and Portugal*: together with the cross-referenced maps, this trusty pair provides a reliable plod through much of the country

Boyd, Alastair, *The Companion Guide to Madrid & Central Spain* (Collins, 1986): scholarly and opinionated, especially for architecture fans

Facaros, Dana & Pauls, Michael, *Cadogan Guides: Spain* (Cadogan, 1987): good advice on bus and train travel, and fine reports on cities such as Barcelona, Córdoba and Granada. Churches and cathedrals covered in some detail. Flippant but well-informed

INDEX